The Diary of Prisoner 17326

The Diary of Prisoner 17326

A Boy's Life in a Japanese Labor Camp

. . . .

JOHN K. STUTTERHEIM

FORDHAM UNIVERSITY PRESS

New York   2010

Library of Congress Cataloging-in-Publication Data
Stutterheim, John K., 1928–
The diary of prisoner 17326 : a boy's life in a Japanese labor camp / John K. Stutterheim.—1st ed.
p. cm.—(World War II : the global, human, and ethical dimension)
ISBN 978-0-8232-3150-8 (cloth : alk. paper)
1. Stutterheim, John K., 1928– —Childhood and youth.
2. Stutterheim, John K., 1928– —Diaries.   3. Prisoners of war—Indonesia—Java—Diaries.
4. Boys—Indonesia—Java—Diaries.
5. Dutch—Indonesia—Java—Diaries.   6. World War, 1939–1945—Personal narratives, Dutch.   7. World War, 1939–1945—Personal narratives, Indonesian.   8. World War, 1939–1945—Concentration camps—Indonesia—Java.
9. World War, 1939–1945—Prisoners and prisons, Japanese.
10. Java (Indonesia)—Biography.   I. Title.
D805.I55S78   2010
940.53′1759826092—dc22
2009016296

Printed in the United States of America
12 11 10   5 4 3 2 1
First edition

CONTENTS

FOREWORD

Mark Parillo

World War II ended sixty-five years ago, and yet more and more works on the subject are appearing in bookstores all the time, many of them personal memoirs such as the present volume. One is tempted to ask what is to be gained by spilling more ink and killing more trees to present such stories to the twenty-first-century reader. It is a fair question.

A good part of the answer lies in the impact World War II has had on world history. Indeed, we are still dealing with the fallout. In 1945, much of Europe, master of the globe for centuries, lay in physical and economic tatters. From east and west the Soviets and Americans, linked in an uneasy alliance, swarmed across the continent to dominate the remains of ruined empires. The story of the erstwhile Allies' falling out and their subsequent bitter, if mostly indirect, hostility forms the backbone of much of the rest of the history of the twentieth century.

Yet it is to Asia that the war has bequeathed its most profound legacy. Japan, like its Axis partners, experienced a smashing defeat that brought with it tremendous loss of life and property, foreign occupation, and the scrapping of the old sociopolitical order. But it was Japan's early victories rather than its ultimate defeat that irrevocably altered the face of East Asia.

Japan's appetite for markets and resources, an appetite that had been growing by leaps and bounds when the government began forcing the nation to industrialize in the late nineteenth century, touched off the war in Asia. Friction with the West, especially the United States, over Japan's aggressive foreign policy measures, including outright war with China, to gain access to those markets and resources eventually prompted the Japanese to seize control of the resource areas themselves.

The most vital resource of all was oil, a commodity in which the Japanese home islands were noticeably poor, while other areas, including most especially the Dutch colony in the East Indies, were remarkably rich. The attack on Pearl Harbor, spectacular though it was in military and psychological terms, was but the prelude to the real Japanese tide of victory. The raid was intended to remove the U.S. Pacific Fleet as a threat to the string of operations planned for the next six months, and in that regard it was an unqualified success. But it was only the opening act of the Japanese plan.

The Japanese victories following the Pearl Harbor raid were enormous in their military and geographic scope. Amphibious forces waded ashore on the Malayan peninsula, and in six weeks they drove the numerically superior British and Indian forces back five hundred miles, until the Allies abandoned the mainland for the refuge of the supposedly impregnable island bastion of Singapore. The Japanese then crossed the Straits of Johore to Singapore itself and subdued the Allied forces there in a week's time.

Meanwhile, the Japanese mounted another major invasion in the Philippines. As an American colony working toward self-rule, the archipelago was defended by a joint U.S.-Filipino force. The Japanese soon overwhelmed the defenders, who withdrew to the rugged Bataan Peninsula on the northern island of Luzon to fight a valiant but ultimately doomed delaying action. The starving defenders capitulated in early April 1942, and a month later a daring Japanese assault captured the last American stronghold in the islands, the small but well-fortified island of Corregidor in Manila Bay.

Having already occupied the French colony of Indochina, the Japanese cajoled neighboring Thailand into an uneasy alliance allowing the passage of troops. Three Japanese divisions moved through Thailand and over its thickly forested western mountains into Burma, another strategically located British colony. Again surprising their adversaries with the speed and tactical excellence of their operations, the Japanese swept over Burma, a land the size of Texas, in six months. They all but destroyed the hastily assembled hodgepodge of British, Indian, and Chinese forces that tried to halt them. The Burma Road, the Allies' "back door" to China, was severed.

And the Japanese, as one would expect, wasted little time in pursuing the great prize, the Dutch colony in the Indies. They swept down both coasts of rugged Borneo, took rubber-rich Sumatra with airborne and seaborne assaults, and overwhelmed a hastily assembled Allied naval force in the Battle of the Java Sea, paving the way for the invasion of Java itself. The undermanned and disorganized Dutch ground forces held out for only a few days. The archipelago's great oilfields were now in Japanese hands.

Onward and outward the Mikado's minions rolled on. Hong Kong, Guam and Wake, Papua New Guinea, the Bismarcks and Admiralties and Solomons and Gilberts, all fell to the rampaging Japanese. By June 1942, they held dominion over perhaps a quarter of the globe, including some of the most richly endowed and heavily populated lands on earth.

The early Japanese victories were all the more remarkable for the ease with which they seemed to be achieved. In many instances, the Allies forces fought with courage and resolution, yet such heroic resistance was all for naught. The Marines at Wake Island turned back the first Japanese assault, but they were overwhelmed by a second one only two weeks later. Filipinos and Americans at Bataan endured starvation rations for months, yet in the end they could do nothing to prevent Japanese seizure of the entire archipelago. Americans, British, Australian, and Dutch warships joined in stalwart opposition to the Japanese invasion of Java, but they were brushed aside for negligible Japanese losses. Indeed, in the first three months after Pearl Harbor the Imperial Navy lost no vessel larger than a destroyer. Japanese airmen ruled the skies, and Japanese soldiers moved so quickly and easily through the tropical terrain that their opponents believed they had a special facility for jungle fighting.

Europeans had dominated East Asia and the western Pacific for so many generations that there had developed a myth of invincibility about them. And whites believed it, too. They had cultivated not just superior weapons but a superior culture. One could give the instruments of order and power—rifles, railroads, steamships—to the yellow and brown peoples, but they lacked the core values and abilities to use them properly to construct lasting institutions and a stable, prosperous society. Even the most successful of these primitives, the Japanese, were but slavish copycats who lacked the originality and vision to be anything more than a pest when white attention was turned elsewhere, like a sly fox that could cause much mischief in the henhouse, but only while the farmer was preoccupied elsewhere. Or so the theory went. That is, until Pearl Harbor and the ensuing rush to ascendancy in the Pacific by the warriors of the rising sun.

The Japanese offensives were so vast in scope and margin of victory that the myth of innate white superiority redounded to haunt the Allies. In the eyes of British, Australians, Americans, and Dutch, the Japanese transmogrified from farcical imitations of Westerners to military supermen. All sorts of preternatural powers were ascribed to them. The Japanese soldier had the night vision of the cat, the cunning of the fox, the stealth of the tiger, the natural ferocity of the wolverine. They had proven insuperable on land, sea, and air.

The great Japanese tide of victory had substantial consequences for the peoples living in the newly established Greater East Asia Co-Prosperity Sphere. They were so remote from the sources of Allied military strength that it seemed likely the Japanese would remain in dominion over that part of the world for a long time. Allied offensives, if they could be successfully undertaken in the first place, had many miles to cross before they would bring liberation from Japanese rule. Pearl Harbor, assuming it could be rejuvenated as a major base, was five thousand miles or more from the new conquests, and Pearl Harbor was itself half that far from the production centers on the U.S. mainland. India, supposing it held out against the threat posed by the victorious Japanese forces in neighboring Burma, was two months' voyage from London, even when the Mediterranean shipping lanes were open. Australia, the only other major base from which the Allies might conduct major operations, was just as far from the United States, provided further Japanese offensives did not capture or isolate it altogether. A reversal of the Japanese conquests of places such as the Dutch East Indies was years away.

Furthermore, there could be no shortcuts to liberation of East Asia and the lands of the southwestern Pacific. Men, aircraft, naval vessels, equipment, and supplies had to be assembled and sent to the far reaches of the Pacific in large quantities before the Allies could mount any sustained drives to wreck the new dominions of Japan. There were layers of strategic locations to be fought through before places such as the Philippines, Malaya, and the Indies could be assaulted.

Adding to the waning hopes of the captive populations was the difficulty of obtaining reliable news about the progress of the war. The Japanese government proved careful about what information it passed on to its own citizens, and the new subject peoples had their news even more carefully controlled. It was hard enough for the interned civilians in the East Indies to know what was happening in the colony itself, let alone what course the war was taking. Every prisoner of the Japanese suffered from psychological isolation along with physical privations.

And widespread physical travails were a harsh reality of Japanese rule. Partly this was a result of simple economics. In prewar days the lands of East Asia and the western Pacific were elements in a vast system of trade, the legacy of the antiquated imperialism of the mercantilist age. The colonies provided natural commodities such as bauxite, rubber, and oil, and they were in turn markets for consumer goods, especially textiles and foodstuffs. The Dutch were no longer the largest trading partner of the East Indies, losing out to the Japanese in the 1930s and then increasingly to the Americans in the last years before the war. The same pattern existed elsewhere in that part of the world; foreign trade, especially with the West, supplied many of life's necessities for the peoples of East Asia. When the Japanese went to war against the West in 1941, the trading pattern was wrecked for good. Japan could not make up the lost imports of food, clothing, and other daily necessities. No matter what policies the Japanese implemented in their newly won empire, for the man in the street there was bound to be hardship borne of scarcity.

For the average resident of the Greater East Asia Co-Prosperity Sphere, life became a daily struggle to secure clothing, fuel for cooking and heating, soap, paper, and myriad other basic goods. But there is no doubt the most pressing need, physically as well as emotionally, was daily nutrition. Officially or unofficially, food became the currency of the occupied territories. As the war ground on, it became the overriding preoccupation of everyday life. Regardless of Japanese policy, hunger and even slow starvation were very real prospects for all who lived under the rising sun emblem. And that included the Japanese themselves.

The Japanese, however, often exacerbated the sufferings of the indigenous populace. This was especially true for those who were incarcerated. Prisoners of war, civilian internees, and political prisoners became the special victims of *bushido*, the traditional Japanese warrior code. It stressed rigid social hierarchy, obedience, stoicism, spiritual purity, and loyalty. A true warrior respected and obeyed his superiors, brooked no insolence from inferiors, and sought atonement for any failure to live up to the code. A failure was a stain upon one's honor that must be purified, and if the failure were serious enough, only blood could wash it away.

Bushido was a product of medieval Japanese society, when the samurai emerged as the elite class just as the nobility—the knightly warrior class—had done in Europe. When the newly risen Japanese government of the late nineteenth century decided to modernize, the samurai were formally abolished as a class. But the new leaders of the government, themselves ex-samurai, encouraged the distillation of the values of bushido throughout the new national educational system as well as in the new national armed forces. With compulsory military service, all Japanese males were indoctrinated into the ways of the samurai. This made for fiercely fanatical soldiers. For their captives, it made for a living hell.

The Japanese soldier was regularly beaten by his superiors, and he was quick to do the same to those beneath him. To the Japanese, imprisonment denoted failure and the moral weakness that permitted capture instead of atonement through death. Prisoners of war were especially despised, since they were reputedly warriors, but incarcerated civilians were not much better in the eyes of their guards. They were the detritus of a society that had failed, and they did not have much value.

The omnipresent consciousness of social hierarchy placed additional emphasis on the symbols and gestures of obeisance, such as bowing to one's betters; failure to comply could bring instant and intense physical abuse. Further, in such an atmosphere strict compliance with all rules and regulations was a symbol of social respect. It did not matter if the rules were set by higher-ups removed from the realities of the situation, if the camp laws were unrealistic, irrational, and the sources of needless suffering. They were the rules, and disobedience transcended legalistic infraction to become an insult to Japanese honor.

In addition, the Japanese used the low regard they felt for their captives as justification for mistreatment in a larger sense. Food, housing, clothing, and medical care were primitive for the prisoners and internees. These people had failed in their obligations to society, so why worry about their daily comfort? Whatever the occupying forces provided for them, adequate for sustaining life or not, was a product and example of the mikado's munificence, for which the disgraced captives should be grateful. If the emperor's warriors had to endure shortages and privation, then prisoners would have to make their share of sacrifices as well. The Japanese lost little sleep worrying about rectifying the difficult conditions in the camps scattered across Asia and Oceania.

Yet another factor influenced Japanese treatment of their captives. When feudal Japan had been forced to open its doors to foreigners in the mid-nineteenth century by Commodore Matthew Perry's "black ships," the nation was militarily backward vis-à-vis the West and thus had to accept the infamous "unequal treaties" imposed by the foreigners. For the Japanese, this was culturally as well as economically demeaning.

Yet the foreigners also had much to which the Japanese aspired: military and political power, modern science, a deep and fascinating cultural life. The Japanese developed a love-hate relationship with the Westerners. They admired them and hoped to copy all that was good about Western life, but they remained fiercely devoted to their own ethnocentric view of the world, in which the Japanese were a divine race to which none could compare. The Westerners were resented for their humiliating treatment of the nonwhite peoples. The Japanese developed a chip on their shoulders, a chip grown all the heavier by real or perceived slights in the decades before Pearl Harbor. The rejection of a racial equality clause in the Versailles Treaty, the unequal warship ratios institutionalized in the Washington and London naval arms limitation agreements, the League of Nations' condemnation of Japanese actions in Manchuria, and the like all further fueled Japanese resentment of the West. When the tables were turned and the Japanese found themselves with the upper hand in the POW and internment camps in the Greater East Asia Co-Prosperity Sphere, there was a special gratification in seeing the white man humbled.

All of these elements—the chronic and widespread shortages of basic necessities, the low esteem in which the white captives were held, the intrinsic brutality of the everyday life of the Japanese soldier, the special resentment felt by the guards for their charges, the prisoners' isolation and hopelessness into the foreseeable future—made for a grim life for those held in Japanese hands during World War II. It was a situation made for sadists, and some did emerge from among the guards. Although the Allies vigorously prosecuted many of the thugs after the war, the inmates' suffering was more than the product of unscrupulous individuals. It was a hell inherent in the situation. It made daily life a horror and planning for the future unthinkable. It took tremendous courage simply to wake up each morning to face a new day.

The humbling and suffering of the 125,000 white Indonesian civilians incarcerated in World War II is more than a tale of the depravity and indomitability of the human spirit under the stresses of war. It is the story of how empires end and new nations are born. It was in the forge of the Pacific War that "Indonesia" came to have meaning and reality.

Well before World War II, however, two major foreign influences began to shape the rough clay of the ethnically and linguistically diverse communities that occupied the sprawling East Indies. Hindus settled on Java and Bali/Lombok, after which Muslims arrived around the year 1200. Islam gradually infiltrated the coastal areas through contact with Arab traders and businessmen. In many places it melded with the indigenous animism and ancestor worship of the locals, and Islam's initial impact was far from remarkable. But over the centuries it came to permeate much of the islands, even penetrating into the interior. A second, much more forceful wave of Islamic conversions occurred in the later nineteenth century. The Muslim faith later played a major intellectual and practical role in the formation of Indonesian nationalism.

The other significant foreign influence on the islands in modern times was the Dutch, who founded a trading station on northwestern Java in 1619. This post, Batavia, which evolved into the modern-day capital city of Jakarta, became the bastion of the Dutch East India Company, the main element of the Europeans' presence in that part of the world for nearly two hundred years. Backed by Dutch troops, the company sought only to maximize profits from exploiting the riches of the East. For many years they ignored the area's hinterlands and expanded their land ownership only as the needs of commerce dictated.

Accordingly, local social and political structures remained in place, and the islands remained a patchwork of independent states, typically run by popularly supported local elites. Some communities were ethnically homogenous, while others were not. There were matriarchal and patriarchal principalities, provinces governed by claim of divine right, and even some Islamic sultanates. So there was no political unification. Neither was the Islamic faith a unifying element, at least not until late in the nineteenth century. Every locale differed in the strain of Islam it embraced, the extent to which it integrated its indigenous religious beliefs, and the fervor with which it practiced the amalgamated faith. Some areas rejected Islam altogether in favor of retaining elements of Buddhism and Hinduism. And, though, there was widespread use of Malay as a language for trade, there also was no common first language across any large sector of the islands. Economic activity varied widely, too, from hunting and fishing to a great variety of agricultural methods and products. Even on Java, the most topographically and climatically consistent place in the archipelago, there was no sense among the inhabitants of a Javanese, let alone an Indonesian, identity. The term "Indonesia" itself was coined by European scholars in the mid-nineteenth century to refer to that vast expanse of sea and islands for which the inhabitants had no name of their own.

When the Dutch switched from almost purely economic to more thoroughly political control of the islands, however, an Indonesian identity eventually emerged. The Dutch East India Company had grown antiquated by the nineteenth century, and the Dutch began to bring the islands under more direct and reliable political control. They used persuasion where possible and force where necessary to convince local leaders to accept Dutch suzerainty. The process began early in the nineteenth century but intensified after 1860. The most severe fighting took place in northern Sumatra, where a nasty guerilla war began in the 1870s and lasted for three brutal decades. But most campaigns were briefer and less bloody than that, and gradually all the reluctant local leaders acquiesced to Dutch hegemony. Those local rulers who were perceptive enough to gauge the Europeans' military capability and their intent to use it submitted without fighting, usually negotiating better conditions under which they might stay in power. Dutch colonial rule thus built upon rather than replaced the hodgepodge of existing political structures in the islands.

This extension of Dutch political power defined what was to become the nation of Indonesia. The Dutch set the geographical limits of today's Indonesia by the extent of their expansion, lumping all the disparate peoples and principalities into the colony of the Netherlands East Indies. The Dutch, too, established the modern-day economy of the area by forcing the indigenous peoples to grow high-value trade crops, such as sugar, tea, and tobacco. The Dutch also exploited native labor for extractive industries, most notably oil.

The system of colonial governance through the local elites had an impact as well. The Dutch were quite content to harvest the wealth of the Indies by relying on local government structures to administer their own districts, including the collection of taxes or profitable trade goods for Dutch coffers. If a prince here and there needed colonial troops to maintain his hold on his realm, the Dutch found this a small price to sustain the flow of money into their pockets. But to keep their colonial masters happy, the local elites often had to deviate from their traditional status of *primes inter pares*, which had heretofore ensured the common man's loyalties by providing him with some sense of a voice in local affairs. The political and economic impoverishment of the average Indonesian under formal Dutch rule created resentment toward the local leaders, to be sure, but also against the Dutch. These were the seeds, if not of Indonesian nationalism, at least of movements for independence.

The wave of liberalism that swept over Europe in the mid-nineteenth century sent ripples across the Netherlands, too. Some Dutch developed ethical concerns about the centuries of exploiting the East Indies and began to call for more enlightened treatment of the Indonesian peoples, including a higher standard of living for the present and more education for the future. Such ideas had little impact on colonial policy for some decades, but, partly because government leaders began to see some practical benefits in quieting discontent among the indigenes, early in the twentieth century the colonial administration initiated new measures for better schools, freer public discourse, and other basic civil liberties. Most Dutch in the islands came to think of themselves as progressive and patriarchal rulers of people still too primordial to care for themselves. Native Indonesians saw the situation, and their Dutch masters in particular, in a different light, as they perceived the chains of imperialism to be distasteful even if now somewhat lighter.

Nevertheless, the lenient policy instituted by the Dutch after the turn of the century allowed many fledgling varieties of independence movements to emerge into the open. Some built on leftist philosophies, others were based in either traditional or "enlightened" Islam, while still others centered on various ethnic groupings. There was much activity on Java, the most populous and central of the islands, and leaders who would become important in the 1940s, such as Mohammed Hatta and Sukarno, first rose to prominence.

But all the organizations, parties, and movements foundered on the continued religious, geographic, and ethnic diversity of the indigenous population. By the 1930s, the Dutch had abandoned their policy of tolerance, and the splintered independence groups fell apart or were disbanded. Colonial rule appeared destined to endure for many more decades at least.

The Japanese conquest obliterated that historical path, just as it did in the other lands of East Asia and the western Pacific. The Japanese proved the white rulers *could* be beaten. The image of shackled European soldiers towering over the squat Japanese warriors who were leading them off into captivity resonated throughout that part of the world. It was an image Asians never forgot, even after the defeated Japanese had departed. It was an image that reshaped the world.

In addition to destroying the myth of white invincibility, the Japanese tide of victory in the early days of the Pacific War directly mobilized the political potential of Indonesia and other lands. Using the gospel of pan-Asianism to further their own efforts to control the resources of East Asia and Oceania, the Japanese preached independence and cooperation. They fostered the establishment of semiautonomous governments and military forces in Burma, India, China, the Philippines, and the Indies. They never relinquished control in any meaningful way to these institutions, but they nevertheless provided political and military training, organization, and experience in places where the locals had heretofore had little.

When the realities of Japanese rule became apparent, enthusiasm for Japan's proclaimed war of liberation waned among Indonesians and other peoples under Japanese rule. In some places, outright resistance movements sprang up. In others, including Indonesia, the organizations spawned by the Japanese ceased cooperating with the conquerors and eventually turned on them. But everywhere the Japanese sun shone, sooner or later it evoked feelings of independence and a sense of self-identity.

In the case of the East Indies, the reaction to Japanese rule was profound. In order to control and exploit the archipelago's many resources, the Japanese made a concerted effort to win over the moderate native leaders by providing training, equipment, and promises of true independence. The Japanese-trained military forces were among the largest throughout the Co-Prosperity Sphere, and Indonesian leaders attended schools and participated in political conventions in Japan. But Japanese rule was hard on the archipelago's indigenous peoples. Food shortages were severe in densely settled Java, and farmers had to abandon their cash crops to concentrate on production. The Japanese soon instituted labor levies, a "blood tax" on the Javanese. At least 200,000 young men were conscripted as "economic soldiers" and sent off to work in Southeast Asia, of whom no more than a third survived at war's end to return home. As the tide of war turned against the Japanese from 1944 on, resistance, both overt and covert, grew.

Japanese rule in the East Indies accomplished in three years what the Dutch had not in three centuries: unification of the peoples of Indonesia. The differences in vision, principles, and methodology that had kept the many groups working for Indonesian independence divided for decades melted away in the blossoming hatred for the Japanese. For the first time, "Indonesia" gained wide adherence as a unifying concept, overriding regional, ethnic, ideological, and religious differences. Two days after the Japanese surrender, on August 17, 1945, Sukarno issued a statement of independence. Much remained for this goal to be recognized by all, especially the Dutch, but there is no question that the Japanese tide of victory and subsequent occupation had galvanized the many peoples of the East Indies into Indonesians.

John K. Stutterheim personally observed this process. But the memoirs of his wartime experiences are not the objective, balanced views of a studied witness to history. They are the story of a teenager caught up in a whirlwind of momentous events. His family was typical of the middling colonial officials that oversaw the colony. His childhood was unremarkable until the vortex of the Pacific War sucked his family into the chaos and suffering of war. He was separated from his father for the entire war, and later had only limited contact with his mother. Facing the trials of adolescence on his own would have been a formidable challenge, but that was only the beginning. He had to learn to accommodate and mitigate the oppressive brutality of his captors, contend with the changing attitudes and actions of the Javanese people he had known all his life, and provide, as best he could, for others who were weaker or less fortunate, including his younger brother. Even when the war ended and he was reunited with his family, he had to cope with the challenges of returning to a life and a world that had been transformed from all he had known as a child. To modern Americans, for whom the early teenage years mostly mean struggling with puberty, acne, and algebra, this is a compelling tale of the triumph of the human spirit.

And yet Dr. Stutterheim's does not treat his past as a heroic epic. It is the simple narrative of a teenage boy dealing with what for him were quotidian afflictions and threats, large and small, the daily struggle for food, clothing, shelter, and relief from illness, fatigue, and brutality. This is, in sum, a grim story of the struggle for survival.

It is in this that we find the answer to the original question: Why yet another book on World War II? The war was for the East Indies, as for so many other places around the globe, the catalytic event in its modern history. Indonesia came to be because of World War II. But besides being the birthplace of new nations and much of the world as we know it today, the war was the pivotal event in the lives of many hundreds of millions if not billions of people. John K. Stutterheim is one such person. His personal story unfolded against the backdrop of those historic times, times that affected an entire generation as well as generations yet to come. It is a story worth telling.

PREFACE

Dedication, I was told, is to give thanks to people who have supported one's attempt to write a book.

My first wife, Loekie Smit, who died on Christmas 1999, always encouraged me during our last years of marriage to get my story off the ground. She herself grew up in Medan, Sumatra, only to be moved during the war to Camp Tjideng in Batavia, Java. Loekie never wanted to talk about her experiences during the Japanese occupation; when I quizzed her, she usually would burst into tears and revealed nothing. By sheer coincidence did I obtain shreds of stories, one where she at the age of eleven was beaten mercilessly by a Japanese soldier whose request in Japanese for an eggbeater she had not understood. Nevertheless, she pushed me to write down my nightmares, even if it was at two in the morning, just to get it off my chest. She stood by me to make drawings and maps and to improve the manuscript. She exemplified the spirit of many in the camps who were determined to rise above their horrific experiences and continue their lives with dignity and grace.

Our five children and my brother's children in Holland have known little about their parents' experiences, and our grandchildren even less. Several episodes came unexpectedly to light with which they were confronted. Our children and grandchildren find it hard to deal with this story, for it comes too close to home, as they put it.

This book will let them see into the depths of their grandparents, and I hope it will give them a sense of the strength and determination we all need to live a meaningful life.

Second, my sincere thanks to a retired teacher, Mrs. Gretchen Russell, living in Gig Harbor, Washington, who spent a great deal of time improving my American English. I benefited so much from her down-to-earth, stern corrections and teachings. How grateful I am for her help when I needed it the most.

Third, this book is dedicated to the boys in Camp Bangkong who did not survive and shared our harsh and difficult experiences. Some of them I had to prepare for burial, a gruesome experience that taught me how difficult it was to stay alive under the circumstances. There is a statue of a small boy with a hoe and ax, dressed in a loincloth, to be found in Bronbeek, Arnhem, in the Netherlands, honoring boys like them.

Fourth, my gratitude to Fordham University Press, which I approached after reading a book it had published about an American soldier in Tunisia, who was taken prisoner by the Germans and brought to a Stalag. He used a hidden camera and took pictures, bribing guards to get film. I was so impressed by Fordham's willingness to publish these pictures that I approached it in the hope that it would publish my memoir, along with my drawings and maps.

Fifth, my current wife, even though she has a difficult time hearing the stories, helped me with my writing and total ignorance about computers, which turned out to be extremely helpful.

My son wrote the following poem:

The Hand I Would Be
I've always known of a stirring pain
In the resilient souls from which I came

I've seen eyes with dust from a hurtful past
Hide ghosts of tears too defiant not to last

I've had hatred towards fairness for not being there
In stories where even my God didn't care

I've only regretted that I could not be
A hand back through time,
        To change it, you see?

In 1993, I became convinced that I had to write my autobiography. Many people who had listened to my stories over the years encouraged me to do so. This was invaluably reassuring, and it was stimulating to go ahead with research and a daunting struggle to master written English, my third language.

My dear deceased friend John Buffalo and I were like brothers. John read my first draft, written in poor English, and encouraged me not to give up and to write down all my memories. Since John had been in the thick of this war, he had a better understanding for what happened to us boys. He himself served during World War II aboard a tin can, a destroyer. He enlisted in December 1941 and was sent straight to the Solomon Islands. Later he served under Bull Halsey throughout the Pacific Theater. His boatswain, who disliked John, sent him ashore on Tulagi in 1942. In a sloop with other sailors, John landed on the beach to explore the island, a Japanese floatplane base south of Florida Island and opposite of Guadalcanal, while heavy fighting was still going on for this base. He and his sloop mates were horrified to see their destroyer suddenly steam away! They were abandoned.

The Japanese navy came down "the slot" to do battle, and John's ship was sunk. A few days later, another destroyer retrieved their stranded group. He remained aboard this ship for the rest of the war and was discharged from the navy in Bremerton, Washington, in 1945. John studied to be a teacher and ended his career as the principal of Stadium High School in Tacoma.

In 1993, my wife and I went to Indonesia to revisit the old places. Evangelist Bob Brodland and his kind wife helped us during our stay in Djakarta. They outlined our trip over the island of Java. In many places, notified in advance by the Brodlands, ministers welcomed us. Among them were the Awondatu family, who lived in Cianjur, close to Bandung, who were so kind as to invite us into their home, while in Magalang we received the help of the Malino family. Victor Malino, a very kind and understanding person, accompanied me on the emotional trip to Camp Bangkong in Semarang, where I took pictures and relived vivid memories of the boys' camp. The people working at the school named Bangkong did not know that their building ever had been a concentration camp. It was a shock to them.

Thanks to all of you, my experiences came together as a book. I hope that students in history will read this story, for few Americans know about the teenaged labor camps created by the Japanese.

The Diary of
Prisoner 17326

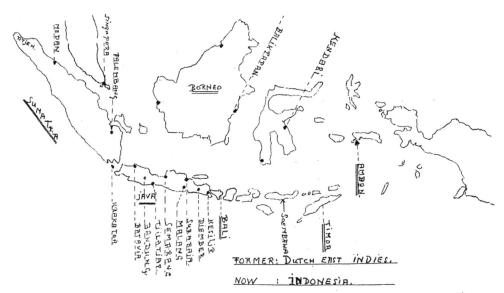

SCALE 1:16725000.

↑ N

ATJEH.
MEDAN
SINGAPORE
PALEMBANG
SUNATRA
BORNEO
BALIKPAPAN
KENDARI
KRAKATOA
JAVA
BATAVIA
BANDUNG
TJILATJAP
SEMARANG
MALANG
SURABAIA
DJEMBER
KEDIRI
BALI
SOEMBAWA
AMBON
TIMOR

FORMER: DUTCH EAST INDIES.
NOW : INDONESIA.

J.K.St.

chapter one

A TEENAGED PRISONER OF JAPAN, NO. 17326

Near noon on the last day of February 1942, a crowd of people waited on the platform of the railroad station at Gubeng in southern Surabaja, Java, for a train going to Malang, a mountain town to the south. With no wind blowing and the sun standing at its zenith, the heat and humidity were stifling. Off to the north, where the Japanese had bombed the rubber warehouses of the harbor, the crowd could see billows of dense black smoke rising, covering the azure sky.

My mother, my younger brother Anton, and I had been waiting on that platform for hours in the hundred-plus-degree heat. Though the Gubeng station had not been bombed, the chaos in Surabaja had delayed all trains along the line.

I was thirteen years old at the time. We were without my father, who worked as an accountant for the colonial government. Owing to his poor eyesight, he had not been drafted in the Landstorm, or National Guard, at the outset of the war, but he had been ordered to stay in Surabaja to supervise the finances of the provincial department. It had been very emotional for mother to leave her husband behind. He was not able to be there to say good-bye. Dad—my mother called him Johan—was short and very strong for his forty-seven years, and he loved to get his boys involved in sports, especially swimming.

A few days earlier, we had been shocked to learn about the defeat of the combined naval forces of Australia, England, the Netherlands, and the United States, which had been battered in the Java Sea. Some vessels that had not been sunk outright, such as the American cruiser *Houston* and the Australian warship *Perth*, tried to escape, but Japanese airplanes torpedoed the *Houston* in the Strait of Sunda, west of Java, later followed by the *Perth* and a Dutch destroyer that landed in the middle of the Japanese invasion fleet off the coast of Bantam and were also lost. Survivors of the battle of the Java Sea were being sent to Tjilatjap, the only small harbor on the southern coast that was still open, to be evacuated to Ceylon and Australia before advancing Japanese columns could arrive.

A jumbo engine hauling a long freight train from Tandjung Perak, the naval harbor, steamed slowly toward us. The brakes squealed, and a hiss of steam escaped from its sides as the train ground to a halt. The short boxcars were painted white and covered by red crosses on all sides and on top. The train was packed with wounded and survivors from the Battle of the Java Sea. I will never forget the horror and agony of that train, the sight of stretchers bearing moaning, burned and wounded men with blood-soaked bandages; the sickly sweet smell of old fashioned iodoform, a disinfectant; nurses in dirty khaki uniforms running around, their backs and armpits stained with sweat; the push of the waiting crowd trying to bring water and food to the cars. More soldiers and airmen, some of them American survivors of a B17 squadron from Singosari, entered the platform and boarded the pitiful train wherever there was room.

After a long delay, the whistle shrieked and the engine moved forward, the big wheels straining, slipping, and grabbing at first, spraying sand on the hot steel tracks, shuddering at the immense weight it had to pull. At every rotation of its wheels it pumped out steam on both sides, hauling off this endless row of boxcars, each crammed with human misery.

I took it all in, each car slowly passing by, revealing a different picture of wounded soldiers, sailors, and airmen through the open doors. Several sat in the doorway, legs dangling, their backs resting against the doorpost. Many smoked cigarettes. Some were wrapped in bandages, and some just stared with hollow eyes. I thought that their eyes went straight through me, as if there was no soul alive behind them, just like statues that could breathe. Slowly, the last goods car with its two red taillights rounded the corner, and the steady chugging sound faded away.

Through it all, my mother said nothing. She just held and squeezed the hands of both her boys. She didn't let go, but she never said a word.

The people who were left behind were quiet, many women with tears in their eyes. Nobody waved. Everyone realized the disaster that had struck.

Finally, people started to move about on the platform. The listlessness and disheartened feeling of the crowd became almost palpable. Anton squirmed free of our mother's hand and spoke up. "Mother, when will our train come?" She had no answer. With no certainty that a train for Malang in the mountains, where our home was located, would come at all, we simply had to wait.

Mother's dress stuck to her shoulder blades. She was covered in sweat. Observing her face, I started to realize how tormented she was, torn between fear for her husband, pain at the sight of those injured men, and hope that our quiet neighborhood in Malang would remain safe.

Finally, late in the afternoon, we boarded a passenger train along with many others who were escaping the chaos of Surabaja. The ride to Malang, a garrison town in the hills, took much longer than the usual hour, but there was little conversation aboard these packed cars, no chatter of greeting and farewell when the engine pulled into the station at dusk.

The next morning, the sky war came suddenly to Malang. I had gone outside into the front yard, and at that very moment a Japanese Zero fighter plane abruptly appeared over the rooftops, so low that I could see the pilot's head. A burst of machine gun bullets hit across the street. Two native boys tried to run for safety, but they did not make it. I looked at their motionless bodies. It was the first time that I had seen dead people. I picked up one of the five-inch spent casings, only to drop it, still too hot to handle.

The Zero did not return. Mother ran out of the house and shoved my brother and I into our sandbagged shelter on the back porch. At that moment the "all-clear" sirens sounded, and we protested being made to stay there. Mother could not be reasoned with at first, but after she calmed down she relented.

A few days later, Mother called us to the living room, where she sat down and emotionally grabbed our hands. With tears in her eyes, she said with great emotion, "Dad and I so far have succeeded in giving you two a happy and peaceful life, but the situation has turned serious, and we face an unknown future. We have to help each other. I recently saw the movie *Gone with the Wind*, with Scarlett O'Hara, and I fear that we have landed in a similar predicament."

At these words, Anton, who was eleven, realized that a change was ahead. His frightened face reflected that awareness, but he was not able to comprehend the total picture. It dawned on me that from here on our lives without major worries were no more, and we were indeed bound for a dark, uncertain, threatening era.

chapter two

DISCOVERING JAVA

Both my parents were born and raised in Amsterdam. Grandpa Stutter-heim was a diamond cutter, but lost his job at the end of World War I, when the diamond industry moved to Antwerp, Belgium. As a result, my Dad had to drop out of high school and started to work in a bank. He obtained his accounting training and started to master several languages. Mother was eighteen when she married Dad, who was ten years older. In 1928, they decided to move to what was then called the Dutch East Indies, where two of Dad's sisters and a brother were living.

His older sister, Aunt Greta, was married to a physician in the colonial army, and they were sent to various outposts. One of them was Poso on Celebes, small and primitive. One night my aunt visited the outhouse during the night. When seated, she felt something cold around her ankles. Her flashlight revealed a large python wrapping itself around the seat and her legs. Quickly, she pulled her legs up and jumped off the pot and started to scream. We still enjoy this story.

I was born on June 14, 1928, in Surabaja, the harbor where the U.S. Navy used to come to bunker for coal. Surabaja used to have many sharks and crocodiles, and it earned its name that way, for in Indonesian *suara* means shark and *buaja* means crocodile.

Dad was an inspector of finance, and his work consisted of auditing county city buildings of various provinces in Eastern Java, visiting each for two weeks. For a few years, from 1930 through 1934, he was stationed in Semarang, central Java, where my brother Anton was born. Semarang was a very hot and mosquito-infested town. East of it were swamps where the mosquitoes thrived. Our home sat against the foothills of Tjandi, the back-yard extending into a Chinese cemetery with markers and buildings scattered over the hillside. When the evening descended, the servants did not dare go close to the graveyard. They told me, "There are *mommohs*, ghosts, roaming on that slope."

Securing a second job, Dad assisted a friend, Mr. van der Knoop, in keeping the books for his import and export business, working evenings and Saturdays. Mother told us that people criticized Dad for having two jobs during the depression, but Dad's belief was that if a person tried hard he could make a living.

Mr. van der Knoop, a stocky man in his thirties, did not have a little finger. Such things intrigue little boys, so I asked him why. He told me that his motorcycle handlebar had hit the brick wall of the gate to his warehouse, shearing off his little finger. Once, even though I was only five, I got to ride on the duo seat of his Harley-Davidson to tour hot downtown Semarang one Saturday afternoon while Dad was working. We drove over Bodjong, the main road, and he pointed out the *warongs*, which were nothing more than semipermanent shaded bamboo stands, where native women were selling food on the roadside. Mother had drilled into me, "Do not eat from the roadside!" Mr. van der Knoop stopped at one of the stands and asked me, "What do you want to eat?" When he saw my puzzled face, he roared with laughter, for he knew Mother's instructions.

This bachelor's office and warehouse were inside an old fort. That really could tickle the imagination of a five-year-old. Dad brought me up there only on Saturdays and forbade me to go outside the gate, where the traffic was bustling in the heat and dust.

As always, I loved to roam and moved under the cooler platforms behind the parapets, which had been part of the outer defenses. Every time I was there, I spotted new merchandise. Grapes and apples came from Australia. The grapes, packed in shredded cork and crated, were found in a large cooled area. Inside the open area of the fort was an old truck used for hauling merchandise from the harbor. Two Javanese men worked for our friend, usually loading and unloading and checking orders. I learned quite fast that being friends with them rewarded me with bruised fruit—grapes, apples, and pears. I wanted desperately to go with them on the truck rides but Dad said no.

Except me, my entire family over the years had suffered from malaria, especially Dad, who once had blackwater fever, so called because blood showed in the urine. For days he was extremely ill, and Mother hovered over him. Thank God for quinine. This was the reason that my parents decided to go live in Ungaran, about a dozen miles south of Semarang in the foothills of Mount Ungaran, where the nights were cooler. We found an old home with high ceilings and generous windows, shaded in front by high trees to keep it cool and surrounded by several acres of land fronting the highway. On the side were *djeroek* trees, with orangelike fruit, and *djeroek Bali*, with fruit the size of a soccer ball and meat like white grapefruit. Mother used to make marmalade with the peels.

When we moved into this home, Mother became annoyed by the sight of thick black rope strung from tree to tree. *Nangkrangs*, big red ants, used the ropes as highways to travel between their large football-size nests, made by them by pulling the leaves together. Mother ordered the ropes removed, whereupon the ants started to track in long lines over trails through the grass. I soon quit running under the trees, for when disturbed these ants started to swarm, and their bite was mean and they clung to their victim. Recognizing the red ants' habits, Mother allowed the black ropes to be strung up once again. The old system restored, and I could play under the trees once more.

The backyard sloped steeply down to a small river. The sewage ran through a concrete ditch, which was planked over, and ran into an extensive, dense, dark-green canopy of banana tree leaves fed by the liquid. Mother always took one bunch of bananas from the trunk, and the rest were given to the servants, who usually sold them.

As always, I was curious. I roamed the backyard. I lifted the planks covering the sewer ditch and found snakes and scorpions, but only chased them away. Once, a large snake raised itself about two feet and looked me straight in the face. This hypnotized me, and we found ourselves in a standoff until Mother came to the rescue. The native gardener, after killing it, told us that this was a small python. Mother told us boys that snakes hypnotize birds in this way.

Dad loved to walk on Sundays, when the family strolled down to the small village, where at best ten European families lived. It was a quiet place. Once, Mother told us years later, I approached a sleeping native policeman, who was supposedly guarding a warehouse, lying in the shade with his hat pulled over his face. I lifted his large hat and studied his face a while, then dropped the hat back in place and walked away. The officer never woke up.

As so many Europeans, we did not own a car. Dad traveled by bus to Semarang, which was not always convenient for him. One morning he was late, and Mother hurried him along. He jumped into his shoes, only to swear loudly, for our puppy had left a messy surprise. After he cleaned that up, he raced along the fifty-yard driveway to the gate to catch the bus, standing under several coconut trees. That morning he must have scared a *blekok*, a relative of the blue heron, out of the tree. This bird has a nasty habit of emitting a white dropping at takeoff. Right on target: "Splat," on his left shoulder. He returned to change his white coat, saying more nasty words as he threw it in the corner. After changing he ran back out the door, only to see the bus passing by. Seldom had I seen him so angry, for he was usually mild-tempered. When he arrived at the gate again, I noticed how he looked up into the trees. I noticed how the servants snickered. Mother could see the humor in the situation better than he and had a good chuckle, but only after he had gone.

I went to school for the first time in Ungaran. Located at the *aloon-aloon*, the center of the village, were a few buildings: the school, consisting of two classrooms, its walls made of *bilik*, or woven split bamboo, its roof of clay tile; the white *mesigit*, or mosque, with its tall sleek minaret; and the post office. An old *benteng*, or fort, guarded the entrance to the aloon-aloon, traditionally a large grassy field at whose center is a huge *waringin*, or banyan tree, with air-roots descending from the branches and forming a massive trunk over the decades. These trees are considered holy, and folklore has it that old witches live in them and prey on little kids at nightfall.

It didn't take long for Mother to realize how much more I loved to explore than sitting in school. The first and second grades were taught by a female teacher in Dutch, in one of the two large classrooms. The pupils were Dutch, Eurasian, and Chinese. As interesting as my new classmates were, the sights and activities outside were more distracting than ever. The bilik walls allowed light and air to pass through in abundance. A huge wooden drum outside the mesigit, horizontally suspended from a tree branch, called believers to attend prayer services. It was fascinating to watch the Javanese men, dressed in sarongs and their chests covered by a *kemedja*, black *kopiahs* covering their short hair, take off their slippers and wash their feet in a shallow basin. Then, barefoot, they would walk on clean flat steppingstones into the mosque, leaving the slippers behind, neatly arranged in rows. I could hear their loud prayers: "*Allah il Allah, Allah akbar.*"

The school door and windows were always wide open. I watched people come and go, such as our neighbor from South Africa, whom we respectfully called Aunt Susie, as she went to and from the post office. I kept track of how many buses stopped at the aloon-aloon. I did anything but pay attention to what was going on inside the classroom.

My teacher became irritated by my inattention and sent me on numerous occasions behind the blackboard, which sat on an old-fashioned easel. Once, after studying the outdoors by looking through the holes in the wall, I turned to fidget with the large hooks holding the easel in place. They were thus loose when the teacher turned and started to write on the blackboard, which caused the entire assembly to crash through the bamboo wall. What a scene that caused. Frantically, I tried to clean what I could. Even so, I took a stern letter home from school that day.

Mother was upset. Obviously I was not ready for school, but I had no choice in the matter. When Mother sat down to discuss my behavior, I melted her with my happy smile, I did not think any of it was important. Once I told her that I had obtained a ten, the highest mark possible. In reality, I had made ten mistakes and could not care less. I would have preferred to walk around, visit the old fort on the other side of the road, and talk to people.

After school at noon, I always walked home, glad to shake off the confinement, and most of the time making a detour and descended along a dirt road, the only other outlet of the aloon-aloon. This narrow rutted track started very near the mesigit, went down straight through two native *kampongs*, or villages, and crossed a small fast-running river. The soil all around was volcanic, rich and red, and would stain my shorts with hard-to-remove soil. Upstream the water came crashing down over one-foot drop offs, spouting through a hole drilled in the center of a polished volcanic rock. Dense underbrush walled the shoreline, branches dragging in the water. Downstream, I joined the *katjongs*, native boys my own age, barefoot and dressed only in black shorts, squatting on the smooth-surfaced boulders at the edge of the river or on the gray rocks midstream. Here we tried to catch tiny needlenose fish, using empty butter cans. One time we were excited to discover a dish-sized green turtle in a sandbank on the shore. The chase was in vain. I asked my companions why they wanted the turtle, and they told me that it tasted great in soup. Then suddenly, "*Oeler, oeler!*" cried one of the boys, pointing at a two-foot-long snake, bright green with a flaming red tail, swimming near us across the river. "*Bisa, bisa,*" they yelled at me in warning. This one was very venomous, so I kept my distance. I wasn't scared of any of the water dwellers.

Just downstream was an eddy in a deeper part of the current where the impressive horns and huge heads of water buffalo were barely visible. Their large nostrils flared just above the water as they snorted. They were cooling off after a day's work in the fields, washing off the mud without any effort from the katjongs. I had a holy respect for these large gray animals. By the time that I saw the katjongs climb on the backs of these fearsome beasts to drive them to the village, I realized that the sun had positioned itself low behind the trees, creating a yellowish glow. It was then time to go home.

At times, it seemed, everything conspired against my freedom. That evening at six, the neighbor's mynah bird, whose perch was on the back patio at sunset, cried out loudly, "Jopie, Jopie, bedtime!" The neighbor's boy had the same nickname as I, Jopie. No wonder I disliked that bird.

In those days, it was actually very safe for a small boy to roam alone through the kampongs and back roads. This, then, was my favorite pastime. Our dachshund usually went with me, but he liked to chase the roaming chickens. The natives did not like that at all, and one time a man threw an *arit*, a small curved knife used for grass cutting, and hit my dog in its belly. Our dog went straight home, where he rolled over on his back to expose his wound in front of my startled mother. She nursed him back to good health while I watched and learned.

In 1935, Dad was transferred back to Surabaja, where we lived for the next few years.

We lived in the large home of his sister, Loes, who was married and had three daughters our age, Loekie, Carla, and Ankie. Aunt Loes ran a fashion-design business exclusively for the upper crust. Uncle Karel imported foods from Australia and stored these products in a refrigerated warehouse. He loved to tell us tall tales. Anton, while leaning with his elbow on Uncle Karel's knee, used to hang on his every word and took it all in.

Uncle Karel had purchased a large gramophone, and the family played classical and opera music. The large, open French doors allowed cool air to sweep through the house, and as we lay in our beds, we kids would listen to the beautiful music the adults were enjoying.

Our big one-month school vacation was always held in October, for that was the start of the monsoon and the hottest month of the year. In October 1936, when I was eight years old, Uncle Karel came up with a surprise, as he often did. He rented a home from a Chinese businessman whom he knew. Uncle Karel told us that it was a primitive four-bedroom home built of bamboo and without electricity, a *tampat*, meaning a place to strike down, and he wanted both our families to go there together. The tampat was located very high in the mountains, just above a remote coffee plantation.

Our parents rented an open-sided Chevy seven-seater. On the back was a large foldout luggage carrier where each family placed a big steel trunk. On top of the trunks sat the gramophone, protected by a rubber sheet. It was no wonder that the engine overheated going uphill on the winding road, but that was no problem to the driver. He just let the engine cool off and then dipped colored water out of the fast-running gurgling creek by the roadside. There was no reason to be in a hurry. We kids sat down at the stream's edge and splashed our feet in the water, enjoying the stop. Native women passed by, walking toward market, and smiled at the sight. Many carried baskets atop their heads, balancing the loads with one hand. Mother purchased a basket full of *ramboetan*, an egg-sized prickly red fruit, from one of them. After removing the rind, we ate the delightful-tasting translucent white flesh, spitting out the grayish-brown pit, and in no time the contents of the entire basket were consumed. We kids threw the red rinds in the water and enjoyed watching them bobbing and floating down the swirling stream.

Our rented home was made almost entirely of bamboo. The main vertical support posts were of teak four-by-fours, but the walls, typical of all major structures in those days, were bilik. The entire structure was brownish and discolored, for no paint was ever used on these structures. The government had forbidden the use of hollow bamboo because rats nested in the tubes, spreading plague as recently as the 1920s. The roof was made of *atap*, dried folded coconut leaves placed in layers like roof tiles. The house had a large living room, four bedrooms, a bathroom, and a kitchen without an outside wall. In its place was a low counter for cooking, so there was no need for a chimney. The floors were no more than packed earth, except in the bathroom, which was concrete. That last room contained a two-cubic-yard concrete cistern filled with water. To bathe or rinse we had to dip the water with a small zinc-lined bucket with a wooden handle inside across, nailed on each end, called a *gajong* and throw the water over our heads. There were two goldfish in this water reservoir to control the mosquito larvae. We had heard stories where newcomers from Europe climbed into this container to bathe, which to us was funny.

Water flowed through a long piece of bamboo, four inches wide and split lengthwise, that entered through an opening in the wall. The water came from a mountain stream at a level above the house and yard, and the construction looked similar to a miniature aqueduct. This stream also went through the backyard and provided water for a small swimming pool, which delighted all five kids. We spent hours in that pool; it was our salvation in the stifling heat. Anton especially would stay in the pool until his teeth would chatter. The stream was also our source of drinking water. Mother created a safe purification system. After dipping the water out of the stream she boiled it; then, when it had cooled, she poured it through a thick layer of fluffy cotton. I was continually surprised to see so much brown sediment on the cloth.

Both sides of the back lawn were fenced off by a row of green hibiscus with bright red flowers topped at a height of four feet. Groupings of wild bamboo were draped against the forest, forming a zigzag back border. The yellowish bamboo reached up to the light and shaded the rim of what Dad called the *rimboe*, the jungle. This always caused a messy appearance at the edge in the back yard, for the long bamboo leaves that dropped curled themselves in heaps against the tree roots. From time to time the gardener would sweep the leaves in a big heap and burn them, causing a slow spiraling path of grayish-white smoke to rise through the tree branches. Fingers of smoke curling upward touched the leaves of the branches, and the warm airflow created ever-changing colors. Above the canopy of the dense, dark tropical growth the breeze curved and dispersed the smoke. The green leaves reflected the rays of sunlight trickling through the hazy particles. A flowering red bougainvillea climbed a post and spread out over a horizontal trellis, covering and shading some reclining chairs and a wooden bench. In the corner of the yard a dark green aloe spread its thick, spongy, elongated leaves, which ended in long black thorns, a popular tool for teenage boys who wanted to goose girls at school. Toward the side of the house was a large waist-high shrub covered with *melatti*, small white flowers draped over small round glossy green leaves. The native women were ardent for the melatti, whose fragrance was also prized for temple offerings, and they would stick a bloom in their hair-bun.

It was an old Javanese tradition to keep pigeons, and the native servants kept several valuable birds in cages at the tampat. Early in the morning these cages, made of fine split bamboo, were hoisted high in the air. The poles used for that purpose were also bamboo, three inches in diameter and twenty feet tall, and several stood like flagpoles at the edge of the courtyard. We could hear the songs of these birds, a soft cooing. The slower and more muffled or veiled this sound was, the more valuable the animal. Visiting wild pigeons came to sit on tree branches close in and took turns sounding off. I would sit there with my feet dangling in the pool and listen to the birds and the water rushing into the pool.

The lights of our airy home were primitive petroleum lamps hung on the walls. At night the pores of the bilik walls allowed light rays to filter through, creating flickering ghostly shadows in our bedroom. In the main living room a large lamp was suspended from the ceiling. This was the first time I had seen the lighting of such a lamp, and was fascinated to see the sock, or mantle—how it at first would flame and then become a fine glowing piece of gauze with a soothing hissing sound.

Barefoot women servants dressed in brown or black sarongs and *kaba-jas*, long cotton blouses closed in front by a clip, worked at the tampat. They had shiny raven-black hair pulled back into a large chignon. After washing their hair they rubbed it with coconut oil, which gave it a steely blue-black sheen. Their earlobes were stretched to fit a graceful one-inch ornament. Many of these buttonlike ornaments contained *sirih*, betel leaves and a piece of betel nut, the astringent seed of the betel palm. The leaves were brushed with slaked lime, and to all this was added *catechu*, the resinous astringent of the *gambier*, a climbing pepper plant, and a chew of tobacco, the entire mixture then crushed and mixed well. The ornaments hid a supply of this addictive substance, which turned their spittle bright red and was bad for their teeth. Often they would spit it out in a long squirt, marking the ground red.

Daily the cook went down to the *kampong pasar*, the village market, to buy supplies. Purchased food was placed in a woven bamboo basket for the return trip. She draped a *slendang*, a long wide colorful cotton strip, over one shoulder and down her back, then wrapped it around the basket resting on the opposite hip. The sling then covered her breasts and met again at the shoulder, where a large impressive knot completed the loop. Our cook and other women would climb the hill barefoot in what seemed to be slow motion, for it was hot and nobody was in a hurry.

The cooking facilities for the tampat were under an awning, and charcoal *anglos*, a small stove quite similar to a hibachi, were used for heating.

Woks were used for almost any type of cooking except for rice. The rice was steamed in a *koekoesan*, a device shaped like an hourglass. The bottom was a funnel-shaped container filled with water, and the rice was placed in an upside-down funnel on top. The steam was allowed to rise through a narrow circular filter separating the two parts. Rice dishes formed the center of most meals, and our cook at the tampat combined many regional spices to give us delicious foods.

After the big midday meal, we all were supposed to rest until about 4:00, although it was hard for us kids to be inactive in this fascinating place. Around that time everybody took a turn for a dousing of water in the bathroom, and after cooling off we would meet for tea and cake on the front patio. While enjoying teatime we could study the hills colored in all variations of green, cascading down to fuse into the coffee plantation not far away and the kampong near it. From this village there was always some smoke drifting up in thin strips among the papaya and coconut trees. The coconut palms reached for the sky, their trunks often rising slightly curved from the red earth before they finally straightened, displaying their clustered green coconuts under the protective bubble of the long green comb-shaped leaves. In the background at the edge of the kampong grew flamboyant trees that formed a dainty, light green wind-swept canopy. Their crowns displayed streaks of small blossoms, a striking orange-red. Behind those trees we could see a soft pastel like picture fading into the hazy bluish-green mountain peaks, partially wrapped in dark low-hanging rain clouds. Our backyard mountain stream rushed downhill, meandering and splashing between boulders and clumps of banana trees, sometimes disappearing from view but showing up again at the border of the kampong.

Sometimes in the evening the monotonous sound of the *gamelan*, the traditional Javanese musical instrument, would drift uphill and surround us, competing with the fragrances of the almost silent tropical night. A series of different-sized brass upside-down bowls were suspended in a wooden frame and made many different brassy tones when tapped by sticks, reminiscent of a xylophone. Other musical instruments, such as the *krontjong*, something like a guitar, accompanied these melodies. Women's singing, in a low key, gently reached uphill. Motionless, I would sit there and listen. A minor echo resounded from the gamelan through the hills around us. To me the music always sounded melancholy, and I wondered what the women were singing about.

One afternoon the wind came up. The air cooled down quickly, and then suddenly we spotted a wind devil, like a miniature twister, sucking up leaves and plenty of debris. I was fascinated by it. Dust twirled around and this twister slowly descended the hill, powerful enough to uproot small trees. This event created consternation among all of us, including the servants, because it was uncommon for that area and a first for Anton and me. Mother said, "Nature is showing its power."

After six o'clock, darkness would set in, and the coolness of the night gave us a welcome touch. Dad would enjoy this quiet scene while smoking a cigar, and Mother would listen to the singing from the kampong while fanning herself with a beautiful hand-painted *kepas* displaying figures of the *Wajang Kulit*, the native shadow plays. Close by, frogs opened up in concert. Sometimes we could hear the native women singing while rhythmically pounding harvested rice in a hollowed-out tree in order to remove the husks. They usually did this work in the evenings when it was cooler, and the singing could last for hours.

One day, as a special treat, we toured the grounds of the coffee plantation nearby. We were seated in two person wooden chairs, and a long thick bamboo pole was pushed through either arm support. This chair had a canopy to protect us from the rain and sun. Four porters, two in front and two in back, carried us along. Where the bamboo rested, they protected their shoulders with gunnysacks. The trail meandered among hills planted in coffee bushes and over fast-running little creeks, which made gurgling noises and splashed down miniature waterfalls. Farther downstream we found tiny bluish fish congregating between rocks where the current was less swift and washed the pebbles. Slender trees with dainty long light green leaves were planted among the coffee shrubs to shade them and, we were told, to put nitrogen in the soil. The coffee shrubs, with their branches bent under the weight of the red berries, benefited from the filtered sunlight, and the *robusta* coffee beans would not sunburn. The women from the kampong picked the beans and carried the filled baskets on their backs to the mill, where the beans were dumped into cement troughs for sorting.

Nature was so abundant and lush in those hills. We could see all shades of green, and the sunrays would filter through the leaves, hitting the rich red volcanic soil. The air was damp but clean. We saw many colorful birds, only partially hidden among the tree branches, making chirping noises and adding to the sense of natural richness.

Here I heard the story of the coffee *loeak*, a small nocturnal predator that particularly enjoys devouring quality coffee beans. After passing through the animal, the dropped beans can be found in piles and are collected by native women and sold for a high price before being processed. These beans were considered a delicacy and were used to produce a special, very expensive coffee. That seemed to me impossible to believe, like another of Uncle Karel's lively stories, but Mother and I read more about this creature, a palm civet, and learned that other Asian countries have similar animals.

Late on another afternoon, out to the side of the house, the servants crowded around an opening in a rotted tree. They had discovered a *rajap*, a termite colony, that was readying the launching of its queens. Large termite soldiers were guarding the exit, while flying termites called *larongs* were taking off. The servants held a small mosquito net over the hole and managed to catch most of the flying queens. They then started a fire and placed a wok on the coals. After busily plucking the wings off the critters, they dumped the insects' bodies into the wok to fry. As the pan filled, the contents began to look like yellow grains of fried rice. The natives squatted down in a circle around the wok, gathered the termites with the tips of their fingers, and ate. The women encouraged me to have some. I cautiously tasted the dish and was pleasantly surprised to find that I liked it. It tasted like peanuts, and Mother thought it must be rich in protein. The women giggled and smiled as they watched my reaction.

Aunt Loes and Dad had extremely good voices, Dad's smooth baritone harmonizing with Aunt Loes' clear soprano as they sang along to the gramophone. I was fascinated by their duets. We all gathered to listen. The songs escaped the small living room and drifted outside through the open patio doors, where the native women sat and listened. In the evenings the adults would play records of classical music by Schubert, Mozart, Beethoven, Verdi, and Puccini, among others. Many times they played operas or operettas and would sing together. The music I most remember, however, included songs by Nelson Eddy and Jeanette MacDonald. We kids took it all in. Their singing penetrated the porous walls so clearly and it thrilled me. Is it any wonder that I remember those pleasant evenings? After we were sent to bed I was unable to sleep, for I wanted to hear it all.

Although Dad could only stay for ten days because of his work schedule, it was clear that this time of relaxing with his family was good for him. The rest of us were able to stay at our little mountain tampat for three weeks. Up in those hills we had a wonderful, cool vacation. I enjoyed the greatness of this mountain countryside and felt I really belonged there. I wished I could stay forever.

But times were changing, even if we had left the newspaper, full of articles describing the progress of the Japanese invasion of China, behind us in Surabaja. Where we were staying there was no newspaper and no radio. The war in China had started in 1937, and the atrocities that had taken place there were at least momentarily out of our parents' minds. Most adults wanted to believe that the invasion of China was not important to us since it was so far away, and they tried to shrug it off as two Asian countries at war with each other and not with us. I could sense Dad's concern with the situation whenever he read the paper, and I dreamed of staying here in this peaceful place, where there seemed to be no worries and no weapons.

chapter three

MALANG

After ten years of work in the tropics, Dad took his earned furlough of ten months in 1938 to go back to the Netherlands by ship.

In those days, a mail ship took four weeks to get to Europe. My brother and I experienced Holland as totally foreign and very cold. After eight months, when Dad became very worried about Hitler's annexation of Austria and the Sudetenland, he decided to return to Java, not realizing what Japan had in store. Our entire family was glad to return to Java, for we considered that our home. Steaming out of Southampton and passing the Isle of Wight at sunset, we saw the brand-new *Queen Mary* pass by, all lit up. What a sight! Aboard ship, at the entrance to the dining room, a large colored wall map was posted with a pin, daily moved to indicate our position. Mother, always the teacher, made us study this map and our progress, as a result we learned a great deal about world geography.

In Lisbon, on the Tagus River, our ship passed the small Dutch cruiser *Tromp*, with a hole in its bow as a result of a collision with a German freighter.

Our ship had painted on her sides in white letters the word "Holland," illuminated by floodlights when we passed through the Strait of Gibraltar. The Spanish Civil War was in full swing, and any unidentified ship would be attacked. That night we anchored under the shadow of the Rock of Gibraltar, which made a deep impression on us boys. When we passed the Strait of Messina at night, an eruption of Mount Stromboli accentuated our crossing. Mother got us boys out of bed to watch the sparks of fire coming out of the crater in a fantastic spray against the evening sky. On leeboard, we saw the twinkling lights of the mainland of Italy. Mother said, "I'm glad you kids were able to see that."

Weeks later, in Colombo, on the island of what was then called Ceylon, we kids had a chance to watch various activities. Ashore were coin exchangers who held cotton cloth sacks in their hands, jingling them constantly. These sacks contained golden coins, and shaking them created gold dust, which was sold separately. On our ship all portholes were ordered to be closed, to prevent coal dust from entering, a very unpopular order in that heat. On the other side of the dock, my brother and I watched the bunkering of coal, loading an old, rusty Greek hulk. On the dock, women were filling rather flat baskets and helped other women lift them on their heads, who would walk toward a gangplank leading up to the Greek's deck. In passing a man, sitting behind a table, would throw a token into their open mouth, only to remove the token after dumping the content of the basket in the ship's hold, and tucked it away in their belt, and they descended on a second gangplank to get another load. My brother compared this busy action to ants at work.

When our ship entered the harbor of Surabaja, Mother stood between us at the railing and with her arms around our shoulders exclaimed in relief, "Boys, we are home again."

My dad was an accountant working for the Eastern Province of Java. He was an Inspector of Revenue whose task was to audit the accounts of all the capital cities of the counties in Jawah Timor, Eastern Java. He would spend two weeks each visit at these various places, to come home to Malang only over the weekends. My dad's headquarters was in Surabaja, a city of one million people. This was the naval harbor, combined with an extensive merchant facility for freight. It had a coal bunkering facility. Before World War II, the U.S. Navy fleet out of Subic Bay used to bunker her ships at this port. Exports were mainly agricultural products: tobacco, sugar, tapioca, tea, coffee, rice, oil, sisal, sulfur, palm oil, kapok, castor oil, rubber, and aloe, to name just some of the bounty.

Dad would take the entire family to the places he had to audit. When inspecting Madioen and Magatan, he would stay close by at a tiny village of Ngerong, where we joined him at the Pasang Grahan, a motel just below Lake Sarangan, a caldera on the slope of Mount Lawoe. The climate was terrific. The pasang was situated on a hill overlooking an Olympic-size swim pool and tennis courts. A road rose from Madioen toward the lake at a steep grade. On this road many old cars would overheat and stop, to the delight of the native kids. Vintage cars turned around to back uphill, for they had no fuel pumps, and the gasoline flowed by gravity.

Mother had picked up our schoolwork assignments from our regular school, to be done during our stay. She always studied with us, for she was interested in learning, especially in geography and history, math, and geometry.

Up there on the mountain our routine was to get up at six, take a bath, and eat breakfast at seven. By that time Dad would descend the mountain to go to work. Then my brother and I would start to study under the tough supervision of Mom. She absolutely meant business; everything was hammered into our skulls: math, Dutch, French, history, and geography, especially that of Indonesia. We learned about the special products of the islands like tobacco, quinine, palm oil, sugar, citronella oil, teak and mahogany. We had to memorize the names of ores and minerals in the archipelago. The animals and birds were distinctly different from each other depending on their location, either belonging to the Asian or the Australian plate—the tapir lives on Celebes, for instance, and the orang utan, the forest man, lives on Borneo and Sumatra in the Asian section.

At 1:00 school was over. Lunch usually would consist of Indonesian food like *nasi goreng*, fried rice with an egg, or *gado-gado*, rice with raw vegetables such as cauliflower, bean sprouts, cucumbers, spinach, cabbage, and fried onions covered by a peanut sauce spiced with hot peppers. An additional dish we loved to eat was monkey hair—fried rasped coconut with peanuts—with fried slices of banana. In the afternoon after a short siesta we would go swimming. On the weekend Dad would pay us a quarter if we swam the entire length of the Olympic pool under water. To us that was a great deal of money, since for one penny one could buy a meal of rice with a vegetable. A new Chevy cost about 700 guilders, the guilder just about the equivalent of a dollar at that time.

By 3:00 in the afternoon the rains would set in, usually to quit after 5:00. By that time Dad had arrived home. Our family would sit on the roofed-over patio, drink tea with a cookie, and cool off in this peaceful setting. A light haze would drift uphill like a faint fog. A bird of prey circled overhead in lazy drifts, looking for food. The rice fields were planted like huge steps down the hillsides with narrow one-foot dikes separating them. Small grooves across the dikes allowed the water to cascade down to the next level. A line of long-necked ducks, *Entoks*, in contrast with the more common short-necked duck, the *bebeck*, would waddle in serpentine fashion over the narrow *sawah* dikes, one after another, making snorting noises as they slowly came uphill. Sometimes one duck would sidestep into the water to burrow its head in the muddy liquid, then come up with its catch and step back into line. A barefoot young native boy would drive them with a skinny stick, displaying a great deal of patience, closing up the line like a caboose. On his head he balanced a two-foot-wide straw hat held in place by a chinstrap. The procession finally entered the main road, there to be joined by a few water buffaloes. These were on their return trip from a bath in the river, sauntering uphill. A very small boy would sit between the horns of each, driving the big fearsome beast, his knees pressed against the skull, feet sticking backwards, to direct and encourage him to go on to the kampong, their village above us, before the sun went down.

After the rain, the frogs started their croaking concert, which continued throughout the night. At bedtime I could listen to it, and it worked like a lullaby. The yellow-red glow of the sunset would shine over the hazy blue-green mountain ridge to the south as the dark rainclouds started to lift over the Lawoe.

In the tropics, the night always sets in abruptly. Soon thereafter we would go inside to steer clear of the mosquitoes, which could spread the deadly malaria.

While we were in Ngerong, my parents wanted to climb Mount Lawoe. They planned to leave around 2:00 a.m., traveling at night to avoid the heat and arriving in time to observe the sunrise. We boys were told to come along. How exciting! This was our first attempt to go to the top of a mountain. We rented small horses, a problem for our tall mother. Her feet dangled from the too short stirrups. Two sailors from a Dutch light cruiser *De Ruyter* were staying at our pasang, and they decided to join us on the climb.

At that hour of the morning it was pitch-black, chilly, wet, and foggy. We had flashlights, but they spooked the horses. It was much better to let our eyes adapt to the darkness of the night. The horses went up the slope single-file on a narrow winding path that circled the mountain peak. Close to the top my dad's horse bolted, for we were passing sulfur vents that hissed in the blackness of the night with a strong stench. Dad was able to stay in the saddle, in contrast with Anton, who was thrown off on the return trip. His stallion smelled the stable at the end of the excursion and galloped away.

We reached the crest of the mountain at about 5:00. It was still dark, and we settled down trying to get some sleep, not easy, for the mosquitoes wanted to make our acquaintance. The sailors lit up cigarettes and Dad a cigar in an attempt to keep these marauders at bay. The rise of the sun was sudden, a huge red ball that appeared quickly. The sky surrounding the sun was a bright yellow-white all along the eastern horizon. We sat there and absorbed this view. The light rays started to sprinkle over the dense forest below us, revealing different colors of green. The mountainside sloped down into an eerie haze.

Upon our arrival back at the pasang, everything was in turmoil. We learned quickly that the Germans had invaded the Netherlands on May 10, 1940. The owner of the lodgings was an older German, Mr. Graber, who had retired from the former Dutch East Indian army. He looked like a ramrod, always the old military man, but quite friendly. He had fought in the thirty-year-long Atjeh War in the northern part of Sumatra. His wife, a native, did the cooking, and they had a five-year-old boy who stole Mother's heart; she was always giving him cookies. The police picked Mr. Graber up and sent him to a detention camp. I noticed that my parents became very quiet at the time. They seemed to realize that hard times were ahead.

Dad decided to return to Malang as soon as possible, cutting short his stay. Mother had a difficult time accepting the idea that the friendly, graying German who had lived most of his life in the Indies was now a dangerous enemy.

chapter four

MERBABOE PARK

After our return from the trip to Europe, my parents established a comfortable new home for us at 27 Djalan Guntur in Malang, Java, opposite Merbaboe Park. This park and the *pasar*, the market, were next to a bridge over the river Oro Oro Dowo. It followed the same route downhill as the important road by that name leading to the heart of the city. The near end of the park was planted in tall trees, Tjemaras, which had fine long needles that would rustle in the wind. The park's center was sunken and planted with bougainvillea, honeysuckle, and cannas where we kids used to play.

Malang was surrounded by five volcanic mountains and built on a plateau about 1,300 feet high, making the nights so much cooler than the surrounding plain. A good cool night's sleep was so important. In Surabaja, even during the night, the high temperature could cause heavy perspiration and sleepless nights. Of these five volcanoes, three were active. Semeru, the highest at 10,000 feet, erupted while we were living there, in 1941. The lava flow was quite unusual, heading so slowly south toward the Indian Ocean that a person could out walk the thick, gooey substance. The area around Malang was dusted with an inch of ash, and since the homes were open, we had a mess on our hands. Everything sounded quite muffled, and no birds to be heard, just like after a heavy snowfall. The ash had fallen in the afternoon, followed by the typical rain shortly after 4:00 p.m., and the yard absorbed the ash very easily. Several minor earthquakes happened at the time of the eruption, but only rattled the doors.

Ardjuno, visible in the northwest, was a tall, beautiful cone; many a painter placed her colorful blue-green appearance on canvas. Kawi, located south from Ardjuno, had been quiet for a long time. Kelud and Bromo completed the encirclement of Malang. Many plantations were draped on the hills surrounding the town, their tea, coffee, rubber, teakwood, tobacco, and aloe brought down by railway for transport to the harbor in Surabaja. South of Malang in Toeren were large fields of cassava, used in making pearl tapioca, in those days heavily used as laundry starch. The

European firms that owned the plantations and factories had to lease the land, since by law they were not allowed to own it.

Three miles north from Malang was a real modern military airfield, built with underground aviation fuel tanks. This airfield was named Singo-sari, after the nearby village. Close by were remnants of old temples built by Hindus who came out of India by the way of the Malacca Straits to settle on the islands of Sumatra, Java, and Bali. One temple was small and looked like a gate with a steep tower. I used to walk through this arch and toward a small dam in a creek where women and their toddlers would bath. There also was a swimming pool nearby tucked in against a hillside. Against the high side, a line of naked female busts hewn out of basalt sat on the edge of the pool. Several must have had water spurting out of their nipples in these earlier times, and I could imagine a harem here. A few miles further on a narrow road led to the old *kraton*, once the elaborate dwelling of a sultan, now mostly in ruins. Predating the Muslim era were two huge stone pot-bellied Hindu like statues that used to flank the en-trance but had toppled and were partially buried on either side of the dirt road leading to it. They were excavated, and one, about fifteen feet tall, was pulled up into an erect position again.

The ancient kingdom of Singosari played a dominant role in Eastern Java about a thousand years ago. I found its history fascinating. In 1200, a Chinese army of the Khan, brought in aboard junks, landed in the Wonok-romo area, which is now the southern part of Surabaja. The Khan's repre-sentative to the Sultan of Mataram in Jawa Tengah, central Java, had been beheaded when he demanded obedience to the Khan, whence the army, which, joined by the Sultan of Singosari, defeated the mighty Mataram. After that, the Sultan of Singosari burned the junks at the mouth of the Kali Brantas, the river that silted the land area on which over seven hun-dred years the current city of Surabaja was built, stretching itself north to the sea. Then the Sultan attacked and massacred the Chinese. The Bata-vian Oil Company drilled and found oil in the exact vicinity where once the junks were burned and sank. The drilling uncovered Chinese coins and other old historical items and remnants of junks. Centuries later Sura-baja was relocated to land deposited by the river and became the naval harbor of Indonesia.

Germany invaded the Netherlands on May 10, 1940. Unexpected prob-lems were created when three bullies in my school approached me and accused me of being pro-German, yelling, "Stutterheim is a German name!" Even though I knew that I was outclassed and outnumbered, I attacked and lost the fight badly. Afterward I picked up my bike and went home, only to be reported missing after the break at school. Mother was quite surprised, for usually I did not fight, but she did not scold me. The next day the headmaster called me in, and I explained that I could not reveal my face after the fight. He accepted that. Within a week I was in trouble again, this time with the minister who taught the Bible class. He claimed that I should have memorized an assignment. But I had no knowledge of it, since it was announced during the hour after the fight when I had gone home. The minister became very upset; his face turned red, and he scowled at me. Some other kids tried to explain the circumstances, but he ordered me to stand in the corner in the back of the class. I never said a word, just picked up my books and walked out to leave the school on my bike. I felt that it was unfair to make me stand in that corner.

By the time I came home I was so upset that my hands shook. I had a great deal of explaining to do, first at home, then the next day in school. Mother told me to go back to school that day, but I refused. She told me that my stubbornness was leading me to nowhere. She held my hand and cried, however I resented that minister so much that even Mother's tears did not make me go back to the Bible class. I really had enjoyed reading the stories in the Old Testament. I finished reading those stories at home, which certainly had Mom's approval.

I received a bicycle with a headlight as a reward for making good grades in school. Elated, I would take the bike and explore the outskirts of Malang and beyond. I reached Singosari and Wendit, two old places about seven miles away. Wendit was a native recreational and tourist attraction. A winding, tree-lined gravel road led to a large shallow lake, its shoreline partially covered by a growing plant, *kangkung,* that would soon prove important to our survival. The Javanese told me that kangkung eaten in large quantities could cause people to go mad. However, at Wendit, the greatest pests were the gray Java monkeys. They swarmed all over to beg peanuts, bananas, and other tidbits sold by merchants in makeshift shanties alongside the road. When the monkeys felt ignored, they turned aggressive. Often they grabbed a visitor's pants or shirt, showing their teeth. I usually gave food to the ones that clutched babies against their chests and was always amazed that these little ones never fell, even if the mother jumped from tree branch to tree branch.

In the foothills of the Bromo crater are still remnants of Hindu tribes, just like the people on the island of Bali. They used to live isolated lives, and many women among them had huge pigeon craws, goiters the size of a grapefruit. It drew Anton's attention when he spotted these women walking on the side of the road. Mother explained, showing us pictures of how the salt was collected from the saltpans of the island of Madura, where the government added the iodine that was lacking in their diet.

Anton was a good student and an avid reader. However, he could display spells of temper, in which he stamped his foot on the ground and balled his fists. My parents were determined to put a stop to this behavior. One way Dad countered this display was to instruct him how wrongly he balled his fists, for Dad used to box in his teens. He challenged Anton to hit him, which made Anton smile. My brother outgrew his disposition and started to quiz dad about his sport activities. He asked Dad, who used to referee soccer games, what it takes to make a good referee. Father's answer was, "Outrun the crowd after the game is over."

Dad was a sports enthusiast. He played ping-pong in the evening and was an excellent swimmer. He was a rather quiet man, strict and conservative, but he loved to dance and at any opportunity dragged mother on the dance floor. Waltzes, especially Strauss, made him twirl around the open spaces; however, it made Mother dizzy, and he loved it that she, a head taller, had to hang on to him. She would be out of breath, but he could continue endlessly.

On the weekends our family would go swimming, often targeting a different pool in different resorts nearby. Malang had a huge Olympic-sized pool, as did the resorts Poedjon, and Tretes, both high in the hills in absolutely beautiful locations. The crests of the hills were covered by green trees, which by an ordinance to prevent erosion could not be cut. This law applied to the entire Dutch East Indies, but things like erosion control were ignored after the Japanese invaded.

Dad got into trouble once for reporting the sultan of Bodjonogoro for inappropriate financial transactions. The governor of Java, Van Der Plas, told him that the case of a person in that position should have been discussed first with him. The sultan got off with a "discussion." Politics and "*adat*," the custom of the people, played a role here. A sultan could not do anything wrong according to Javanese custom. Instead of being annoyed by such limitations, Dad chose to accept such cultural differences gracefully.

In Malang, one of our neighbors was a naval officer, the commandant of the Dutch frigate *Soemba*. He invited all neighborhood children to watch some black silent movies when Santa Claus's birthday came around on December 5. Most of the silent films were about his ship, and the captain told us about the various scenes. Several were made in the eastern part of Indonesia, revealing Japanese fishermen within the three-mile zone, at that time considered territorial waters. These ships were boarded and inspected. The captain told us that many of these fishermen were actually ranking naval officers studying the coastlines. There were also cartographers aboard, making detailed maps of the coastlines. Some of these maps were far more up to date than ours, he told us. The maps were usually found in the main cabin, hidden in a secret compartment. He told us that they had to break open walls to find them. One part of the movie showed the Japanese captain being held at gunpoint against the wall while Dutch sailors were cracking open and splintering a hidden compartment. A triumphant showing of a map followed this scene. Another scene that fascinated me was when *Soemba* had three Japanese fishing boats in tow. Their bows were like dolphins riding the waves, and it seemed as if our ships were really able to protect our waters. We were told that some of the fishing vessels were confiscated, but most of them were released after they paid a fine for fishing in our waters.

Our host said that Japan was getting ready for a possible invasion. He also expressed the opinion that the Dutch navy did not have a sufficient number of vessels to patrol all the long coastlines. The distances were simply too vast. At the time I did not believe him. He told us how old our warships were, and certainly there were no capital ships, only two small cruisers and an escort cruiser, about eight destroyers, and mostly old submarines of the "K" class. Additionally, there were a few frigates and mine sweepers. My friend Bob Tuizinga, also present, had received from his dad, who was the captain of the hospital ship *Op ten Noort*, the British book *Jane's Fighting Ships*, and the naval officer urged us to look at this book. It contained up-to-date information on all the navies in the world, and we were awed to see the pictures of the huge ships of Japan with their pagoda superstructures.

This evening fired my interest in naval vessels. Afterward I shook hands with the captain and thanked him. When I came home I could not stop talking about this movie and all we had discussed. That annoyed my mother, who was not the least bit interested in those stories. However, we studied Jane's book. World War II had started in Europe in September 1939, when Germany invaded Poland, and when certain warships were mentioned in the news we had a good idea how they looked like. My knowledge of warships surprised Dad. Again, so many adults I knew expressed their opinion that Japan really did not have the ability to conquer Southeast Asia. The Japanese war products were made of inadequate materials, they said.

Dad discussed with mother and me the visit of a large Japanese delegation under Yoshizawa Kenkichi during June 1941 to the capital, Batavia. The newspapers mentioned the developments of these economic discussions. Their minister of economy, Kobayashi, remained aboard the ship *Nissho Maru* anchored in the harbor, Tandjung Priok. The delegation politely stated that Japan was in great need of products found in the East Indies, since it had been at war with China since 1936. Japan had just taken over Indochina from the French Vichy government. Japan wanted oil, bauxite, copra, tin, rubber, quinine, and timber.

In the end, the Japanese proposal was quite aggressive. The request meant no less than economic surrender, impossible for Dutch government in exile in London, in close alliance with the British, to accept. Furthermore, the Japanese intended to bring in their own laborers to do the work. They proposed to include Japanese soldiers to "protect" their workers. The Dutch government was willing to trade, but not under those conditions, and the Dutch leaders were especially appalled by the idea of accepting imperial troops.

The Japanese consul in Batavia, who participated in the discussions, tried to soften the blow by stating that this trade surrender was in the best interest of the Indies. After the Japanese invaded Java in 1942 this consul let it be known how the Dutch could have saved themselves a great deal of the harsh treatment during the occupation. Later on some of the Dutch doubted that their treatment by the Japanese would have been different. In any event, *Nissho Maru* lifted her anchor at daybreak and steamed away in order to save face by avoiding the Dutch government's rejection of the Japanese offer.

Throughout the Dutch East Indies there were more than seven thousand Japanese citizens, who had officially received an equal status with the Europeans, in contrast with the Chinese. Most of the Japanese on Java were storekeepers. In Surabaja, for example, we had all shopped at the Tjijoda hardware store. Within a week of the departure of the *Nissho Maru*, just about all the Japanese living in the Indies closed their stores and left. Several returned after the invasion as officers, with the advantage that they could speak Dutch and Indonesian.

The Dutch government started a campaign against espionage and posted signs stating: "Watch for the Moesoeh Mata," the enemy's eye. They also campaigned against *chabar angin*, news by the wind, or wild rumors. Posters appeared showing a gathering of chickens while a rooster stood in the background holding his wing behind his ear to listen. Written on the poster was the admonition, "Leave cackling to chickens."

The disappearance of our Japanese neighbors and the government warnings should have been a sinister hint about what was going to happen. Instead, life went on as before. The attack on Pearl Harbor came six months later.

During 1941 the days in Malang were peaceful, even if there was a war going on between the Netherlands and Germany. The only evidence of that war was when Dutch warships came to the Indies or our merchant ships were reported sunk in the Atlantic or, closer, in the Indian Ocean.

We children felt safe to go anywhere. We were free to converse with the local native people. As teenagers, we would play soccer in the fields on the outskirts of Malang and explore the surrounding areas. There was nothing to fear.

We had servants, but mother insisted that we two boys do all our own chores, such as pick up our toys, clean the bookshelves, and collect our dirty clothes. Our female cook had been with us from the start. She was excellent at preparing both European and Indonesian food. She was married to our gardener, and they had one little boy. They lived in the servant quarters. She always helped me to put my little garden together. In the backyard I raised tomato plants and brown pole beans, and I planted a *zuurzak* tree that produced football-sized fruits, quite sour and a delicious ingredient in our homemade, hand-cranked ice cream, a Sunday treat. Daily she would make her trip to the market one block away in order to buy our food. To our dismay, our cook developed festering boils on both sides of her neck. These worsened slowly, so mother took her to the doctor. The verdict was disastrous: this was open tuberculosis, extremely contagious. Of course, this was horrible news for her, but also frightening for Mother, for our cook handled our daily food.

Mother told her that she had to go to a special hospital for treatments and my parents would pay for it. The woman refused, stating that going to a hospital would mean going there to die. This was true, since the natives waited so long that it was often too late. When they finally entered the hospital, it seemed they came there to die. Mother had to let the cook go, and they both cried. When the cook and her family returned to their native village, I thought she would surely die there.

We had a Lionel O-27 train set, a very expensive item in those days, set up on wooden slats. Anton and I made hills out of sawdust, and when cleaning up, stored the sawdust in empty kerosene cans. We had seven hundred toy soldiers and some forms to pour our own lead figures. Then we painted them. We exchanged the forms with other kids. The supply of lead became a problem, so I climbed up the roof, where the valleys were formed by curved lead plates. I cut off the soft edges and felt very triumphant; but when the rains came Dad found out, and I ended up with a glowing rear end. Another disaster happened when I poured boiling lead into a form and some splattered on the back of my left hand. I tried to shake the hot lead off, but it stuck sizzling to my skin. I covered it with butter, but I could not hide the injury. That was the end of our soldier production.

Some friends of my parents were appalled that we boys played with war toys. They were dead set against it. I answered angrily, and I had to apologize and was sent to my room. That evening I told my parents that the entire episode was unfair. Dad told me that I should have kept my opinion to myself.

At the edge of our neighborhood, where all the streets were named after mountains, ran a narrow-gauge "sugarcane train." The tracks ran through a narrow, shallow ravine with a bridge high above. During harvest time, each afternoon at 5:00, to the delight of the neighborhood kids, the small, waddling, smoke-belching engine would approach the bridge, blowing a warning whistle. Its speed was slow and its approach noisy, for it was pulling thirty sugarcane-loaded cars uphill. Upon seeing us, the engine driver would shake his fist, knowing what we were up to. We would sit on the railing of the bridge and time the jump to land on the stack of canes on the cart, grab several of them, and roll off the train sideways. The art was not to land between the carts.

Among us boys it was a daring, highly dangerous form of excitement. The most daring was my neighbor J. Dutry van Heaften. Bob Tuizinga was there, too, but he was too heavy to jump. Anton was not present, since I was too concerned that he would leak the story by accident. We cut the canes in four-inch sections with my Swiss army pocketknife. While we sauntered home we would suck and chew at the end of the cane, enjoying the sweet taste. Our little group became popular for passing out pieces of cane, and by the time we hit Merbaboe Park there was a noisy crowd savoring our booty.

When Dad was home he taught me chess. We usually played in the evening or late afternoon, when he had a single beer each day. I enjoyed the game immensely. He was very patient and taught me how to anticipate an opponent's move.

At this time new stamps were issued to promote Islam, the predominant religion in the islands here, but Mother and I also discovered Filipino stamps with an overprint of the commonwealth. This brought up the topic of a possible commonwealth for the Dutch East Indies, which was still a colony. At that time there were close to seventy million inhabitants, of whom a quarter-million were Dutchmen. Dad was quite reserved in his opinion, but I knew he loved the country and its people. He surprised me by stating that he wanted to retire in the hills above Malang. Mother agreed with the notion of settling in a bungalow in Batu with a rose garden.

Many Dutchmen would not agree with my parent's idea of gradual self-rule for the Indies. Mother believed that the Volksraad, the representatives of the Dutch government in Batavia, should be given more autonomy. One moderate member of the Volksraad proposed in 1936 to declare equality of the Indies with the Netherlands, and in ten years, independence. A clear majority agreed with him. Finally, in 1938, the Dutch government replied, rejecting his proposal. As a result, the Indonesians had nothing to gain by fighting the Japanese, in contrast with the Filipinos, who had that promise of independence to look forward to. Mother also felt that a member of the royal family should come to the Indies to show their interest, but this never happened. Many Dutch people shared this feeling about the faraway Indies, for in those days, a KLM flight took five days, in contrast with a boat trip of thirty days.

My cousin Greetje, Dad's niece, was married to an officer in the Dutch Air Force. They were stationed in Singosari, five miles from our home. Her husband was the captain of a Glenn-Martin bomber. Once, while attending a swimming event, my cousin was called away. One of the bombers at Singosari had crashed. All crews were called up to take to the air immediately. This was done to overcome their fear. Again it was a warning that war could happen at any time.

chapter five

WAR

Close to the sugar cane tracks lived the family Bruinvis, very good friends of our family. Wim Bruinvis taught gymnastics at the high school. He was tall and skinny and had a good sense of humor. Annie, his wife, and Mother were very close friends. She had two baby girls, Truus and Lieneke. Often in the evening they would come over to play ping-pong at our roofed-over back patio, where we had excellent lighting.

Early Monday morning on December 8, 1941, while Dad and I were playing chess and Mother and Anton were playing cards in the front room, we heard bicycle tires braking in our gravel driveway. Wim Bruinvis ran up to the porch, trying to catch his breath while standing between the wide-open sliding doors.

"Did you hear?" he blurted. "The Japanese attacked Pearl Harbor and smashed the American navy." Deep, astonished silence followed. Dad took a deep breath and said, "My God."

Dad, for a reason I do not recall, was supposed to leave later that day by train for Eastern Java, but after this news he decided to go to Surabaja instead. Mother grabbed Anton and pulled him onto her lap, which Anton resisted. Dad and Wim turned on the radio to receive further information.

My world turned upside down. I had been in the eighth grade for sixth months, and found the school now confiscated by the military.

Wim was drafted in the Landstorm and sent to Batavia. Dad had to stay in Surabaja, for the ministry was short on personnel due to the draft. Dad's eyesight was poor, and he did not qualify for military service. He moved in with his sister Loes, who owned her home and an established business. Annie and Mother became even closer friends.

Soon we heard about the daily bombardments of the harbor, Tandjong Perak, and the city of Surabaja.

After the Japanese struck at Pearl Harbor, not a soul in the Indies could expect neutrality any longer. Our mother country, the Netherlands, her government in exile in London, immediately declared war, and belated defensive preparations were set in motion in the islands. It was naive to think they would be at all effective against the powerful Japanese forces. Drastic changes faced each family every day, from food supplies and school schedules to the sudden absence of most able-bodied men from our communities.

During the months of December 1941 and January 1942 the situation in the Indies changed at a fast rate. The radio was used more than ever; our family became news-hungry. At first, the initial war activity took place in the far away outlying districts, including Singapore and the Philippines. The Japanese were winning every battle, but what was worse and a shocking surprise to us was the speed of their advances toward the main island of Java. It seemed that nothing was able to stop them. Nobody, from the governor on down, knew what to expect.

It took the Japanese only three months to succeed in occupying the vast area of the East Indies. They entered from three directions. The western approach, moving past Singapore through the South China Sea into Southern Sumatra, aimed for oil-rich Palembang. Initially, Japanese paratroopers tried to seize the oil fields, but they were defeated.

However, Japanese troops landed at the coast and the Dutch were overwhelmed. At the same time, they occupied the island of Bangka, effectively sealing off the southern escape route from Singapore.

The northern spearhead came down the Makassar Strait, targeting the oil centers, the island of Tarakan, and the harbor of Balikpapan on the east coast of Borneo. Radio broadcasts informed us about the tragic developments in the Strait. The island of Tarakan was weak in its defenses, and a lonely Dutch minesweeper was lost there. Four old American destroyers, four-stackers of World War I vintage, withdrew through the strait heading south. The defenders destroyed the oil fields and installations at Balikpapan, enraging the Japanese when they realized they had not gained the oil installations intact. This meant that their warships had to burn heavy, crude oil, high in sulfur. Most of the defenders lost their lives and even civilians were murdered at those locations. Hearing about the killings gave us even more cause for fear.

The Japanese also came at us through the Spice Islands, forming the eastern part of the pincer, to land paratroopers at Kendari, a large new airfield on Southern Celebes. From there they could reach Eastern Java by air. Their army and navy fanned toward the islands of Ambon and Bali.

After they conquered these strategic places, the shipping lanes to Australia were blocked. Again the radio related accounts of the heroic defense of Ambon by Australian and Dutch soldiers. It took the Japanese days to take the island, and they lost a ship in the harbor. This news was heralded as a boost to our morale, which was at a very low point.

Mother decided in February to go visit Aunt Loes in order to be close to Dad. We boys joined the train trip. We spent many an hour in my aunt's sturdy bomb shelter. The radio station close by was hit, and we realized that the risk was coming closer all the time.

We boys would stand in the front yard watching the thick clouds of the burning harbor. Mother forbade this out of fear of shrapnel, dragging us away into the dwelling.

My aunt's house was large and she had several naval sailors as boarders. From them we heard the daily worsening news. One of the sailors was aboard the destroyer *Piet Hein*, which later sank in the Bali Strait.

By the end of February, Dad and Mother decided that Mother and we boys had to go back to Malang, where it probably would be safer, especially after the defeat of our allied navies on the Java Sea.

The Japanese and Korean troops in Japanese service landed on March 1, 1942, on Java. One group invaded west of Batavia and the other one made for Djapara east of Semarang. Singapore had surrendered on February 15, and there was utter chaos among the British, Dutch, and Australian armies. Many refugees from Singapore came to Sumatra, while British army units went to Padang on the west coast of Sumatra and the RAF fled to Palembang. General Blackburn brought Australian troops to southern Sumatra only to move on to Java. All that was happening was a delaying action to give the Allies time to regroup.

At the Battle of the Java Sea, the combined navies of Australia, the United States, Britain, and the Netherlands suffered tragic defeat. There was no air coverage, and most of our ships were lost. As a result the entire northern coast of Java was exposed, and the Japanese entered Bandung, the headquarters of the Dutch army, on March 6.

Two days later, the Dutch East Indies surrendered. When the radio announced this news we listened silently to the national anthem with tears in our eyes. Then the radio went silent.

In our area, Japanese shock troops pulled up from Kediri coming over the pass and entered Malang from the Southwest. They rode bicycles with solid tires. They wore *fundoshi*, or loincloths, tennis shoes split at the big toe like a pig's foot, and five-flapped caps that covered the napes of their necks. They looked dirty and primitive, a ragtag army, but they were the victors. Rifles were mounted to the bicycles. Other infantry pulled artillery uphill with ropes by hand, no horses, no trucks. The officers walked alongside them and whipped their own men.

They scared the hell out of the women, for we had been told of a rape that took place in Ngawi, when a minister's wife was used by an entire platoon while her husband was tied to a post. This incident happened when the Japanese were on the way to Malang. Almost instantaneously, every woman started to wear long pants to avoid showing their legs to the invaders.

In front of our home was the beautiful Merbaboe Park, where the troops parked their trucks, made their cooking fires, and bivouacked. They placed a guard right in front of our home, which, though my mother did not like it at all, was actually a safeguard. The next morning one soldier came to us and spoke only Japanese, made it clear that he needed a broom, he made that kind of motion; he bowed when leaving, to return the sweeper a few hours later. Again he bowed. We did not know how to respond.

After about a week they started to pull up stakes and left one Dutch disabled truck behind. That afternoon three Indonesian teenagers started to take the wheels off. All of a sudden the Japanese police showed up, arrested them, and beat them while they were dragged off. We learned the next day that they were hanged at the aloon-aloon from the huge banyan tree. They were left there to rot in the rain for an entire week, and in the terrific heat the bodies started to sag and fluid went to their legs. The smell was such that everyone avoided the area.

The intimidation of the population was thus very effective. We had heard from the escaped British forces what took place in Singapore. This was confirmed after the war. The Japanese beheaded several Chinese and placed the heads on bamboo stakes adjacent to their guardhouses. On other locations several severed heads were displayed on a shelf. The guardhouses were placed at strategic locations, and the Japanese made everybody stop and face the guard to bow. People could not avoid seeing this monstrous display.

We realized that tough times were ahead, but we could not dream how bad they really would be.

Immediately the Japanese demanded all Dutch money to be turned in, especially silver coins. The banks were closed and all savings confiscated. They told us that the year was 2602, and not 1942.

Everybody was supposed to receive an identification paper printed in solid Japanese characters.

The last islands to be occupied were Lombok, Soemba, Soembawa, and Ternate. The only place not occupied by Japan was Merauke on the southern coast of New Guinea, located opposite Port Darwin in Australia. The Dutch flag was never lowered in this tiny outpost.

Such were the sudden developments in the former Dutch East Indies that changed my pleasant childhood in this beautiful, peaceful country.

chapter six

UNCERTAIN TIMES
IN MALANG

One day at the end of March Dad returned from Surabaja by train. He had lost his job, which was not surprising, since the Japanese were replacing Europeans with their own staff. As the train entered the Malang station, it slowed down and Dad noticed that the platform was crawling with Japanese soldiers. He did not trust what he saw because he had heard about other men who had been arrested on suspicion of being members of the Dutch military trying to blend into the civilian population. Dad decided to leap from the rolling train as it slowed to enter the yard. He landed in the bushes and rolled, but unfortunately tore his right calf muscle. After crawling through the perimeter fence he flagged down a Demo, a three-wheeler with the motor built over the front wheel, whose driver brought him home.

His arrival created quite a bit of consternation. Mother called a doctor, who examined him and announced that he would have to stay off his leg for four to six weeks. Events were challenging our family on every side. The only good thing about Dad's injury was that we enjoyed the many weeks while he was home. However, our financial situation became precarious for my parents' savings had been confiscated. Mother's response was to buy sugar and djeroeks, similar to oranges, and make orange marmalade that she sold in our neighborhood.

During this time Dad listened to Radio Australia, which was strictly forbidden. The Japanese had sealed all radios with wax to cover their dials. Dad found a way to heat the wax to loosen and put it back in place afterward. He would sit under the vanity table in the bedroom, surrounded by stacked pillows at night, because there was less chance that people would visit us then, since a curfew was in force. In any case, shortwave was always better received at night. Once he became very excited, for he heard of the ferocious carrier sea battle in the Eastern Solomon Islands on August 24, 1942. He tried to tell us how significant this was, for it was the first time that the Japanese had not won a sea battle during the war to date.

Within five weeks Dad was able to get around, and he found a job close by, doing accounting work.

Other smaller actions of the Japanese had a powerful negative effect on us kids as well. Layangan, kite flying, which so many people enjoy world-wide, was a teenage national pastime on the island of Java. All kids used to make kites, tying two pieces of thin bamboo like a cross with iron thread and covering the frame with a special lightweight paper. We used over-cooked rice as glue so the paper folded over the thread would stay in place. The real sport was to fly a kite high up in the air and make it dive behind another to cut the line. When the severed kite would whirl down to earth, all the kids would run after it to catch it. Anton and I pounded glass in a mortar and added glue. After a thorough mixing we dipped our fingers in it and ran the thread through them to give the line more cutting power. The sport and competition was worth the discomfort to our fingers.

The Japanese banned kite flying. They did not say why.

The Japanese paranoia that we came to know very well turned also against the Boy Scouts and Salvation Army. Apparently this suspicion was based on the use of uniforms and ranks within these groups. The Boy Scouts disbanded rather quickly; no parents were willing to risk their children being arrested by the Kempeitai, the Japanese military police.

The new police force, after all Dutch members were eliminated, became an extension of the Kempeitai. This helped to accomplish what the Japanese were obviously aiming for, a steadily increasing confinement and intimidation of all Europeans.

One day in September 1942, when Dad was away at work, Mother learned through the grapevine that all white men had been arrested. Exempted were Germans and Swiss. Even Swedes were taken, even though Sweden was officially neutral.

At age forty-six, Dad found himself behind barbed wire in a large building located on the main highway to Surabaja. We were able to visit him there, allowed to stand close to the barbed wire and talk. Mother had a real problem giving him a kiss through the barbed wire, and she started to cry, which made my Dad extremely uncomfortable. Dad would hold her hand with both of his but hardly said anything.

After Dad's incarceration we had to turn in all radios. A week later the Japanese methodically searched all homes in the European community. It was frightening to us when they found a burned-out radio tube in our drawer. Mother had the greatest problem explaining to the Japanese officer that it had burned out. It was a close call, for the Kempeitai always got involved in cases that suggested spying or communication off the island, and usually people picked up by them never came back.

Another incident that shocked our community came with the arrest of our Dutch Reformed minister. We kids played with his two children, since the family lived just down the road. We learned that the minister had been involved in trying to create an underground railroad to get people who were pursued by the Japanese out to the Indian Ocean where they could be picked up by a submarine.

Once the Kempeitai picked him up we never saw him again. After weeks without a word from him we became to believe that he had been killed. The Kempeitai used to put their prisoners in pig crates and stack them on trucks, then transport them to Surabaja, where they were loaded aboard a ship and at night dumped at sea. Nobody ever survived.

Mother was a strong and capable woman, and she comforted herself about Dad's imprisonment with the knowledge that at least he had not been picked up by the Kempeitai. After about one month we were allowed to see Dad again through the barbed wire. This second visit was no easier for Mother, seeing Dad confined and losing weight, but her own determined will was leading her and she firmly told us that our family would survive this separation. She cried a great deal after she came home from this last visit, but outside the fence she tried to keep her spirits up for Dad's sake. We were able to lift a rolled up one-inch thin mattress over the wire to him, which Mother had made and Anton carried. Many women made those for the anticipated transport to Kesilir, an isolated spot at the eastern-most end of Java. We knew where he was sent because the men had been told what their destination was.

One morning a Japanese officer walked into our front door and bowed. He spoke some English and informed Mother that he came for a visit. Then he set down on our large couch and said, "When our troops moved into your park I spotted you as good looking woman and I decided to visit you later on." He demanded whiskey. Mother walked to our side bar and showed him a totally empty drawer. As a precaution she had poured all alcohol into the drain. She told us two boys in Dutch, "Do not leave the room." Then she turned to the officer and said, "I do not serve uninvited guests."

The officer got the message, stood up, and, without saying good-bye, left.

Mother suddenly sat down and released a deep sigh while her hands started to shake. Anton ran up to her and gave her a big hug, while I told her how I admired her for standing up to this officer.

A few days after Dad was taken away, I was riding my bicycle through Oro Oro Dowo, alongside the river by that name, when a Japanese guard stopped and arrested me. Although I was only fourteen, I was already six feet tall and towered above him. He was clearly convinced that I was an adult. Other people who knew me and witnessed this arrest alerted Mother. She swooped down with my birth certificate. Pushing this piece of paper literally in the guard's face, she pointed and tapped her finger at the impressive stamp at the bottom and eventually got it across to him that I was underage. The guard could not understand a word of her argument, and neither could we understand what he was trying to say. The flustered soldier waved his arm and clearly was reluctant to let me go, but in the end he gave in to my Mother's will. It had been hard enough for her to see Dad go; losing one of her boys might have been too much to bear.

Even after that episode I wanted to see what was going on in town; the thought of staying close to home was unreasonable to me. One day, a neighbor boy named Frans and I went by bike to the railroad station in the early afternoon. We stopped to look around in front of the government building at a roundabout. Then, as we passed, a Japanese guard stopped us. At first we ignored him. Then the man yelled at us and threatened to shoot by raising his Arisaka rifle to his shoulder. He was furious. Next to him was a flagpole with the Japanese flag. He made it clear that we had failed to bow to both him and the flag. We did not understand his Japanese, nor did he speak Malay. He gestured that we had to place our bikes against a tree. He pointed to where we had to stand and face him, a five-foot-tall man who held in his left hand a rifle with attached bayonet that reached at least a foot above his head. He bowed and gestured for us to do the same. After this demonstration he swung his right arm to hit Frans in the face. Quickly we bowed in imitation. As a result he missed us, and he screamed, turning purple in rage.

I took off my glasses, for it became clear that we were going to get a beating. He hit us hard, again and again. Then he forced us into the hot sunshine, where we had to stand to attention. As sunset approached he hit our faces again, and made us bow deep to him and the flag. Then, abruptly, he motioned that we could leave on our bicycles. We were perplexed when he let us go. It was dark when we arrived home to find our mothers frantic and in tears, not knowing what happened. We decided to avoid all Japanese posts in town.

All streets in the district we lived were named after Indonesian mountains. In December 1942 this area was declared to be the region where all Europeans had to be relocated. The implications were significant. Our area became a camp, christened in Dutch De Wijk, "the neighborhood." The size of this newly formed camp was about one mile wide and two and a half miles long, completely surrounded by a barbed-wire fence fifteen feet high. Several gates were established, but the most important one was adjacent to the bridge and pasar. Here, in the market, we were allowed to trade freely with the Chinese and Javanese who could enter this restricted area. Months later, when the gates finally were permanently closed, armed Indonesian guards were posted. We called them Hei-Hos, from the Japanese *hohei*, meaning "foot soldier."

Gradually, all Europeans from the surrounding plantations and small towns dribbled in. By the time everybody had arrived in De Wijk, its population was estimated at ten thousand, all women and children. This included the Europeans from Djember, a town in Eastern Java, centrally located among so many plantations. They were brought in early after the adult men had been removed and sent to Kesilir.

chapter seven

KESILIR

In October 1942, Mother told us that she had obtained a permit for the three of us to travel to Kesilir, where Dad was imprisoned. At last we were allowed to visit him.

It was a onetime occasion. A number of other women from Malang were also allowed to travel with their children on one designated day. Mother had to secure a special permit, written completely in Japanese. Even though we were short on money, she somehow produced enough for the railroad tickets. Where she got this remained a mystery to us, but most likely she sold one of her few pieces of jewelry at the market, where many Chinese traders were always present. On one hand, she was so very determined to see Dad, but on the other hand she was quite anxious, not knowing what was ahead of us. Mother had never traveled far by herself, and the presence of the hostile Japanese forces was continually unnerving. We figured the distance to be about 190 miles. The farther east we went the more primitive the travel would become. Mother anticipated difficulties where she would have to make quick decisions. She would have no one to turn to, since Europeans were no longer living east of Malang.

Before the war, Kesilir was a stretch of land in development, carved out of the forest with the intent to establish an agricultural area. The Japanese caught on to this project and brought many Dutch civilian men to the primitive settlement as a slave labor force. Several plantation specialists were among the men, and the Japanese, who recognized their value, placed them in charge. The circumstances were extremely austere. The forest had to be cut down, simple housing set up, and land brought under cultivation. All this work would have been a real hardship under any conditions. The men's shelters were nothing more than rectangular boxes, with four corner posts, woven bamboo walls, and a roof of *atap*, the dried leaves of the coconut tree. The floor was packed dirt. At first the men slept on the ground. Thin homemade mattresses that could be rolled up instantly in case of a move elsewhere provided their only barrier against the ground.

Later they were able to construct bamboo beds. Water had to be boiled in order to make it safe, and outhouses had to be built.

We had never heard of Kesilir before Dad was removed there, so Anton and I studied our detailed map in an attempt to become familiar with the course of the railroad and our destination. Located at the very southeastern end of Java, the area was just south of a river named Kali Serail, which flows east toward the Strait of Bali. Escape was almost impossible. The forests on the west and south border were forbidding, and crossing the river in the north meant entering the native settlements. The natives were so afraid of the Japanese that they would betray any escapee. On the eastern side were the coast and the sea with its well-known and powerful currents.

Kesilir was quite a distance south of Banjuwangi, on the east coast of Java, where the ferry crosses over to the island of Bali, clearly visible in the distance. The map showed that we had to go east at Bangil and travel through Pasuruan and Probolinggo, following the beautiful coastline with its white beaches. Pasir Putih, White Sand, was one of them. Pasuruan was one of the places that Dad had to inspect before the war, and he used to swim and dive there for shells. Once he took us there and challenged us to dive without equipment. That was a major effort, but he wanted us to be fit. The sea was clear and coconut trees were cradled along the shoreline, their roots exposed by the waves. The tree trunks revealed notches on both sides all the way up. These had been made by *katjongs* using machetes so they could climb easily in order to cut coconuts. At Probolinggo the tracks headed south to centrally located Djember, the capital of the province by the same name. Djember was well known for all the rich plantations, especially those growing robusta coffee and tobacco. We would have to get off at Rogodjampi before reaching Banjuwangi and go south to Bentjuluk, close to the Kali Serail.

Early one morning in Malang we boarded the express luxury train, cooled by bars of ice inserted above the windows, and headed north to descend into the lowlands. After about an hour we arrived at Bangil, halfway to Surabaja. There we left that first train to board another one heading east. This train was substantially less comfortable, with wooden windows that would slide up and down. This train was a people's express, pulled by a steam engine. An inexpensive way to get from here to there, it stopped at most towns, with wooden benches stretched out on both sides of the carriage our only seating. Most of the passengers were common natives heading for the market in Probolinggo, some with their children, and all their produce in *kerandjangs*, baskets. Among the items for sale was *durian*, a large watermelon-sized fruit with a coarse thorny skin and a very strong odor. The taste, however, is excellent. Many other colorful fruits were available, including starfruit and *mangistan*, a brownish hard-shelled fruit the size of a tennis ball. They, like the durian, were delicious, but the mangistan was full of marble-sized pits. Anton and I always joked that a bite made us think of a mouth full of loose teeth.

Fortunately, the windows of the train carriages were wide open, because other items headed for market were *trassi*, a small dried fermented fish, and shrimp, whose penetrating odor was one of the strongest smells ever to find its way into our nostrils. For the natives trassi was a major source of protein. Overhead, stowed in the luggage nets, were tattered crates, over-stuffed burlap bags, old luggage, and round baskets, made of woven bamboo, full of live chickens and some ducks. The animal droppings sometimes leaked through. Mother remarked to us in Dutch that before the Japanese occupation these animals had to be stowed in the baggage car.

The surroundings of Djember were beautiful, the hills covered with huge plantations. After pulling out of Djember, looking north, we had a marvelous view of the brown barren top of Mount Idjen, an active volcano whose crater was full of water containing sulfuric acid. Years earlier the Dutch government had made an artificial drainage canal to the sea, for otherwise the acidic water would destroy the crops. At the rim of the crater natives placed wooden sticks in the highly concentrated overflowing fluid to let the sulfur crystallize out against the wood. Natives carried this harvest in two tall, slender baskets each on a yoke across their shoulders. The wooden sticks were bundled in the tall baskets, which made the crystallized sulfur stand out above them like a bouquet of yellow flowers. From the train we could see some carriers with these loads descending the hills in a long single line like ducks. In their villages they would sell these sulfur sticks to Chinese businessmen, who in turn sold the sulfur for many uses.

By afternoon we reached Rogodjampi and transferred onto a narrow-gauge goods train. In addition to some small boxcars, a few carriages were attached behind the saddlebag engine. These wooden passenger cars were short, quite primitive, and dirty with ash.

This time we were heading south. The wood-burning engine belched the worst type of smoke and cinders, while the train clattered over rickety track and moved slowly because of many small bridges and long curves stretching around the dark forested hills. I stuck my head out of the open window, only to have my hair singed by hot pieces of coal. This "toy" train shook from left to right, like a hula dancer. The scene displayed the lush countryside so typical of the entire island, and the sunset made the foothills glow.

We arrived before six o'clock in the small village of Bentjuluk at the end of the line, still three miles from the Kali Serail, the final barrier to Dad. No hotel or motel to be found. Nobody wanted to accept white people in their home for fear of appearing to be pro-European. We did not know what to do at first. Slowly we walked down the main street, carrying our belongings and the pack with food and clothes for Dad, which seemed to get heavier in the heat with each step as daylight faded. Finally we found an older Chinese man who allowed us to lie down on his patio, just a few feet away from the road. Clearly he felt sorry for my mother, who looked tired and uncertain. He gave us a *tiker*, a thin mat made out of fine woven split bamboo.

The floor, made of concrete, remained as hard, just the same, but it was clean. However, the tiker did not chase the mosquitoes away. The man also brought us a traditional native citronella coil, which burned down slowly overnight and kept the mosquitoes at a distance. Furthermore, we were allowed to use the outhouse. We had to squat over a hole in the center of a concrete slab, the hole flanked on either side by a raised footstep. There was of course no toilet paper, but instead a bucket of water for cleansing.

We were tired and tried to absorb all the experiences of that day. I admired my mother, for it took guts to undertake this trip under the current hostile circumstances. We still had no idea what was ahead of us, and we wondered as the evening settled over the village, there on the floor of the patio. Finally we had a chance to relax and watch the villagers' activities, listen to the peculiar noises, and inhale the dust and smoke. In the distance, frogs opened up their concerts. I always loved to listen to them, especially in the rainy season, and we were actually supposed to be already in the monsoon, which this year was delayed. The sounds of the frogs always gave me a psychological "cooling" sensation. In the distance, with alternating intensity, we could hear the rhythmic drumming sound of women pounding rice in a hollowed-out tree. The evening wind brought us a melody as they sang. The young voices drifted through the cooling air of the darkness, and while the drums sounded repetitious, the clear human songs penetrated beautifully, a bit slow and sad.

It became clear that many natives passed by just to look at us, to see the *belandah*, the white people. This did not bother us in the least; nobody had any bad intentions. Anyway, there were no lights, except for chance rays darting through the open windows of the homes lit by petroleum lights, and all we saw of each other were shadows.

The night sky slowly revealed its stars. We could see the Southern Cross, and we talked about the beauty of all that. Mother told us about the Northern Hemisphere's star groupings, such as the Big Bear and the Big and Little Dippers. Finally we unwound a bit.

Through the open door and window we heard the Chinese family eating. The rattling of dishes and, worse yet, the penetrating aroma caressing our noses reminded us of our empty stomachs. Anton said that he was hungry, and Mother clearly became uncomfortable about his complaints, since she had no food for him.

A Chinese man came down the road, preceded by a katjong who hit two pieces of bamboo together in rhythm: *tek, tok, tok.* Usually street vendors would use a *klontong*, a rattle, but not here. The man carried a yoke of bamboo; on each end he balanced a bamboo frame, one containing cooking ingredients, the other a coal fire. He asked Mother if she wanted to eat *sate kambing*, pieces of goat meat speared on a bamboo stick and roasted over a coal fire. Some hot spicy soy sauce was added. Well, if you are hungry, you fill your stomach; so we did, and we loved every bite. It was too dark to see what we ate, but later on we heard it was goat bowel! When the Chinese man informed Mother about the content, she just giggled.

The next morning we had an early awakening. The local roosters crowed, and many villagers were already on the go. The sky was clear and the sun promised us a hot day. We felt quite stiff after sleeping on a hard floor. The air was scented with wood fires over which the women were frying rice in a wok. Quickly we purchased some cakes and downed them with hot tea.

Mother thanked the Chinese man for allowing us to sleep on his porch. He wished us a safe journey.

Our next challenge was to try to reach Kesilir as early in the day as possible. The best means of transportation was by *dogcar*, a horse-drawn, two-wheeled buggy, also called a *sado*. It has two seats across the carriage and a shared back support. Mother haggled with the driver over the price. After they agreed on the amount and the service, I sat up front next to the driver, my mother and brother on the backseat. Shafts on either side of the horse were angled slightly upward, so that the carriage was about fifteen degrees lower in the rear, giving a steady downward view to those in back. The wheels were large, with metal bands that made the ride quite stiff and noisy, and a canopy protected us from the hot sun. A small and rather skinny horse was harnessed to the sado, and his trot was encouraged by the driver's whip. The road was of poor quality, in contrast with well-maintained asphalt roads in other parts of Java. Mother remarked that the future would reveal more of this neglect. The dips and bumps in this out of the way corner of Java showed that increased traffic and neglected maintenance already had become a problem.

A Japanese truck passed us, leaving a dust cloud that we had to tunnel through for the next ten minutes. We could see the fickle course of the Kali Serail in the distance, well marked by dense groves of trees.

We arrived quite early at the lone bridge. This bridge, the width of one car, was built of white stone. The span stretched about sixty feet, hovering over a deep rocky gorge with rushing brown water, an effective barrier for the men imprisoned here. The Japanese guard inspected our permit. He pointed across the bridge toward a field, obviously cleared in the recent past, where we were allowed to sit on the grass. There was absolutely no shade. At the bottom of a nearby slope where the ground was damp, we spotted a stand of young banana trees and an adjacent terrace of recently planted *ketella*. This was Kesilir in the making. We crossed the bridge and turned to the right. On the left was the Japanese guardhouse, with a few trucks parked alongside. In the field Mother spread a white cotton sheet on the grass and placed her basket with the goodies she had saved for this time. Mother had been looking forward to this reunion and wanted to celebrate.

The sun was already getting hot. Other Dutch women and some kids joined us, choosing their own little spots. We did not know what to expect; the sober surroundings were intimidating and we were anxious to see Dad. We spoke in whispers, and the children in each group stuck together, unusually quiet.

Suddenly a group of men came over a slight knoll. The men stopped and looked down toward us, some shading their eyes with their hands. A few waved in recognition of their families. Nobody ran. They just walked. Many had clearly lost weight.

Then Dad came into view, and right away we noticed how much weight he had lost. His shirt was wrinkled and not very clean. He was wearing shorts folded at the waistline, and we spotted ulcers on his legs. His feet were stuck into homemade sandals. Always reserved, he tried especially hard under these circumstances to contain his emotions. After he embraced Mother, who was shocked at his appearance, he looked at Anton and me silently for a long time and nodded his head, swallowing hard several times. He sat down next to Mother and held her hand. He told us that malaria had struck him again, but that he still had some quinine pills left to control his fever attacks. Dad was usually not very talkative, and he had trouble expressing himself as he struggled to control his deep feelings and his anxiety.

Mother handed him some goodies, and his eyes really popped out of his head at the sight of the smoked sausages. Clearly he had not seen such food in months.

He offered us some water out of a bottle. It tasted awful. He told us they had to boil the water after dipping it out of the river. We learned that they had built their own bamboo barracks and were clearing brush and burning debris. They were working under the leadership of a former planter who knew the place and were struggling to eliminate the acid soil conditions.

What shocked us most was his description of a traitorous Dutchman in their midst who was in league with the Japanese. This Dutchman, Van Den Eeckhout, had been a participant in a mutiny in 1929 aboard the old cruiser *Seven Provinces* off the coast of Southern Sumatra. Protesting a salary cut, the sailors locked up their officers and set sail through the Sunda Strait. A military airplane dropped a bomb on the ship, and several mutineers died before the ship surrendered. Dad said that Van Den Eeckhout had organized a group, the Asiatic Brotherhood of Indo-Europeans, that was willing to collaborate with the Japanese. Dad said that they knew who these traitors were, and that there were very few followers.

Our conversation was limited because we had so little time. After an hour and a half the Japanese guard gestured with his rifle butt by way of telling us to go home. Only ninety minutes for all this effort and anxiety. The farewell was very difficult. Mother had trouble tearing away from Dad. Anton and I stood aside quietly to give them some time together, resulting in little time to say good-bye. The guard rudely interrupted and drove us away, driving the butt of his rifle between Dad and Mother but not hitting them.

By now the sun, at its zenith, was making us perspire profusely. It was especially hard walking back in that heat, crossing the bridge again, and looking for our sado, parked among all the others. Many women cried on the return walk. Mother walked proudly but fought to hold back her tears. Then we faced another surprise when the sado drivers suddenly increased their prices for the return trip. Many women became angry and raised their voices, but to no avail. Mother decided to pay up, for she realized that walking would make us miss the train connection.

The return trip went much more quickly, and we made it home to Malang on the last evening train. That meant an arrival at midnight. Mother was very quiet but told us that she was grateful to have seen Dad. We boys were extremely tired and especially glad to find a good bed. But that night I could not help wondering what Dad slept on.

After this visit we did not hear from Dad for three years, and many times we wondered whether he could still be alive.

chapter eight

THE FINAL DAYS OF DE WIJK

A Japanese commandant named Ikada was put in charge of De Wijk. Every month more restrictions were applied.

Once several women approached Ikada about the increase of restrictions in our camp. They called the place "our concentration camp." Ikada smiled and said, "You do not know what a concentration camp is!" He also stated that he received word from Batavia's leaders about the internment of the Japanese civilians in the United States and how mistreated they were. It became apparent to the women that he saw our imprisonment as a form of reprisal. We understood his answer fully only later on, after we were transported to Lampersari, in the town of Semarang.

Most of the mixed-blood people, the "Indos," were left outside the camp, and the ones living inside had to leave. The Japanese judged the Indos by skin color; if they looked more than 50 percent white, they had to be in camp.

The women inside the camp desperately tried to maintain an organized structure to support their self-esteem and family values.

By this time no one had any means of communication with the outside world, and we didn't know anything about the progress of the war.

The Japanese forbade us to organize a school, so it was done in secret. There were many teachers willing to participate, though there were hardly any schoolbooks. We formed classes of six pupils moving by bicycle between the teachers' homes. Our camp school system caved in when suddenly all bicycles were confiscated and teachers were told that the Kempeitai was going to get involved.

Every Dutchman owned a bicycle, and when these were all turned in, Merbaboe Park was cluttered like a dump. We tried to sabotage the bikes, mostly by cracking the spokes of the wheels. After the bicycles had stood for two weeks in the rain, coolies stacked them on trucks to haul them out of camp.

Then the order came to remove all pianos. We boys had to load even the grand pianos on trucks, which was extremely heavy, done all by hand. Again, we destroyed as much as possible, bending the strings inside. Next were the sewing machines and iceboxes. People were supposed to turn in any gold, silver, jewelry, and money still in their possession. Most of them did not do so.

Mother had met an evacuee, Mrs. Dickie Berendsen, and her baby girl and invited them to live with us in the garage. Dickie was very young. She was married to Dr. Henne Berendsen, a veterinarian. She had met him in the Netherlands while working in a hotel. She was extremely shy, nicely innocent, and came straight from a farm. Henne was assigned to Madoera, a dry and dusty island, mostly producing beef cattle. Being quite religious, she had a hard time getting used to the local customs, which blended Muslim and indigenous beliefs. For instance, every year a Karapan, a steer-racing event was held. Two steers shouldered a beam tied crosswise, an end dragging on the ground. A driver stood on the beam and held on to a pole marked by a colored banner for identification. While the race was on, only the banners were visible above the dust. Although Islamic law forbade it, the betting was heavy, and to hasten his team to victory the driver would lift the tails of the steers and push a paste of ground up red peppers up their anuses.

Dickie abhorred the event and the place. When her husband was drafted at the start of the war, he advised her to go to Malang, where it would be so much safer.

Our former neighbor Annie Bruinvis, already a very good friend of Mother, and her two young girls, Truus and Lieneke, moved in with us from outside the camp. Wim, her husband, had been drafted and sent to Batavia.

These three women formed a tight-knit group inside the camp, which helped them survive.

Heart-rending was the order to turn in all pets, cats, dogs, birds, and rabbits. We said farewell to our two white poodles, knowing that most likely they were going to be put to sleep. The Muslims outside camp considered them unclean, just like pigs and snakes. The Japanese claimed that their action was to prevent rabies. Anton cried when he had to turn over our rabbit.

Eventually, our two-bedroom home filled up with seventeen people, Mother and us two boys sleeping in the study. There was only one bathroom. Living so close together created problems, especially getting along with each other.

The last family to move in had a boy of fourteen, my age. He was the strongest kid in camp. All of a sudden he contracted pneumonia and was the first in camp to die, a terrible dose of reality I had a tough time accepting.

Mother informed us boys, with tears in her eyes, that she had no more money. On my own initiative I went to the pasar to talk to a Chinese milkman. I convinced him that I could bring his milk bottles to the houses of his customers. He made his bicycle available, and we loaded the bike with pocketed gunnysacks hung over the frame and handlebars, which made it difficult to steer, especially going uphill.

I brought milk to the backdoors. Once, while doing so, I heard giggling and words I did not understand. When I turned, I saw a mother and her two teenaged daughters stark naked showering. They were Swedish, from a neutral country, but they were nevertheless incarcerated. I did not know how fast to retreat.

In addition I managed to get other jobs. I repaired books at the clandestine library in the former building of the Masons. On the side of this building was a spacious tower, where in the afternoon the female physician held office hours. I cleaned up afterward.

Anton delivered bread on a tricycle, where the box was located between the two front wheels. In the late afternoon he picked up dirty linen and stuffed it into the breadbox, to be brought to the Chinese laundry outside. Mother had a fit when she discovered what he was doing and made him line the box with a clean sheet.

My friends and I still managed to be kids, even within the surrounding barbed wire. I discovered a means of transportation, a pair of roller skates, to get to the Mason building more quickly. Toward dusk we boys entertained ourselves on the skates. Several boys would make a human chain by holding hands, and the lead man would head downhill first. At the bottom of the slope he would suddenly turn and stop. This created a catapult action, and the last kid was jettisoned with enormous speed.

Even as a small boy I had relished my freedom to roam and explore, and the months of confinement in De Wijk began to chafe. Once I climbed the steel ladder inside the tower to look far into the outside world, seemingly functioning normally. This created a sickening feeling. Often I would nose into the medical books, with a special interest about malnutrition, until the nurse, a friend of Mother's, caught me not working. All she said was, "It probably does not matter anymore, for the rumor has it that we all will be shipped out."

Soon afterward, Commandant Ikada ordered the block leaders to tell us to be ready for transport. The order stated that we were to be shipped in sections, each week one group, usually a block. This amounted each time to about a thousand women and children. The air became tense with questions and anxiety. How would the men find their families if we were moved? Would there be sufficient food for the huge number of people, and who would provide it? What kind of medical care would be available? Most important of all, would families and friends be allowed to stay together wherever we were taken? Of course, none of these questions were answered, except by time.

It had been almost already a year since we traveled to Kesilir to see Dad, and we had not heard from him. The Japanese had taken nearly everything of value from us. It was a constant struggle to get enough to eat. Still, we were in our own community, seeing our neighbors and friends daily. Anton and I had some freedom to roam in the many acres that were surrounded by barbed wire, and we could still see our beloved Merbaboe Park. We could pretend that we still had some control over our lives. That was all to change now, and quickly.

Every person was told to have ready one piece of luggage. The older teenaged boys loaded the transport trucks, stacking them high with steel trunks, the day before the people departed.

We boys clambered on top of the trunks. A Hei-Ho, an Indonesian guard, sat down next to the driver, and the truck drove to the railroad station where we unloaded the freight and coolies transferred the trunks and smaller luggage into the boxcars. We would wave at the Indos, Chinese, and Indonesians, who responded in kind.

I made the trip to the station frequently, since our family was second to the last one to be shipped off. Over the last few weeks it had become very quiet in this extremely large camp, where ten thousand women and children had lived for almost a year. When I walked through the deserted streets, my hollow steps echoed against all the abandoned homes, with open doors and where furniture and belongings collected dust. I talked to myself: "Here the pharmacist used to live, and over there the Swedish people where I delivered milk." The hair on my neck would stand up, and I would race home to see familiar faces again.

We heard reports from others that Indonesians came through the barbed wire to help themselves to belongings left behind in the homes. They operated usually in small groups and were not afraid when I ran into them, since I was alone. Once they came toward me with clubs, and I fled.

In our home was a widow in her seventies, Mrs. Malu, who occupied a small storage room adjacent to the kitchen. She was shy, stooped, and thin, always dressed in black. We found often that she was hungry, for she had no money, so everybody tried to give her food. She would thank us sincerely with her quavering voice. She was very religious, and that seemed to help her cope with her circumstances. Once Anton snickered and remarked about her black outfit. I was shocked to hear Mother say, "Those are the only clothes she has. She had to flee from her home when the Japanese attacked." Anton and I discussed this, realizing how hard it would be for her when we were moved, and we approached her. We said, "Madam, we want you to go with us to one of the empty homes and get you a solid trunk. We will help you find decent clothing and pack it for you." At first she refused. Finally we convinced her that if she did not take the clothing, somebody else would. Upon leaving Malang she had a trunk with her name on it. That piece I loaded on the truck with great satisfaction.

Another woman, nineteen-year-old Greta, lived in the servant's room. She had been married to a naval lieutenant for only a few months when the islands were invaded. He escaped to Australia. It seemed to me that she was always crying, holding his picture. I felt so sorry for her, but Mother told me that I really could not help her. When the day of departure came I noticed her sitting in front of her trunk, crying. The trunk was packed but for her white bridal gown in her hands. I told her that I had to take her trunk. No answer. "Why do you want to take your gown?" I asked her. She stared at me and whispered, "If my husband comes back I want to put this on again." From my perspective this made no sense. I grabbed the dress and stretched it out in the lid of the trunk and sat on it to close it tight. Later on I talked to mother about this episode. Her response was, "Poor lonely woman."

Mother, who was so steady and helpful with others, was in tears herself over our forced move. She did not know what to try to save, but she did salvage a large stamp collection by pulling all stamps out of the albums and placing them in manila envelopes.

Just this act of saving valuables would have been rewarded by a severe beating if the Japanese had discovered it. She also saved many family pictures. All the tin cans with food were packed. Mother's group had very little jewelry, and they hid that in the cloth belly of a toy mouse that was treasured by Mrs. Berendsen's daughter, one-year-old Jettie. During searches this little girl held on to her mouse for dear life, and it went unnoticed.

The morning of our departure was an emotional one. We left behind our home and most of our belongings. It was hard to believe that we would be able to hold on to the wonderful memories of our peaceful, happy years there, especially when we had to cope with harsh treatment at the hands of the Japanese, but somehow we did.

The day before we left, the Japanese guard had announced that each person had to take a small basket filled with food. Unfortunately nothing was said about liquids, and that turned out to become a major problem during our entire trip. The commandant specified the measurements of the basket, and he came down that evening to measure the baskets, inspecting each home, only to go into a rage if any were oversized.

Mother had packed one large basket for the three of us. She almost received a beating when Commandant Ikada saw it. That night we repacked it into three small ones. Mother had the foresight to carry a large bottle of water. She had learned that from the Kesilir trip.

One woman with three toddlers prepared the tiny baskets and stuck a bamboo pole through each handle. Then each child swung the bamboo over his shoulder, looking like a classic hobo's bundle. Attached to the end was a red pouch with a streaming banner that read, "We three little mice are leaving, we don't like this home anymore." This mother was like many, trying not to frighten her children and attempting to maintain a sense of humor as well.

At daybreak the trucks arrived, staffed by drivers and Indonesian guards. Three Japanese sergeants arrived in a separate car and immediately started to scream out orders, which only created more confusion. There were more than a thousand women and children milling around, adding to the distress and anxiety. The Japanese started to scream what sounded to us like, "*Tenko, tenko, bango!*" We did not know that this meant roll call and number. We were pushed into a lineup three deep in front of the Merbaboe Park. Women cried, and kids called for their mothers. Clumsily, everybody tried to get in line, friends wanting to stay together. It was pandemonium.

The Japanese soldiers made a mess out of our count, and as a result the woman in charge, the block leader, started to count heads while a toddler sat quietly on a portable potty, watching the tumult.

The women and children were loaded on the trucks, standing room only. I was one of the last, since I was helping the old ladies and lifting the little ones up to their mothers. Mother complained to her friends that I was only fourteen years old and yet tried to shoulder so much responsibility.

Just before getting on the truck I saw a wonderful opportunity. I ran to the flagpole and lowered the hated Japanese flag, which displayed a white field with a central red ball, the symbol of the rising sun. In passing we had always been compelled to face it and bow. I ran to the smallest room of the house and draped the flag over the toilet seat. I looked at this draped toilet with unbelievable satisfaction, then turned and ran to the truck to join the others. I did not tell Mother what I had done.

chapter nine

THE TRANSPORT

We were packed in like sardines. After helping the others I was the last one to come aboard, which gave me a good view of the passing surroundings. The trucks drove at a good clip, not slowing down going through the curves, so that our tightly packed group swayed back and forth with every turn.

We arrived at the railroad station in Malang. Japanese troops were everywhere. After our arrival, one truck at a time was unloaded, the women and children kept together and then herded to the northern end of the building. "*Lekas, lekas!*" the Japanese ordered, using the Malay words: Hurry up!

Several fourth-class passenger cars with blinds over the windows were waiting for us. They were of the old style, with a small entry platform on either end of the coach and three benches stretched out over the entire length of the car inside. One bench, centrally located, was without back support. Some cars were equipped with an enclosed primitive bathroom, a hole in the floor where one could see the railroad ties pass underneath. There was a handle on the wall to hang onto. There was no toilet paper, no water, no lock on the door.

The compartments were soon packed with people. In that heat everybody became thirsty, but water and other liquids were in very short supply.

Our train sat motionless in Malang for hours. The temperature inside the carriage climbed. Little kids started to become restless, and there was a great deal of crying, with mothers trying to calm their toddlers and encourage them to sleep. One woman thought to distract these little ones and started to tell stories.

One woman attempted a joke: "Japan arranged a sightseeing trip for us through our beautiful Java." Another quipped, "But since we did not pay, the windows are covered to restrict our view." But as time wore on, many settled into a deep silence.

Mother had cooked rice the evening before and placed it in a one-gallon tightly closed aluminum container. That morning, by lunchtime aboard the train, it had turned sour in that heat. She threw the rice out but regretted her actions the next day when she started to realize how valuable that rice had become, even in its sour state.

The heat became oppressive. One woman started to take off her corset. Clearly she was overdressed, as if she were planning to go to a fancy tea party. She and her husband had owned the biggest jewelry store in Malang, which had been taken away from them by the Japanese. With her were her three small boys, who appeared to be intimidated by all the commotion. They sat close together like three scared little chicks. There were several other women who had also dressed up. Some people said that they had done so to impress the Japanese. It seemed foolish under the circumstances and certainly extremely impractical. As a teenage boy I felt very uncomfortable and out of place among all those women.

Sitting out on the platform of each train carriage was a Hei-Ho, a native Malay guard in the service of the Japanese. I heard the Japanese sergeant in charge walk alongside the train taking head counts. The Hei-Hos did the actual counting inside the cabin and reported to the sergeant in Japanese. This translation into the other language created a problem, and as a result the soldiers had trouble getting the numbers right, which made it necessary to repeat the process several times. Finally the three Japanese in charge of the transport moved forward to their headquarters in the first car, right behind the steam engine.

Around 11:00 the train finally set in motion. It was apparent that we were heading north, in the direction of Surabaja. I opened the door, went outside on the balcony, and started a conversation with the Hei-Ho. At first he was upset that I was outside the cabin but I pointed behind me and told him, "Too many women." I promised to go inside at stops or if the Japanese guard should appear. He smiled in agreement. He would rather talk to me than be bored. A short skinny fellow, quite young, he said he had taken this job only because there were no other opportunities. His family lived in Kediri, west of Surabaja, and he was homesick.

I heard many complaints about the Japanese from him, that they broke promises made when he signed on and that he had been forced to buy his own uniform. Most offensive to him was that the Japanese did not trust the Hei-Hos, and he showed me his only weapon, a bayonet stuck on a piece of bamboo.

The train trip was extremely slow. A ride from Malang to Surabaja, a distance of sixty miles, normally took ninety minutes. However, our train became sidetracked every time a scheduled one passed. In the little town of Bangil, now in the lowlands, we had a long layover that became difficult to tolerate in the heat of the afternoon. The air inside was stifling, but since we were at a standstill I had to be inside. The compartment was dark. Many women started to shed clothing to a bare minimum, and at just fourteen I felt shocked and embarrassed. Mother and Anton became quite listless because of the heat. Many kids fell asleep, but some just whimpered and complained of thirst. The smell of wet diapers dominated.

Another stop in the middle of the afternoon was in the familiar Gubeng train station of Surabaja, our stopping point when we were going to visit Aunt Loes. How different a situation this one was! Here we were again, near our Surabaja home, but sweltering in this stifling heat in a packed car, not knowing what our destination was. I listened to the noises of vehicles crossing the viaduct. I used to stand in freedom on that same viaduct, spanning all those railroad tracks, waiting for the night express to come in. Now all I could do was let my vivid imagination recall this old vision. Those happy days were gone.

By late afternoon we pulled into the classification yards at Tandjung Perak, the harbor area of Surabaja. Slowly our train picked its way over the twisting tracks, rattling over switches, and scaring the grazing goats tethered on the embankment. We passed a platform where coolies were loading timber on a few flatcars. They stopped their work to stare at our passing engine pulling the blinded coaches. Finally our locomotive slowly came to a stop at the far end of the yard. As far as one could see, the numerous tracks looked sizzling hot, and the air above them vibrated. The locomotive was uncoupled. I stalled for time on the platform, but then crawled inside the sweltering coach as I had promised. We heard the engine again setting into motion with hissing steam, only to realize that its sound gradually faded in the distance. The carriages remained in the hot yard.

I became more aware of the intense smell of sweat, food, and diapers. The sun went down and we were enveloped by darkness. There was a war on, and no lights were allowed anywhere since the Japanese wanted to protect the harbor. The surrounding area became quiet, apart from animal sounds. In the far distance we could hear motors, probably coming from the harbor. I heard the Japanese bark orders at the Hei-Hos, who answered that everything was in order. Then quiet descended on us again. The windows stayed covered. One person complained about the darkness, but somebody else responded, "This is better, given the state of undress of some of us in this heat."

The lack of space meant that many toddlers were asleep on the floor. Going to the toilet was a slow process as we tried to feel our way through the crowded car. Again, after the Japanese in charge had inspected the train, I went outside and sat on the steps with the Hei-Ho, who "drank his cigarette," the Malay expression for smoking. I could make out the dark silhouettes of boxcars with their wheels quietly resting on their steel railroad tracks.

Around eleven at night everything became extremely quiet, and the sea wind started to cool us off. This wind also brought us the muffled and distant noises of a typical tropical night, twitters of chirping insects and birds that seemed to alternate their calls, the sudden passing flutter of a bat overhead. The sky was dark and cloudless and full of twinkling stars. The pointing Southern Cross was clearly visible. I left the train door ajar for some air, since nobody could see that in the darkness. The emotions of the day took their toll, and I rested my head against the wagon compartment while I sat on the steps. I noticed that the Hei-Ho's head was nodding as well. He looked awfully young to me. As always, mosquitoes started their engines to look for blood. I was so tired that I did not even attempt to slap them.

Half-asleep, I was rudely awakened by sirens. Searchlights reached for the sky, scraping the dome of the night. We heard the drone of airplanes. The Japanese in charge ran alongside the train yelling commands to the Hei-Hos to make certain no lights were visible.

I crawled inside the car door but left it open. All of a sudden we heard explosions over the harbor. The bright light of a flare illuminated the sky and then slowly faded. We were completely helpless in these train cars in the middle of the yards, which made tempting targets.

Quiet descended again. I tried to doze off, but that did not last long. Around 2:00 a steam engine came slowly toward us, hissing and making chucking noises. Again there was yelling. Heavy footsteps passed by. More commands came, then and the lurching of train cars being coupled. Then came a sharp whistle and our train came slowly into motion.

We appeared to be moving west, but I could not be sure where to. The Hei-Ho did not know either. The direction could be either Kediri or

Semarang, where we had lived briefly when I was young. After several hours the locomotive slowed down for a small station and in passing I was able to read the name Bodjonogoro. I knew the map of Java very well thanks to Mother, and this told us that our destination was Semarang or beyond.

Semarang was an old harbor town with a long history of pogroms against the Chinese, which had occurred prior to the 1900s. The Chinese were craftsmen, owners of stores, and traders. East of town were swamps infested by malarial mosquitoes, making the entire area unhealthy. The harbor had a shallow entrance, so ships of any size had to stay outside, lying in the roads. Central Java's export of plantation products went through this town, brought in by the railroads.

We arrived in the Semarang station after the sun rose on our second day of travel. The guards drove everybody out of the railroad cars, again shouting "*Lekas, lekas!*" After all the hurrying we were made to stand there on the dusty platform in the hot sun for hours. This was rough on the little ones, who cried for water. A conductor for the railroad came forward with a container filled with coconut milk and squatted down to give them a drink. A Japanese guard ran forward and ordered him to stop, but when the guard was confronted with all those small faces desperately trying to get a drink he relented, turned, and left. The Indonesian conductor smiled and tried to comfort the children by rubbing their heads. When this compassionate man stood up there were tears in his eyes. He said, "Every week I see more people with little kids on this platform. *Kassihan*—a pity." The mothers thanked him, and one said, "God bless you. I will pray for you."

chapter ten

LAMPERSARI

Lampersari was like Malang only in that it was a holding area for thousands of prisoners, most of us Caucasian, but including many Indos. Many other women and children had arrived in this camp before we did, and they had already faced the necessity of creating some kind of tolerable situation for themselves. There was a camp hierarchy of sorts, and some of the women were more or less in charge. It was now our turn to be newcomers, to figure out the odd rituals of this new camp, and to resist or resign ourselves to the situation.

We were told that our luggage had already been sent to Lampersari, an older and smaller native neighborhood of Semarang, and apparently our destination. Later that morning trucks finally pulled in to the train station, and we were all loaded on board, then driven through town toward the bottom of the Tjiandi hills. The trucks rumbled into Camp Lampersari, entering on an adequate oil road itself also called Lampersari, which was lined by shade trees. Dirt roads branching off on either sides of this main route revealed *kampong* homes, small dwellings constructed of bamboo. It was dusty, dirty, and sweltering. Here we were ordered to climb out of the vehicles. Surprisingly, our luggage was there ahead of us, and although many small parcels turned up missing, the heavy baggage arrived intact, being more difficult to steal. At this point, to our amazement, the Japanese walked away and left the distribution of all new arrivals up to Lampersari's internal organization.

Several women who appeared to be in charge at Lampersari started to divide us newcomers into small groups in order to get quartered. We were to be added to homes already occupied, reversing the situation our family had experienced in De Wijk. I noticed right away the impoverished conditions of the welcoming committee. Most of them were barefooted and dressed in old faded shorts. A few were wearing homemade cotton checkered blouses, which had clearly once been tea towels. Some people were housed in the tiny bamboo huts we had seen from the truck, which actually were not deserving of the word "home" but instead were a sort of tumbledown shanty. If the occupants were lucky, the roof would not leak. These bamboo dwellings were a part of the area known as Blimbing, the Malay name for starfruit. Before the war this kampong had been declared uninhabitable because of the many waterborne health problems. The bamboo homes were thus neglected and in the rainy season stood in about six inches of water. Apparently the Japanese had systematically cleared a native section of town, than surrounded it with a double row of barbed wire, with a three-foot-wide passage between for the guards. This perimeter defined a new and harsher prison camp, where we were expected to endure or die.

We were somewhat luckier in our housing assignment, and Mother and her girlfriends were able to stay together. A young girl took us down Lampersari Road and made a right turn at the end. This was another oil road, Sompok, that we had to walk down until we reached the double row of barbed wire. On the other side of the fence was the Sompok school, but since the outside fence was covered by woven bamboo we could hear the children at the school yet not see them. On our left was a small brick three-bedroom home, sitting on a rise at an elevation of roughly four feet, and partially hidden by a huge shade tree. This bit of elevation enabled us to see part of the school and the kids across the road.

I was beginning to feel the true oppression of imprisonment, an awareness I had been able to ignore with even a small degree of freedom in Malang. The opportunity to see Javanese kids in routine activities convinced me that there was still another world out there, so different from ours. I continued to hope that a better time would be in our future. Never before had I realized what a privilege it was to go to school as a normal being.

The terrible primitive circumstances were devastating to our group at first. There was a great deal of discouragement, and somber and defeated feelings seemed overpowering. Mothers with small kids were overheard to sigh, "How in the world can we survive these circumstances?" One person in our home complained, crying, "What did I do, God, to deserve this?" Mrs. Berendsen answered, "He always has a reason. He will show you the way; be more positive in your belief." Mother knew what was needed, and told this frightened woman to pull herself together for the sake of her children and get busy.

The sense of responsibility to someone else, especially to the children, was reason enough to fight for survival. Women without children had a much harder time finding the will to live.

This small house was the first of three homes in a row, together surrounded by barbed wire on three sides. They formed a tiny peninsula of the camp and stuck out like a finger, pointing at the foothills of Tjiandi. The first dwelling was our destination, where we were directed to one small bedroom meant for the eight of us. Some ladies came and half-heartedly welcomed us. We could hardly blame them, since our arrival meant more people crowding into the rooms. They offered us lunch, which consisted of only a cup of tapioca starch without anything added or mixed in. Worse times had arrived, and Mother, Anton, and I all remembered the sour rice we had thrown away the previous day. From this time on we had for breakfast a ladle of plain tapioca starch, just like that used to starch a collar.

In the crowded room, our two steel trunks were placed alongside each other and became a bed, with our mattress on top. We were able to suspend our large mosquito net from the ceiling. This was not at all an easy task given the primitive tools in our possession, but it was crucial, since Semarang was notorious for its malaria.

Most people had to sleep on primitive mattresses on the floor. And at least our roof did not leak, but water seeped in through the window cracks when rain and wind would hit the panes. This home had one regular bathroom and a kind of outhouse in the back.

Even the old kitchen without a ceiling was occupied by three persons: a grandma, her daughter, and her little granddaughter. Their mattresses were on the concrete floor. From the rafters black silver-dollar-sized spiders looked down on them, giving them goose bumps. They also complained about the nocturnal rats that visited and displayed so little fear. The girl would waken all of us at night, with her screams piercing us to the very marrow when a rat walked over her little body. At that time none of us could imagine that rats themselves would become hunted for food. Later on the rats disappeared, since no more edible garbage was to be found. However, there was no choice but to live under these circumstances or die. We had to learn to make adjustments fast.

Time had an odd way of passing under the Japanese occupation. On one hand, each day seemed filled with our struggles to cope and thus went by quickly enough. Yet, since we could only measure time in terms of our captivity, each week and month passed interminably slowly. The Japanese had been on our island for seven months before they got around to taking Dad away. Mother, Anton, and I had remained in De Wijk for about a year under increasing hardships and food shortages. Thus our arrival in Semarang in September 1943 marked our second year of bowing to the Japanese flag. We had been absolutely cut off from any contact with the rest of the world, and we didn't know anything of the progress of the Pacific War. In our efforts to overcome each day's difficulties it would have been very meaningful if we had known more, but we faced another two years behind barbed wire, the second of them with our small family further divided. Death from starvation and malaria were real threats to our determination to be reunited.

Mother soon went to work in the camp kitchen in the Benteng, which was an old defensive structure up the hill, where the camp commandant had his headquarters and where any food supplies were stored. It was in this central kitchen that our daily ration of tapioca starch was prepared. Gradually we started to adjust ourselves as much as possible to the dehumanizing routine of this camp life. After several months most women found they had learned to cope. As the year 1943 rolled on, the conditions in camp worsened, but the unhappiness gradually cleared, and we tried to look for something to laugh at or listened to foolish rumors about the progress of the war.

There had been other deaths since that first shocking death of my friend in Malang from pneumonia. The family in Malang whose parents had objected to us boys playing with war toys was soon compelled to deal with a great tragedy. The mother and her two small children were sent to Camp Halmaheira, another women's camp in Semarang. She was adamant and refused to eat rice or tapioca starch, and perhaps she was without a close friend who could encourage her. We heard through the grapevine that she was the first woman to die in Camp Halmaheira, and she left a one-year-old boy and five-year-old girl behind. I felt so sorry for those kids, who were now completely dependent upon total strangers.

German women who were married to Dutch nationals were allowed to leave the camp. Japanese law stated that these women were still German, and thus protected. To my knowledge, none left. The Dutch women had no quarrel with them; they were completely accepted and integrated.

Lampersari tested everyone's ingenuity, and many found clever solutions. People quartered in those Blimbing "houses" struggled with many problems, one that their mattresses could not be placed on the dirt floor. One solution was to drive bamboo spikes into the dirt, than bamboo or wooden planks were placed across and tied with rattan. Once Mother sent me to help an elderly lady, the wife of a minister, to try to solve this problem. Mother had known her well in Malang and had received so much emotional support from this true believer after Dad was taken away. She was gray and worn, but kind and appreciative, and she never complained. We were somewhat successful in building a sort of bed. She insisted on paying me, handing me fifteen navy beans even after I objected. I took the beans home and shared them with Mother and Anton, but this gift shocked me with the realization that we might actually starve.

In that section of Blimbing the septic tanks overflowed during the rainy season, a situation aggravated by numbers, since each tiny home contained about twenty people. We tried to deal with the problem by digging a common ditch that led to a small creek that disappeared under the barbed wire.

Throughout the war we often found the actions and decisions of the Japanese completely irrational. One such tragic example involved an elderly Indo couple living just outside the barbed wire of Lampersari. The Japanese decided that he had more than 50 percent European blood, and so they threw him in Lampersari. His wife remained in their small home just outside the fence. Every morning he would walk slowly alongside the barbed wire, talking to her on the other side. She often would throw some food wrapped in a banana leaf and stitched together with narrow bamboo pins. With his shaky voice he always thanked her in Malay. This great enemy of Japan was all of a sudden shipped off to a male camp. His wife could not understand his absence and daily called for him. Some of the women tried to explain that he had been moved, but she insisted that he should come talk to her and often she would still throw food over the barbed wire. After some time she quit trying to contact him.

Camp language slowly emerged in our daily routine. The women used very few crude words, seemingly determined to keep up a certain standard in front of their children. We boys were scolded many times for doing the opposite, especially if I used a profane Japanese word.

For the roll call we used the Japanese word *tenko* or the Malaysian word *kumpulan*. Smuggling through the barbed wire was *gedek*, and was a very common occurrence in the early months. *Bolos* meant to walk away, something we often had to do as a form of passive resistance to the Japanese.

There were duties to be fulfilled, such as cutting grass, *babat*, and the *babad* group had the chore of cleaning the entrails of an animal brought in to make soup for the seven thousand people in camp. Their work assignment gradually faded along with our food supplies. Another expression was "table-speech," when a Japanese officer stood on a table to give us yet another lecture.

Listening to those speeches under the hot sun was at the very least a nuisance. Of course the speeches were delivered in Japanese, and not understanding anything was boring. Sometimes the translation revealed a repetitious pattern; the commandant was not an inspired speaker. The toddlers would sit down and hang on to their mothers' legs.

The Japanese admired people who tried to learn their language. Mrs. Van Der Poel, who spoke Japanese, was an important person in camp. She had lived in Japan before the war when her husband was assigned there as the Dutch ambassador, and her skills helped us all. The women in camp respected her, in part for her ability to control her emotions, and she was subtle enough to ridicule the Japanese without their realizing it.

If the Japanese heard us use the word "Jap" they became outraged, beating the person who used that word and cautioning us to show more respect. Yet it was impossible to have any respect for these soldiers. Most of them were peasants, without any education, who had never seen a white woman before. They were slovenly and drenched in sweat. Only with difficulty did they learn enough Malay to communicate. They insisted that we use "Nippon" to refer to them. The result was that we called them Nips.

There was a deep chasm between the women and the Japanese. The women despised the guards and acted independently, strengthening the internal organization to make the camp function. The commandant seemed to be relieved, for it was apparent that he could not handle his responsibilities well. In any case, most Japanese officers were unhappy to be associated with a prison camp, especially one containing women and children, and he was no different. He never passed up an opportunity to show his contempt for the defeated white people. Any foreigner, *gaijin*, was inferior to him. For their part, the women totally rejected any attempt by the Japanese to explain rules or customs. No bridge was ever established over this chasm. The women were determined not to cooperate at all, and this defiance made the commandant complain constantly. The Japanese guards considered the women only as *furyo*, prisoners, deserving of no regard under their particular code of honor. It did not matter that they were civilians and women.

One thing that most women did participate in at one time or another was the smuggling that went on. A few had some money or valuables that they had managed to hide during previous searches, and most families had brought clothing and linens. Smuggling was severely punished, but women desperate to feed their children would sometimes sneak through a drainage ditch under the barbed-wire barrier. Occasionally items would change hands when native drivers pulled their oxcarts in front of the Benteng. As the first year in Lampersari passed both the items and the opportunities for smuggling gradually diminished.

The kitchen at the Benteng was supposed to supply our food needs, but the amount made available by the Japanese authorities could not possibly feed the huge numbers of women and children adequately, and women tried to preserve their own foodstuffs, either brought with them or smuggled in. *Gedekken* was the term for an exchange through the barbed wire, most of which was covered by woven bamboo. These transactions were usually made during the night, for daytime activities were too easily detected.

Many women went to a designated open field to start their small fires for cooking. The problem was that when the woman was alone there and forgot an ingredient for a meal, she had to walk quite a distance to get it. Upon returning she often found that her food or wood had been stolen. It became a necessity to cook in pairs. Many injuries occurred, and there was no shade at all. Some women who boiled water during the midday for tea became ill with sunstroke, or a pan would tip over due to its shaky foundations and cause a scalding burn. The simplest efforts were difficult here.

Anton was now thirteen and I fifteen years old. Since we needed a safe cooking space and firewood, I became inventive. I tied a rock on a rope and threw the rock over the high tree branches that came from outside of the barbed wire inside to our space. By pulling on the rope I broke branches off and then collected the fuel. I also assembled some tools, including a small saw, an ax, and a pair of pliers. These were highly prized tools, and we were not allowed to have them. We got them in any way that we could, stealing or mostly by barter. We called it "organizing." I got the ax from the Hei-Ho guardhouse at the main gate. I stuck it in my belt as if it were mine and walked off with it after a brief conversation with the guard. Afterward I had the shakes, but I was so very happy to have this tool.

Since Lampersari was at the edge of the foothills, the terrain was quite uneven. Our grassy front yard sloped upward rather steeply. Into this rise I dug an upward trench, collected many abandoned red bricks, and built a safe oven consisting of three levels, each one higher than the last. I would start the fire in the bottom so that the heat draft would pull upward, heating three spaces at the same time. This was an effective way to conserve wood. Mrs. Bruinvis expressed her appreciation, since she could obtain warm water for the little ones.

Later on the open field for cooking fires was identified as *"dilarang keras,"* off-limits. We became totally dependent on the central kitchen at the top of the hill for our food. In desperation we still built fires, though, our only way to get warm water. The central kitchen could not supply warm water for all the people in the camp due to a shortage of containers and the chronic problem of wet firewood. We needed warm water for tea or coffee, if we had any, and to cook food illegally obtained by trade through the barbed wire.

Finding firewood became an increasing problem. Once Anton helped me at midnight, by moonlight, to pry loose a slanted support beam that held a corner post of the barbed-wire fence. These posts consisted of *djati*, teak, heavily tarred. The removal was a very difficult and dangerous task, especially with our primitive equipment. We waited until the guards had passed, walking between the double rows of barbed-wire fencing. Then, we got the support post loose with a crowbar. To our astonishment, we discovered that the area where the beam had been attached to the post was without tar. A pale oval surrounded by pitch-black wood was clearly visible even in the dark. This realization scared us, for we knew the early morning Japanese patrol would spot it in no time. We decided to cut the post up, right then and there. This was another big effort, and we were running out of time.

After that job was accomplished, when we could already see the early red glow of morning, we had to find a hiding place for the firewood. At this point we finally realized what a monster of a problem we had created. If the wood were found, the least punishment we could expect was a severe beating—but most likely far worse if the Kempeitai were to be called in. In desperation we used some charcoal to blacken the white spot, but without much luck. We took the split-up pieces of wood to the back of the house where the outhouse, a concrete slab covering the hole in the ground, was located. In the middle of the slab was an oval gap flanked on either side by a raised footstep. I reached into this hole and dug sideways, making a shelf large enough to store the sticks. Quickly we hid them inside.

An hour later a tremendous commotion told us that the guard had discovered our mischief. The order came, *tenko*, and everybody had to line up in blocks in the street. Looking down the long Sompok Road, I saw nothing but people standing on the hot asphalt. We lined up three deep. The assembly included toddlers and babies, all wilting under the hot sun while the Japanese barked orders. All the homes were emptied. The agitated Japanese and several Hei-Hos swarmed all over the area, but they never found the wood.

Mrs. Van Der Poel was called to translate as we were lectured and threatened. The commandant, Hashimoto, stood on a crate to be able to see over all of us tall whites. Whenever that happened I could not help but enjoy the sight. Here was a man who proclaimed to be of a superior race, and yet looked so pitiful, for he was very angry and red in the face. He held his left hand on the scabbard of his sword and gestured dramatically with his right. Drops of sweat were visible on his forehead. His cap slid backward, and his brown shirt was soaked with perspiration. Mrs. Van Der Poel stood next to the commandant as he told us that somebody had committed a hideous crime, and he threatened us with hell and doom. Every time she translated a sentence, she said, "Heeee saysssss" in a very sarcastic way.

The commandant finally gave up. By then it was noon and blistering hot. But even so we were lucky. Mother discovered our actions only after the *tenko*, and we got a lecture. Her lips trembled at the thought of our possible punishment by the guards. I told her in my defense that our three families needed the wood desperately. This group consisted of we three, Mother's two girlfriends, and their three little girls. The three women looked at us in resignation, and not another word was said, for they realized how important our wood was. We were lucky not to have been caught, and Mother looked to her friends for reassurance that we really were safe after all.

On another occasion I climbed a tree about three yards up. I had my legs slung around the trunk and was cutting a branch. This branch suddenly broke off, and I fell backward, with my legs still clasped around the trunk of the tree. My back and head hit the tree hard and knocked me out.

I found myself on the grassy ground, and the back of my head hurt fiercely, but otherwise I was okay. Unfortunately, this incident created quite a commotion. Several women fussed around me, claiming I was hurt. I did not need the attention and felt quite embarrassed. But at least I had the branch to carry home.

In the first month or two on the Sompok Road there were some evenings that we listened to organ music. Many women would stop and sit down in the grass, and found joy in listening, for the music enabled them to forget all their misery for a short time. A Dutch family from Semarang had been put in this camp in the early days and brought a small organ and other belongings of a kind forbidden to us later arrivals. The mother would play after sunset if she were in the mood. With door and windows open, the music would drift toward the people sitting on the lawn. One evening, when making rounds, the Japanese commandant heard these notes and he stormed into the house, smashing the organ. He seemed satisfied and grinned. Then he announced in Malay, "Now you have firewood."

In front of the room occupied by our families was a porch with a leaky roof, with walls only three feet high. More people arrived in the camp, and two women with an eleven-year-old girl were quartered on that porch. They brought two cabin trunks and two mattresses. The trunks were placed side by side and they covered them with mattresses stuffed with kapok. Inevitably, leaks in the roof caused the mattress to get wet. After rooting around a bit I found some broken roof tiles, climbed the porch roof, and kept on rearranging the tiles until the leak only showed up very close to the lower rim. However, these poor women still had a problem if the wind came up. The rain streaked in from the side over the three-foot wall. A suspended cloth would catch and direct the water downward, and that helped a bit, but the heavy rains of the wet season were hard to combat. Their wet mattresses were very difficult to get dry again, even in the hot sun.

In the house next door lived a distinctive character in camp. She was middle-aged and always wore a sort of one-piece overall, but most notably she had a radio. I never knew how she managed to keep it in camp, for Hashimoto, the commandant, had warned us that possessing a radio meant the death penalty. She must have already lived in the area before Lampersari became a prison camp. Eventually the Japanese realized that a radio was being used in our end of the camp. This prompted an unexpected raid. At 6:00 in the morning the Japanese guards came storming down the road, flanked by Hei-Hos, all screaming *"Tenko, tenko!"*

I watched as the woman with the radio approached the one-inch-thick steel pole rising from the septic tank in our back yard. This was the vent, reaching up twenty feet and ending in a round metal platform about ten inches across. She calmly climbed the pole, placed the radio on top, descended, and took her place at roll call. The Hei-Hos went all over the area and scattered and ripped everything apart, searching for that radio. The Japanese officer in charge, tiring of the wait, started to lean with his back against the vent pole. Every time he moved, the top would sway as in a breeze. As if I were in trance, my eyes never left this radio. We felt as if we were sweating blood. It was so remarkably quiet that I could hear the tense breathing of women standing close by. Small children sense danger so well, and even though they were not always required at *tenko*, they were at this one, and they stood there very quietly through the tedious search. This seemed to be instinctive with the youngest ones in camp, in contrast with the teens, who were more rebellious.

As abruptly as the guards had shown up, they left, without a radio. On our part there was no cheering, just a great sense of relief. We dripped beaded sweat as we moved, barefoot, back out the full sunshine, finally able to leave the street of sticky hot asphalt.

This amazing woman, the owner of the radio, also climbed telephone poles and tapped wires so that we could have extra electricity. We made devices to boil water, using two plates, one copper and one zinc, which were separated by rubber and hooked up to wires. This was then submerged in water. Our contraption created numerous problems such as short circuits or fires. Sometimes a blue flash shot out of the plug or the fuse box, but by now we had to try any trick in the book in order to cope.

Always on a small bicycle, the Japanese commandant moved about to patrol the streets of Lampersari. At the sight of the Japanese the little boys would sing *"een aap op een fiets, hoe vind je zo iets,"* freely translated to mean, "A monkey on a bike, how do you like!" At first the man really took pride in getting the attention of the kids. However, when he later learned what their words meant, he tracked down the mothers of these kids and gave them a severe beating, hitting their faces with his fists. One little boy embraced his mom, crying, "Why, mommy, why?" For days these mothers had blue bruises. It must have been hard for the women to teach their children to be submissive when they themselves were defiant.

A teenaged girl making rounds and ringing a bell would announce special happenings. She would cry out news such as, "There is a special food ration today," or bad tidings such as, "Five hundred women must show up for work." The women always listened carefully, because they knew they had to respond.

Months passed, with time moving fitfully, and every day something worse seemed to happen. Hunger became a severe problem, complicating the many illnesses because it delayed their healing. Toddlers who developed diarrhea started to run a high risk of dehydration, further threatening their emaciated little bodies. Mother had learned from a frightening experience when I was less than two and had a severe case of diarrhea, suspected to be a form of cholera, and she was aware of some simple basic remedies. In the tropics many women had to become aware of infectious diseases. They taught each other various home remedies, using good common sense. When the little girls in our group were stricken by diarrhea, we made a primitive solution. We boiled water with green tea and added rice, ground eggshells, carrots, some salt, and cinnamon, which Mother had brought in the form of rolled-up dried bark. Most of these ingredients had an astringent in them to slow down the bowel, and that was one of the reasons hot water for tea was more a necessity than a tradition. Bananas were hard to come by, but we knew they worked well to compensate for potassium loss.

A fifty-year-old nurse made rounds, although in a camp of seven thousand she could not get very far. It was too much to attend to, but she tried to remedy many simple ailments. She walked everywhere with a big bag filled with supplies slung over one shoulder, but she did not complain.

The nurse collected snails and dumped them in boiling water. This triggered a shrieking noise that gave the observers goose bumps. The goo, including the ground snail shells, was fed to the sickest kids, giving them a bit of protein. The sight of these little emaciated children, lying listless with hollow eyes, was heartrending but common. It was another kind of pain to witness the suffering of the mothers, sitting there totally helpless, not knowing how to combat the unforgiving conditions. Even though we knew that the Japanese often took a liking to the smaller kids, our guards seemed to be untouched by their suffering.

If a child became so ill that the so-called hospital in our camp could not handle it—for example, in the case of facial abscesses—permission was asked to admit the patient to the city hospital outside the camp. If the sick one were lucky, Commandant Hashimoto would grant the transfer. In the case of a child, the mother was not allowed to accompany him or her to the hospital. Sometimes for weeks no word would come. The child might suddenly return, or a death announcement would arrive. Those mothers went through agony.

One day I had to work on a very dirty floor, and Mother reminded me that I still owned a pair of tennis shoes. They really did not fit too well anymore, and I had become so used to walking barefooted anyway, but I obeyed her wishes. As a result, I developed a blister on my left heel that grew in twenty-four hours into a dollar-sized tropical ulcer, something serious under very sanitary conditions and much worse in camp. If such ulcers got out of control, the whole foot could become involved and might require amputation. The hallmark of a tropical ulcer was always distinctive; it never developed a crust but rather remained an open sore, with pus oozing out constantly.

These ulcers, caused by viruses, could eat away muscles, tendons, and even bones. If the ulcer were accompanied by malnutrition, the result could even be death.

In camp we treated these deep ulcerations with a strip of gauze soaked in iodine. Used as a tamponade, this gauze was crammed into the wound. I also frequently soaked my foot in salt water, since salt was the only thing we never ran short of. The nurse came daily to use silver nitrate sticks on my ulcer to burn it out. This nurse repeatedly told me, "One teaspoon of salt to a quart of water." Since I could not work, I missed out on the little extra bits of food that came with extra duties.

One night I was awakened by a strange sensation on my foot. We were not allowed to have lights at night, but I struck a match, a costly, hard-to-get item, and saw a myriad of tiny golden-colored ants crawling over my heel. At first I panicked, but it soon dawned on me that these critters were actually cleaning the wound. I resigned myself to letting them go on about their business. It took three weeks to heal, and I was lucky at that. It left me with a bluish, not very sensitive coarse spot on that heel. My foot gave me trouble for years to come.

Through the determination of the camp prisoners rather than our Japanese captors, a hospital of sorts was established, staffed by several nurses and volunteers, and headed by a female physician, Dr. Willemse. We were also lucky to have a Hungarian surgeon, Dr. Markovitch, who had an excellent reputation. He had been trained before World War I in Vienna, when it was still one of the top medical centers in the world. Several physicians had left Austria when the empire lost the Great War and fell apart, many coming to the Dutch East Indies. They were allowed to practice because they had served first in the colonial army and had a great deal of experience. This Hungarian surgeon had to move with us boys later on to another camp, but he was not allowed to practice medicine there. We were fortunate he was able to help at all in Lampersari. Once my mother chopped off a fingertip with an ax when she was splitting wood, and he crafted a skin cover that healed perfectly.

These physicians were excellent, especially considering the circumstances—poor sterilization and no access to all the proper tools, for starters. There was no surgical room, just a scrubbed table at best. The nurses and doctors worked under horrendous conditions, with few medicines and less food for themselves and their patients.

A large bamboo structure, which had been a horse barn before the camp existed, was converted into a hospital, for it was the only available space large enough to function as such. The building was dug into the hillside, the same hill that was crowned with the Benteng, and extended with two overhangs beyond the tiled roof. These large lean-tos had zinc sheets of metal roofing, one on the western side, covering the entire length of the building to shield the main room from the hot sun, and the other one on the southern side, toward the top of the hill. The second one reached over a concrete-lined ditch, which ran across the high part of the hill and was about five feet wide and five feet deep.

The inside of the hospital consisted of one huge room, its space reaching to the tiles of the roof and the floor nothing more than packed dirt. The walls had no windows, making this room cavernous and dark. Hot air would drift through the wide entry door to rise to the bare roof tiles. Where the walls and the roof met there were slits that allowed the hot air to escape, taking with it the stench from this malodorous place. Steel beds lined either side of the long, gloomy hall. In the later months of the camp these beds were each occupied by two or three patients, many of whom suffered from diarrhea. Diapers made out of cotton sheets were used for these patients, who were often too weak to get out of bed. There was a shortage of bedpans as well as everything else.

The nurses and the women volunteers who worked with the many ill and dying were saints. Dr. Willemse, the physician, was very competent and of course overworked. Besides the lack of medicines, there were no adequate dietary foods, and for several hours during the day there was no water coming from the only tap located outside the building. The bedpans were emptied in the ditch up the hill. The linen, after being washed, was clipped on a clothesline outside, where the hot sunshine had some disinfectant effect.

The harsh reality was that many patients were there to die.

Many very ill toddlers, whose mothers had already tried everything they could, were also kept in this structure, four or five across in a large bed. There were few cribs. Quarantine was often a dire necessity but was almost impossible to accomplish. Many of these youngsters were so ill that they required spoon-feeding. They were usually dehydrated, listless, and feverish, with dry lips and eyes sunken in their sockets. A child with polio might be lying next to one with meningitis or amebic dysentery. If special foods arrived in camp, such as milk and bananas, most of it was rushed to these sick toddlers.

One German woman, who had been married to a Dutch planter in charge of a plantation above Djember, had four children. The eldest was in Holland to study, and because of the Nazi occupation she had no knowledge of his whereabouts. She also had two young teens, a boy and a girl, and a baby who was born in Camp Malang. As a toddler in Camp Lampersari her youngest became terribly ill with meningitis and was placed in the camp's hospital, where he had to share a large crib with two other little ones suffering from the runs. His mother guarded her infant day and night at his bedside. On the second day she went outside to cry out and vent her anguish. A woman who was an "original" from Semarang noticed her suffering and placed her arm around the woman's shoulders. After hearing the details she spontaneously offered a small crib that she owned. Now at least this very ill little boy was better protected from other diseases. Finally the child, although extremely weakened, recovered somewhat and was taken home, but the nurses confiscated the crib. I couldn't help but wonder if possibly this mother asked herself what would have happened, had she, as a German citizen, opted to stay outside the camp; maybe her little boy would not have contracted meningitis.

Our small group had not been there very long before the rainy season arrived. The monsoon created real problems for the entire camp. The intense downpours with the heavy raindrops would drum loudly on the zinc roofs. The sounds were deafening and added to the somber mood, especially in the hospital. This relentless pounding water heightened the sense of confinement in the gloomy and cavernous room. As always, the first rains of the season came down like a flood and remained constant for one or two weeks. The rushing water swept sticks, bamboo, coconut, and palm leaves down the ditch and piled all this debris up under the hospital latrine. In no time it dammed up and water started to run in all the wrong directions. It even started to wash away the dirt steps at the lower entrance to the hospital. The nurses called us boys from our work at the Benteng up the hill to help.

Daylight was fading fast. We were working under dark, low-hanging clouds and had to solve the problem before the sudden and complete darkness so typical of the tropics, as abrupt as turning off a light switch. Upon our arrival at the ditch we stripped down to our shorts. Going into this powerful current was not easy, and we felt no sense of adventure. Two kids, while lying on either side of the ditch on their stomachs, held on to the others, forming a chain, and we started to poke with bamboo sticks into this pile of debris, which was mixed with the feces of patients who suffered from all sorts of diseases. Our tools weren't much help, since the bamboo sticks broke easily. We were scared and did not dare to submerge our heads. When a large hole finally developed in the obstruction, the forceful pressure of the water gushing through it almost swept us downstream. However, we had succeeded in knocking this jam loose. One nurse stuck her head out of the hospital patio door to thank us and say, "Good job." Then she noticed us, all five boys stark naked, standing in the rain to wash off, and cleaning our shorts. She blushed in her embarrassment, and holding her hand in front of her mouth, ducked back inside.

With increasing numbers of sick people, a decreasing food supply, and the hostility between the Japanese and the imprisoned women, tensions continued to mount. One woman observed that the Japanese definitely knew how to keep conflict alive and seemed to enjoy keeping the women on edge. They never knew what to expect from one day to the next; in that respect, camp life was never monotonous.

Even during the rainy season it was hot and sunny until afternoon, when the rain rushed in. We tried to use the sunshine to our advantage. One day a tall, heavy-set nurse, the mother of two small children, was hanging her laundry on the line just below our makeshift hospital. The commandant's Japanese assistant, Karimoto, happened to walk by three times in a row. A frail, emaciated woman, just released from the hospital, bowed to him on two of his passes but failed on the third attempt. Karimoto began to scream and knocked her off her feet. Slowly she tried to get up. After witnessing this assault, the sturdy nurse approached Karimoto to tell him that the frail woman had just been released from the hospital. His answer was to slap her face, which enraged the nurse. All of her suppressed emotions and tensions exploded. Towering over Karimoto, she hit him back so forcefully that he fell, and she jumped on top of him. She continued to beat him, pushing him into the muddy ground. He stood no chance in the face of her rage. The other women realized that this could mean the death penalty, and they dragged her away.

Karimoto had been totally dishonored, defeated by a low-ranking white female prisoner, and he withdrew, only to return with help. The Japanese soldiers' ensuing treatment of the nurse was an example of controlled brutality. She was set on a chair and whipped, even after she became unconscious. She was then locked up in solitary confinement and did not regain consciousness for days. The penalties for the entire camp were severe as well: three days with no food for anybody. Finally some women were permitted to go to the beaten woman and help feed her, and after about three weeks she was allowed out. A strong and determined woman, she was alive, but she had to be hospitalized to care for her infected skin. This entire episode shocked many of the women, and they thanked God that she was not killed. As their mother was carried off, unconscious, her two little children bowed deeply before the Japanese, as they had been drilled to do.

This woman almost certainly was not given to violence before the Japanese imprisoned her. Life inside the barbed wire was like that. Social change involved all ages and people from varied circumstances. The small children had no concept of what a daddy was. They had seen photographs, but the images meant almost nothing to them. Questions such as, "What is a daddy, mamma?" were particularly painful to many mothers. Later, after Japan's surrender, many fathers did not even recognize their children after an absence of over three years.

At the base of the hill below the hospital was a small bamboo home, closest to the commandant's quarters. Two young women lived there, and it was not crowded as other dwellings were. We couldn't help but notice that the Japanese guards frequented the home of these women, who, according to gossip, had come from the Surabaja harbor area. Rumor further had it that they had served the naval red-light district. Apparently these women were paid in food supplies, and other women in our camp shunned them. These two girls insisted that by entertaining the camp commandant they kept the Japanese from bothering other young girls in camp. At first their statements were met with scorn and ridicule, but we learned how true their arguments were by the end of 1944.

A group of Japanese officers entered Halmaheira, another camp in Semarang, and showed papers that had been issued in Batavia, which they claimed gave them permission to remove young girls of seventeen to service officers in a nearby bordello. These poor girls were hauled off. The regular guards stood aside. The next camp these officers hit was Lampersari. Again the regular guard stepped aside. When the unfamiliar officers started to grab some of the girls, other women exploded, and hundreds of them defied the Japanese, creating a shield with their own bodies around the young girls. They absolutely refused to yield. As the hours ticked away, more women showed up. It became clear that the Japanese camp guards were not going to interfere on behalf of either side. Finally the officers gave up their attempt to kidnap the girls and left. We later learned that these officers had been acting on their own initiative.

The exhausted women were in tears. Some went on their knees and thanked God; it was easy to imagine what those girls would have suffered without the courage and determination of the older women. Our society within the barbed wire protected its members in unexpected ways.

chapter eleven

THE BENTENG

The Benteng, the storage area and food depot, was the nucleus of Camp Lampersari. Located on a hill, it was some sort of military barracks or warehouse out of the previous century. The Benteng was almost square, with a large atrium in the center of the wooden structures. On the roadside was a huge entry door, opening to the outside world. Flanking this entrance were the headquarters of the Japanese commandant and a large food storage area, where sacks of tapioca and rice could be stacked up to two floors high. Not far away from this door, but outside the barbed wire, was a smaller building we called the Tangsi, where the Hei-Hos were quartered.

A five-foot-high fence enclosed the commandant's quarters, and it was easy to see over it. On the western wall were two large barracks. The southern side was partially open and sloped down toward the hospital at the base of the hill and the actual camp. Dirt roads scattered from that point on and led into the main part of Camp Lampersari. Salt bags were stored between the barracks under a lean-to, unguarded, since very few people would steal salt when hungry. All other food products were locked up.

Located on the open side of the Benteng was the makeshift camp kitchen. It was large and grimy, resisting all efforts to keep it clean, and contained nothing more than open fire pits built out of concrete blocks. The kitchen was roofed over, an open structure without a chimney, so that the smoke, and there was always plenty of that, especially when the girls had to use wet wood, escaped on the sides. A chronic shortage of matches compounded the problems.

The barefoot girls found themselves stepping through cinders and ashes as they worked. They tried repeatedly to sweep the ashes down the hill, but their efforts were in effective. No walls protected the women and girls from the monsoon rains or wind. The cooking utensils were equally primitive, consisting of large oil drums set up over the concrete blocks confining the fires, which were usually stoked with green and often wet coconut wood. Those who worked in the kitchen had to be there early, by 4:00 a.m., to get the fires hot enough to cook the tapioca starch and the rice on which we subsisted. They stirred this food with oars and doled it out with the shoulder blade of a cow. Work continued throughout the day, with the last shift leaving at seven in the evening after all the dishes were washed.

There were sixteen pig-iron woks for cooking rice, each one three feet across and about a foot deep. Nobody bothered to wash the rice first; it was too much work and there wasn't enough time. As a result, we had to evict dead bugs from our meals.

Older women worked on long tables cleaning vegetables adjacent to the kitchen. A small kitchen for the hospital patients was located under the eastern roof of the fort, but as time wore on there was not much difference between their rations and ours.

Natives brought in supplies by horse cart, with Hei-Hos standing guard over the delivery. The standard foodstuffs, never in sufficient quantity, were rice, tapioca, some sugar, and occasionally vegetables. On rare occasions we received bones and entrails of beef, hardly any meat, used for the hospital diets. Equally rare were supplies of fresh fruit, milk, or eggs, so that protein, vitamin, and mineral deficiencies became a common problem for nearly every camp inmate.

Conditions, the weather, and the indifference of the Japanese defied efforts to keep the kitchen area clean and safe. Girls who worked in the kitchen suffered injuries—abraded, bruised shinbones when drums would slip and tumble, burns from flying cinders. Standing in front of a hot fire during a noon tropical temperature resulted in dehydration, and smoke irritation of the eyes was also a common problem.

Older women, including my mother, were in charge in the kitchen, and several teenage girls did the hardest physical work of maintaining the smoky fires and stirring the food. The kitchen was the domain of the girls; no boys were tolerated. After rations had been distributed, some of the little girls would crawl inside the drums after they had been turned on their sides to scour them before their next use.

Those women and girls who worked in the kitchen originated from all walks of life. Some girls had been in wealthy families and had never been asked to work so hard, but they discovered a great determination within themselves. Those who continued to labor in the kitchen were hardworking and spirited souls, and it was amazing that they could cook for more than seven thousand people, day after day. It would have been a terrific task under normal conditions, but it was truly astounding considering the conditions at Lampersari. Not all girls were able to stand up to this extremely heavy work in the kitchen, for the circumstances were too difficult. Some were unable to resist the temptation to feed themselves more, at a high cost to others, and gradually the responsible ones were sifted out like the grain from the husk. Their workday would always start with a struggle at 4:00 a.m. Sometimes it was a comical sight to see three girls on their knees fanning a feeble fire by frantically moving a woven bamboo *kepas* up and down while blowing hard. Dust and smoke encircled them in no time, so that only their bare stained feet were visible. A triumphant yell would follow at the detection of a flame. Their smeared smiling faces drew our laughter. The next step was to haul water from the sole water spigot just outside the kitchen floor. The five-foot drums had to be filled with water and carried back. Two girls used a long three-inch-thick bamboo pole, stuck through attached rings, and lifted the drum back to its place on the concrete blocks.

The crew was dressed in cut-off shorts, since skirts were absolutely impracticable. They wore tight halter-tops, and dirty scarves to hold their hair back. We could always identify these crews by their chronically red-rimmed eyes.

The young women's early morning work coincided with their observation of a tradition of the Japanese officers, who were not a bit embarrassed. Each daybreak they walked stark naked to the bathroom for a dousing with water. Still undressed and dripping wet, the Japanese men would then return to their quarters to grab a towel and dry themselves. The early kitchen crew had a front-seat view at this parade. At first the girls snickered, but they soon lost interest.

At times a wind would blow through the open side of the Benteng and help fan the fires. When that happened the smoke drifted into the commandant's quarters, to the girls' great satisfaction. Even though it enraged the commandant, he could do little about it. The women in leadership positions repeatedly told him we needed dry wood, but the situation never changed. We worried, however, and with good reason, that he would order them to stop cooking. We desperately needed our own little fires elsewhere in camp.

We now had a new and harsher commandant, Yamamoto. He was adamant about two items, both irrational under the circumstances. For one thing, he resented women washing clothes, even though they were then lectured about not keeping clean. He felt that they should do other work. He also objected to women making fires of their own. Down the slope of the Benteng was a large tree, where the commandant had a seat fashioned, high up in a fork between branches. At times he would sit there to detect possible smoke spirals from the open field below and down the hill. He made it a habit to hurry down, but usually by the time he arrived, the hot spot had evaporated. The women's yelling of "*Kiotsuke!*" meaning to stand at attention, was an alarm signal that went from person to person down the road like a chain reaction, outpacing his walking speed. By the time he arrived in the field, any fires were doused and pans had disappeared.

All the teenage boys had to work in the old fort. Some of our duties were unloading supplies that arrived at the gate of the Benteng. Because there were thousands of prisoners in Lampersari, the supplies delivered were in great quantity, but there was never enough. When bags of tapioca arrived, we had to work very hard. These bags were loaded on oxcarts that pulled up very close to the wide gate in such a way that the animal ended up in the shade of the tree branches, but the cart's tailgate was exposed to the full sunshine. The drivers squatted down in a semicircle to smoke and catch up on the latest gossip or converse with the Hei-Ho guards.

A bag of tapioca weighed 220 pounds and was solid as a rock. The tailgate of the oxcart was let down and stayed horizontal at a height of about four feet. Two boys stayed inside the cart to upend each sack, quite a demanding job. I was hardly ever in the cart, though, because I was strong enough to be one of the carriers. I would turn my back toward the cart and place my feet apart, then bend my knees to receive the bag over my right sweaty shoulder. I then had to straighten out my knees, balance the bag on my shoulder, and start to move forward at a quick trot, building up speed to climb the stairs formed by stacked sacks, all the way up to the attic floor. We were not allowed to load the attic floor itself; the tapioca bags were too heavy for the floor to support them.

One day, after unloading the tapioca, we found eighty-pound burlap sacks filled with sugar up in the attic. We did not dare to cut them open but could not pass this opportunity. We cut brass curtain rods to about five inches and filed one end into a sharp point. Then we determined which bag of sugar was dry, and I would lean against the burlap. I had deep pockets in my shorts and pulled the brass rod partially out, poked the sharp end into the sack, and let the dry sugar fill up my pockets, all the while appearing to be casually leaning against the stack of sacks. The only noticeable difference after I was through was that the dry sacks were substantially thinner.

Forty-four-pound bags of salt were stacked close to the kitchen and had to be carried a long way. The burlap for salt was rougher than that used for sugar and rubbed the skin of my shoulder open. Salt on sweaty, naked skin was very painful, so I always tried to have a cloth to protect the skin of my neck and shoulder. Often we would sit down to catch our breath, and we perspired plenty, but somehow we never considered taking extra salt in all that heat. I had heard too many stories that salt was poison for people with hunger edema, and I tried to stay away from it.

Once I carried one hundred bags of tapioca in one day. Many boys collapsed doing this brutal work, totally exhausted, or worse yet, while trotting up the stairs of tapioca bags their knees would buckle and they would fall on the sacks or down to the floor below. Many bruised knees and elbows were a result. The stronger kids just had to take over.

The Hei-Hos' supervision of us was usually extremely lax; often they stood in the shade of the trees at a distance from us. This opened up a chance to talk to the oxcart drivers, and sometimes we could trade. I would hand them a shirt or handkerchiefs in exchange for small things like duck eggs or a *gula-jawa* disc, since large items were difficult to conceal. *Gula-jawa* was unrefined brown sugar, poured hot in a coconut half shell, where it cooled down as a disc, trapping bottle flies and many other impurities in the process. Once I hid this prize inside my shirt, where my sweat dissolved some of it. Yet, upon arrival at our home, our group hugged me for bringing them this sticky brown mass. The bottle flies were just evicted.

Vegetable carts were our favorite to unload. We always told the driver that we would clean the cart. We did a great job, and cabbage leaves and broken carrots were our booty. Occasionally a *sado*, or dogcart, would bring in vegetables. The driver would feed his horse by placing a bucket full of hay, corn, and carrots on the ground. When the drivers went to the bathroom, I would push the horse's head aside to grab the carrots. Whenever I had the chance to do so I tried to bring carrots, hidden in my pockets, for the three little girls in our "family." To them a bit of carrot was like candy. It always gave me a great deal of satisfaction to see them savor it. When no carrots were to be found and I entered the house empty-handed, the little ones just looked at me sadly but without complaint. Their big eyes were almost more than I could bear.

One early morning several boys and I were unloading wood for the kitchen. The wood was delivered in *tjikars*, large wheeled ox-drawn vehicles, and it was dripping wet, which meant that the fires in the kitchen would belch a great deal of smoke. The commandant, Yamamoto, whom we nicknamed Ian the Hitter because he seemed to enjoy beating women, had just settled down behind a table outside his building but inside the five-foot fence. On the table stood a bowl of steaming rice. The telephone inside his quarters rang, and he went indoors. I saw my chance and jumped over the fence, grabbed the rice bowl, and climbed back over the barrier. Alerted by a small dog, the commandant saw me, came rushing out, and grabbed me by the foot. I was dressed only in shorts. The commander grabbed a dog whip, a rattan stick with a short leather loop at the end. I had to stand at attention as Yamamoto circled me and started to lash me. The leather loop plowed into my skin. He hit the crooks of both knees until all the skin was gone and raw flesh showed. At first I did not feel anything; anyway, I was determined not to give a peep. I felt so insulted by this short man with the golden teeth and mean grin that I had to control myself not to hit him with my fist. Here I was, fifteen years old, six feet tall, towering over this small man. At the time I was still quite a strong kid and was tempted to tackle him, but my brain told me self-restraint was my only choice. The penalty for attacking a Japanese officer was usually death. The biggest disappointment of all was that I could not eat the rice, and I was so hungry.

Every morning Yamamoto called me out of the *tenko* and made me bow and do deep-knee bends so the wounds would open and blood would run down my calves. He would stand there and smile, for he knew that the succeeding days were painful ones. Once he poked with his dog whip at the back of my knee and knocked loose some scabs. Flies were attracted to the raw spots, and I could not get rid of them. After about a week, bored with my impassive response, he quit calling me out of the lineup. I had never allowed him to see how badly it hurt. It took a while, but I washed the debris of the sores with saltwater, and to my surprise the wounds healed without scars.

Initially all concentration camps in the Dutch East Indies were under the supervision of Japanese civilians based in Batavia. In 1944 an order came from Tokyo that all camps were to be placed under army rule, including the camps in the eastern Indies, which up to that point had been supervised by the navy. This worsened our conditions significantly and seemed to explain why commandants changed camps more frequently. Each change in leadership seemed to make conditions worse.

The army officers who were now in charge of the camps hated to hear complaints or see requests appear on their desks. Their indifferent responses and hostile attitude irritated the prisoners. When they could not handle a problem presented to them, their response was usually to ignore it. For example, if a mother complained about the conditions of some sick little kids, the Japanese would order her to dress the little ones and put socks on them, knowing well that these mothers had none, and obviously ignoring the real issue of malnutrition and poor medical care. A lecture would then follow, the recurring theme of which was advise to the women to sacrifice themselves for their children. The officers wrote this speech down in their records and considered the problem solved. Nothing else happened, since the commandant considered he had done his duty. If the request were about adults, the commandant would look on unemotionally and quietly respond, "All of you may die in this camp. There is plenty of room in the cemetery."

It became obvious that the Japanese soldiers were unhappy in their assignments here. Some had been sent straight from service in China and were homesick. They hated the tropics, the heat, and their inability to communicate properly with the natives. Further, it was obvious that they considered guarding women and children as less than glorious duty to their emperor.

Especially when reminded by our camp leaders about international law regarding the treatment of prisoners, our captors would sincerely explain that Emperor Hirohito would handle any such rulings and order them to carry out related actions. "But no such order has arrived," they would point out to us. They would then turn to the complainers and say, "You prisoners are ungrateful. Now you will be unhappy, for you will be punished." The women felt cheated by their response.

During inspections of the overcrowded homes the Japanese would say, "Your house smells bad; you should be ashamed." However, no action was ever taken to try to do something to eliminate the smells or the larger problems of overcrowding and poor sanitation. Again the real issues were ignored, and blame was incorrectly placed on the prisoners. We gradually realized that this was the predictable reaction to any attempts to improve our living conditions. I often heard the women complain to each other about this indifference; the adults trying to care for their children must have felt particularly helpless. The Japanese response to requests for help or supplies often was "*Mada, mada*," which, Mrs. Van Der Poel explained, meant, "Don't bother." These Japanese themselves always tried to be clean, but they saw no correlation between their standards of hygiene and those of their prisoners.

On many occasions the Japanese would hold *razzias*, raids, mostly looking for Dutch coins and jewelry, something they had done right from the start. More than one mother had hidden money inside her child's cloth dolls. While everybody was lined up and inspected, these toddlers clamped their dolls against their chests. For reasons that we could not explain too well, the Japanese always took their frustrations out on tall women, especially if they were redheads, and beat them savagely, often with no justification at all. At roll call, these women chose to stand in the back row.

After we had been in camp for several months, in June 1944 it was announced that all boys aged ten and older had to be quartered in the barracks of the Benteng, the younger ones together in a large room and the older ones in another room with bunk beds. There were two boys of eighteen who, for unknown reasons, were not shipped off to the adult camps— but then, little the Japanese did made sense to us. Although the camp was large and very densely crowded, we boys could still manage to have some contact with our mothers and sisters. We were not restricted from descending the hill to help or visit people all over camp, but we were often prevented from doing so by our work assignments. Sometimes these jobs put a boy in close proximity to a family member, as was the case for Anton and me, since Mother worked in the kitchen at the Benteng. For others it was harder, especially if family members were assigned a duty clear across camp. As hard as it was for my mother not to have Anton and me with her, her truest sympathies were for the families whose boys were only ten or eleven. It seemed that the Japanese were determined to undermine all efforts at any stable social structure that we prisoners tried to establish. The Japanese considered ten-year-olds to be adults; at least that was the explanation given to us.

Not so many months after this move, the commandant took the next and final step to separate our families. One of the eighteen-year-olds, tall and skinny, who was fluent in Malay and Javanese, made plenty of deals with the Hei-Hos. Javanese is a far more complex language. He was nicknamed Pantas, the Malay word for handy, although it was not entirely chosen as a compliment. He was a good friend of another eighteen-year-old, a broad-shouldered fellow nicknamed Tegap, meaning "strong." He was taller and acted as a backup for Pantas, and he had a swagger to his walk. Pantas bought *gula-jawa* and eggs from the Hei-Hos, which he in turn sold for money, jewelry, or linen. He usually approached the Hei-Ho guard at the main entrance just before he was going off duty. Pantas handed him the linen that the guard stuffed in his shirt, and the soldier pointed at a sack with food stashed behind a tree. Pantas and Tegap were able to feed themselves adequately from the profits.

Eggs were especially prized because of the lack of protein. Raw green salted duck eggs were the best because they did not break easily. The natives placed these duck eggs in salt to let them cure, and the eggs turned greenish and the inside became slightly glassy and rubbery. They became a precious item, especially for mothers with small children.

Nearly everyone disliked Pantas, the smuggler. He bragged about how he ran his operations, and he and his sidekick Tegap never shared anything, showing no compassion even to small sick children. At one point he had his eye on a seventeen-year-old girl who started the kitchen fires at four in the morning. After some effort he had sex with her at that dark hour in exchange for several duck eggs. Their tryst took place on the stack of gunnysacks filled with salt, and after he was through he came back to our quarters in the Benteng to brag about his conquest, but then started to complain about a sore crotch. His scrotum had scraped over the gunnysacks and salt had rubbed into his skin. He noticed the soreness, but in our dark room no lights were allowed, and he could not determine the real problem. When daylight finally arrived he was able to remedy his problem. He soaked his testicles in a pan filled with water, which indeed gave him some relief. We made many remarks about his "salted experience." Some boys said that pepper should have been added to make it complete.

Even though many rough jokes were made about this episode, most of us felt sorrier for the girl than for anything Pantas might have suffered. She had to be so hungry to agree to Pantas's proposition. Fear of pregnancy had diminished, for almost all women had quit menstruating as one consequence of starvation.

We also had to serve night duty, called *fushinban* by the Japanese, as guards of the interior of the camp. We never understood the reasoning, and we figured this to be another layer of harassment. We had to work shifts of two hours, three boys per shift, one inside the Benteng, one at the outlet, and one at the bottom of the hill. Every night a Japanese guard checked us. If he caught one asleep the boy would receive a terrible beating. We yelled at the top of our voices in case we needed to wake up the next guy to be inspected down the hill, and we informed the inspecting soldier that everything was in order: *"Fushinban ijo arimasen!"*

Even when we were exhausted, a good night's rest was not always possible. Some kids had to get up in the middle of the night, quite often in a rush, due to diarrhea, since dysentery was a recurring problem. No lights were allowed, and so kids stumbled over the others in their haste. Some kids started to come down with malaria.

In September 1944, the boys in the Benteng were assembled for roll call. This one was held exceptionally early, at five in the morning, official Japanese time, which was two hours ahead of us. Normally tenko was held at seven. Several Japanese and Hei-Hos appeared. After the *bango*, the head count, the Japanese told us to collect all our belongings because we boys were to march to a different camp. That turned out to be Camp Bangkong, which until then had been a women's camp. The women there were being moved to Camp Halmaheira, another female camp of five thousand, also in Semarang, close by.

My brother and I collected our meager possessions. I was glad to have a rucksack and a large mosquito net for the two of us. Everything happened so quickly. Before we knew it we were lined up in blocks, carrying our few belongings. The order came and we marched off, three abreast, through the wide-open gate. In a glimpse I saw Mother, standing at the side of the gate, with tears in her eyes, waving. She happened to be working at the kitchen, or she, like so many other mothers, would not have even known that we were being sent away.

.

chapter twelve

CAMP BANGKONG

When we marched through the gate of Lampersari, the older boys first and the ten-year-olds in the rear, we had no idea what our destination was. A ten-year-old who looked far younger then his stated age was the very last one. Before he got into motion he discovered his teenage sister, who worked at that early hour at the fireplace fifty feet away. Upon seeing her brother, she ran to the formation and kissed him good-bye, for she had taken care of this kid since their mother had died a few months earlier. A Hei-Ho behind the lineup, armed with a wooden rifle tipped with a real bayonet, hit the girl on her back with the wooden butt, and he scraped the boy's thigh with the tip of the bayonet. The youngster jumped and tried to catch up with the column while limping, blood showing from his exposed thigh. All along the trek he had trouble keeping up with the others while his lips quivered and he tried to prevent tears from running down his cheeks. How lonely he must have felt.

In a long line in rows of three, hundreds of us kids streamed toward the bridge over the canal. We were under no circumstance allowed to break ranks, and as a result the little injured boy was on his own. Ahead of us the Japanese in charge rode a bicycle. Silently we said farewell to the Benteng, which had been our most recent home, and the Tangsi nearby.

Anton stayed with me. He did not talk. Neither did I. We had no idea where we were heading as we crossed the bridge, and soon found ourselves entering the old Karreweg, or wagon trail. That early in the morning many natives were on the road to work, with a yoke over their shoulders supporting flat baskets hung on each end, called *pikoelans*. They stared at our column silently and with obvious curiosity. Women carrying a child in a *slendang* resting on their hips stopped at the roadside to watch and gestured to each other.

Mother's efforts to pack wisely when we were first moved from Malang were again appreciated. Draped over my rucksack I had our mosquito net, which was big enough for both Anton and myself to sleep under, something critically important in mosquito-infested Semarang. Small quantities of yarn and thread and a needle helped us keep together the few pieces of clothing we had. Anton and I each had a two-inch-deep enamelware container with large hooked handles and one knife, fork, and spoon apiece. I also carried my two larger knives, which I used for working with wood. We had no money by this time, although some of the boys still had a few carefully hidden coins. Medicines like quinine were long since used up, and few of us had any soap left.

We found the distance to our destination not to be great. The Japanese soldier and the two Hei-Hos who had marched at the front of our column stopped at the rear gate of what they called Camp Bangkong, whose name in Sundanese meant "big frog" or "toad." We marched up to one of the two back entrances, adjacent to each other. The gate that we faced was a filthy and dilapidated entry made of wood and bamboo, clearly used for supplying the camp with wood and food. Deep ruts from supply wagons tracked all the way into camp. A large garbage pile, waiting to be cleaned up, was just outside the gate. My heart sank into my toes at the sight of this compound that appeared dark, stark, and gloomy. I could not help wondering why this was happening to us.

Bangkong had been a Catholic school attached to a convent. The school, whose grounds were the size of a football field, was now surrounded by two rows of barbed wire. The front side of the compound had a barrier between the church and the school buildings on both sides, reaching sixty feet in height, which was covered with woven bamboo. Part of our sunlight was taken away, making Bangkong darker and, to some of the younger boys, more sinister. The front gate of the school opened on to a main road, Djalan Bangkong.

Bangkong, and Lampersari as well, were not isolated, but had been established areas of Semarang before the Japanese came with their barbed wire. Thus the roads at either end of Camp Bangkong were heavily traveled. On Djalan Bangkong, opposite the entrance to the camp, were numerous two-story buildings occupied by businesses. It was apparently to keep the workings of the camp hidden from the community that the tall barriers were erected, but this made no sense, since we were marched along public roads daily to work in the fields. Furthermore, the Japanese had demonstrated repeatedly that they were not concerned with the reactions of the natives or the Chinese who were outside the camps. However, as we had seen already in Lampersari, many things the Japanese did made no sense.

Not far past Bangkong the town thinned out, and most of the roads dwindled to footpaths. Beyond a large swampy area, uninhabited, lay the Tjandi foothills on the higher side of the only road, the Deitjonghan, where one building existed, the high school. The Japanese now used this school for an officer-training program. The Deitjonghan was on the perimeter of the fields we soon found ourselves working in. From these fields we were able to see the Tjandi hills.

The original Bangkong school and convent had been efficiently laid out. Standing perpendicular to the two roads, the Karreweg and the Djalan Bangkong, were two long buildings, running parallel, sandwiching a large two-towered church and the *aula*, the gymnastics hall. Toward the Karreweg were multiple bathrooms. The two long buildings contained classrooms on the first and second floors, and along the entire length of the buildings were extensive verandahs. The upper floor had a long, wide balcony reaching out ten feet. Between the church and the buildings were large open sandy spaces used for assembly. As the camp population grew, up to 1,400 boys could be found during *tenko* in these commons. Adjacent to Bangkong but outside the compound itself was the housing for the Japanese commandant.

Standing barefooted and sweating on the hot asphalt of the Karreweg, we were counted, a slow process, since the soldiers had trouble with their calculations. It took four head counts before they were satisfied, and then they gave the order that we could enter Bangkong. We passed the makeshift kitchen, built against the outside wall of the *pendopo*, a large roofed-over area. Against that wall were stacked concrete blocks with spaces between them. Fires were built to heat tall oil drums, balancing precariously on the blocks. This entire work area was totally exposed to the weather except for awnings, which were intended to protect the stokers from the rain. Often they had to stand between the oil drums to stay dry, only to inhale the smoke. It was Lampersari all over again. The *pendopo* was next to the back gate and was eventually occupied by sickly elderly men, especially those suffering from tuberculosis.

We had attracted a small crowd of Javanese youngsters gawking at us from across the road just before we entered the back gate. Many of us became uncomfortable, the more so after we had marched through the gate and entered the largest sandy area, alongside the church and aula, that became our parade grounds, for it was here that we always had our numerous daily tenkos. Again we were counted. It was at this point that we got our first ugly taste of the new camp management. It was so hot and the uncertainty of what to expect made us all fidgety. One boy, Leo, whom I had known only slightly in Lampersari, immediately attracted the attention of the guards because of his nervous and silly grin. He was barely fifteen years old and was often awkward in his manner. Perhaps the guards thought he was taunting them, but in any case, they took this opportunity to teach the rest of us strict obedience. The guard standing in front of Leo demanded that he bow deeply, and he concluded Leo's efforts were not good enough. With two hands alternating, the guard slapped him on both sides of his face. He made him bow again and the beating was repeated. Finally the guard tired of beating Leo and moved on with the counting. Leo's face was bright red, his neck was swollen, and his ears glowed brighter than the sun in the sky. This nervousness was ultimately to be his undoing.

Slowly the mass of boys was divided into groups called *hans*, each containing about one hundred boys. A *hancho* was appointed for each han, assisted by a *komicho*. My brother and I ended up in Han 2, Classroom 5, downstairs. The bigger boys were mostly assigned to Han 1 and Han 2, but younger brothers could stay with their older brothers. We realized later that this meant more and harder work for the younger ones. There were a few boys already in Bangkong, and we learned from them that their mothers and sisters had been transferred to Camp Halmaheira earlier that same day. Later that morning more boys joined us from Halmaheira.

On the twelfth and thirteenth of September, a contingent of young boys arrived by truck from Karangpanas and Gedangan, also in Semarang. In addition, the Japanese brought in about fifty old men, who kept mostly to themselves. The arrival of the boys and old men from Karangpanas caused chaos while they were moved around.

Karangpanas means a place that is hot. It was close to Tjandi. The 2,600 women who had been there were moved to Halmaheira and Lampersari. The 3,700 women from Gedangan, a very dark camp close to the sea, where buildings were totally enclosed, were moved to Lampersari, where the new arrivals were at first troubled by the bright daylight. These two camps had been convents and boasted of terrible conditions. Karangpanas became known as the infant's graveyard, so many epidemics occurred. A measles epidemic took nineteen emaciated infants, followed later on by meningitis and poliomyelitis, demanding ten more young lives, some of them the younger brothers or sisters of our roommates. Recurrent requests for hospitalization at the city hospital were finally granted after many weeks had passed. The Karangpanas commandant made the sick women work, for in a speech he stated his belief that one-third of the camp reporting ill was faked. All these women were eventually sent to Camp Lampersari.

Eighty boys from Bangkong, including Anton and me, went by truck to Karangpanas on the twenty-eighth and the thirtieth of November and the first of December to provide the needed labor. There were about a thousand cabin trunks belonging to the women to be loaded on trucks. I often had to hoist these big trunks by myself, and I was surprised that the bare skin on my back remained fairly well intact.

We were not allowed into Lampersari as I had hoped, thinking we might see Mother. Teenaged girls did the unloading. As a special reward we received a small meal of pork ragout and some sugar. As good as it tasted, I would have gladly traded the food for a few words with Mother.

Back in Bangkong we realized to our surprise that some of the original occupants, nuns, had been allowed to remain in what had become a boys' camp. Additional nuns arrived from the various female camps until there was a total of forty-five of them. They ran the makeshift fifty-bed hospital. There was also an attempt at an apothecary, occupying a small room adjacent to the hospital, which was run by a pharmacist, but it was poorly equipped. There was but one bathroom and one faucet for the entire hospital.

The church was converted into sleeping quarters for the little boys, even below the altar and the sacristy. Teakwood bunks had replaced the pews. We were told that in Japanese culture a ten-year-old was considered to be an adult, but they seemed painfully young to us, who were only a few years older. There were even two orphaned nine-year-olds among us. The presence of the nuns was critically important and a godsend to these littlest ones. We others had to sleep on the tiled floors of what had been classrooms.

The camp, housing at least 1,400 persons, measured 73 yards long and 130 yards deep. Along one side of the compound were four rooms set aside for the sickest boys and old men, where the nuns spent most of their time. Adjacent to the left tower of the church was the walk-in clinic, staffed by nuns and a physician. Three physicians had come with us from Lampersari. The chief of medicine, the Austrian Dr. Neuberger, had been in charge of the female Camp Bangkong and had practiced in Semarang for a long time. As a matter of fact, he had delivered my brother Anton. There were eighteen physicians in Bangkong, but only three were allowed to practice.

At the far end of the same long wall were several smaller rooms used for various functions, administration, storage of vegetables, storage of rice, the jail set up for those of us who might choose to challenge our captors, and a storage room for tools that was opposite the pigsty. Near the front gate was the guardroom, where the Japanese and Hei-Hos would gather to take turns patrolling our camp. Adjacent to the guardroom stood the most horrific room in the camp, the death room, where so many boys and old men ended their stay in Bangkong.

That first evening Anton and I started to get acquainted with the other boys in our classroom. We had to learn to work and eat together. We tried to learn where people had come from and what their experiences had been. In the first few months there were twenty-seven boys to our room. At a later date our group had to absorb far more boys, filling the room to a crowded thirty-eight. We finally realized that we were on our own, not able to fall back on or consult with our mother. During our stay in Lampersari, even when we were quartered in the Benteng, we had been able to talk to Mother or ask her opinion when she was at work in the kitchen, and sometimes we visited her in her room on the other side of the camp. Anton and I never cried, though, and from there on we never discussed our separation from her.

We slept on the floor under a large mosquito net on two skinny dilapidated mattresses that had been left behind. The space assigned to each of us was sixteen by forty-eight inches, including the storage area for our belongings. Our rucksack hung from a nail in the wall. During the day we pulled the mosquito net up to the ceiling and rolled our mattresses up toward the wall to cover our possessions. The only footpath through the room was one tile wide, eight inches, in between the mattresses.

A few kids were assigned to work in the kitchen under the supervision of a forty-year-old man. Most of the older men worked at the vegetable tables with some of the very young boys. However, it became immediately clear that in Batavia the Japanese high command's intention was for us to work in the fields. The camp commandant made it known that every day, even Sundays, at least four hundred boys were to report at the parade grounds for work.

Our daily work followed the same routine for most of our time. In the tropics the sun comes up at six o'clock and that was our waking time. We all tried to get to the bathrooms, only fourteen of them for 1,400 persons. The kids who had to work in the fields had priority over the ones who stayed behind. Each of us tried to wash or shower in a hurry. The spacious shower stall, hastily erected by the Japanese, was nothing more than a long perforated pipe hanging overhead; the water ran continuously from six to seven-thirty in the morning. More than twenty boys were able to shower at the same time. The *kedek* (woven bamboo) walls only covered from sixteen inches above the ground to five feet. Shorts and towels were hung over them. During the day the faucets were turned off.

We dressed quickly in shorts held up by a belt. This belt was very important for several reasons. Attached to mine was my prisoner number, 17326, printed on a scrap of cloth in East Indian ink. Although this number gave me a feeling of resentment at being dehumanized, I wrote on the front of my forbidden diary, "Bangkong, Han 2, Room 5, 17326." In defiance of Japanese efforts otherwise, that thin diary was a continued attempt to maintain a sense of myself. During the day I stuck it inside my thin mattress.

Hooked to our belts was a zinc cup with a large handle, and a small enameled pan with an ear attachment for hanging on the backs of our belts. A spoon was stuck in our belts, also in back, and sometimes while we walked the spoon would clank against the enamel pan. There were no shoes, no shirts, usually no hats.

After showering and dressing we stood in line to pick up our breakfast, a large cup of tasteless tapioca starch just like we had been given in Lampersari. By now I knew how poorly that empty meal sustained me. Assembly was always at seven. Before our line up we had to get a *patjol*, an Indonesian hoe, from the *goedang*, the storage room opposite the kitchen. We lined up in blocks of forty boys, called patjol hans. When the Japanese or Korean guard walked by with his Hei-Hos we had to yell *"kiotsuke!"* and *"keire!"* and, of course, we had to bow deeply.

The Dernier brothers were then put in charge. taught anyone who paid attention about the frailties of human character. They carried a card on their belt with the words "Hancho, Indo-Belg." They were Belgians, so we were told, in their early forties, and had held some kind of minor positions in Surabaja before the war. Johan, the older, recognized my name and told me he knew my Dad. His inquiry about my well-being dripped with honey, but there was no bit of honesty or sincerity in the man, and I immediately disliked him.

Here in Bangkong, the Japanese discovered each man's weaknesses quickly. They found that the Dernier brothers were so fearful that they would gladly bully the boys in their charge. They were responsible for keeping all the boys working in the fields and didn't hesitate to beat a child if they thought it might gain favor for them with the Japanese.

We marched off through the front gate onto the asphalt road, patjols over our shoulders. Many blocks further down, the column of about four hundred teens turned on to a cool, shaded, rather pretty road, known as Djalan Siwilan. This road ended in swampy fields where we were put to work at the site of our first major labor project. We built a narrow dirt road that connected with Djalan Siwilan, and which led us further into the open, marshy fields beyond. This snaking, muddy track, totally built with our sweat, was just wide enough for a truck. On this route several bridges had to be built out of coconut tree trunks. Where a ditch traversed the road, by laying the trunks parallel, we made a bridge. The gaps we filled with rock and mud. These trees were very strong, but they rotted out rather quickly. The Japanese boasted that their bunkers were built out of those trees and withstood bombardments very well.

During October 1944 the rains were sometimes heavy, and our road was flooded at points, so that supply carts with their steel wheels bogged down. The Japanese guard in charge, whom we nicknamed Easter Egg due to his shape, and two Javanese *mandoers*, from the Portuguese word for overseer, were going to remedy this drainage problem. A group of taller boys was called to work on the digging of a ditch across the road. I tried to slip away, but Easter Egg grabbed me. When he sensed my reluctance, he kicked me hard in the thigh.

Working with a hoe in the blubbery soil was exhausting, but finally we dug the ditch. Then an army truck arrived, loaded with coconut tree trunks, but it also got stuck. As a result we had to unload and roll these trees to the ditch. First, with great difficulty, a bulkhead had to be made to protect the side from washing out. Without mechanical help, we then moved the logs into place on the supporting bulkheads to form another small bridge. While supervising this project, Easter Egg, in agitation, sank knee-deep in the soggy mud of the ditch, and a flow of the most horrible Japanese words left his mouth. The mandoers had to pull him out. The mud-covered and soaked Easter Egg was comical to look at, but we did not dare to laugh. He certainly had lost his composure. I noticed a smile on the faces of the mandoers, who were actually the ones in charge of the construction.

The wind had come up when the order finally came to go home, and we skinny boys, dressed only in wet shorts, shivered. Tired and hungry, we marched to camp, while the rain washed the mud off our skins.

If there were warm water we would receive a cup to make tea, a real treat able to lift our spirits. Some boys would always stand next to the gate upon our return, and often they would yell, "No tea." Many heads visibly sagged at such a disheartening welcome. All patjols were to be counted when turned in and locked up for the night. Sunset was at six and the lights were turned off early.

The fields we were to work lay against the foothills of Tjandi. On top of a knoll in the corner of these fields was a bamboo home, which we were made to build for the Japanese in charge, who could then oversee the fields from his window. The thatched roof and awnings were made of *atap*, folded dried coconut leaves. On the side, overlooking the fields, a long section of the wall could fold down horizontally toward the outside to rest on foldout legs. This enabled the guard in charge to observe us through his field glasses while he was seated in the shade of the awning.

Upon arrival in the fields our column of boys had to be counted again at the unofficial parade grounds, which was really only an open field. After dismissal, everybody ran to the ditch to urinate, since the watery breakfast of tapioca starch had now completed its route through our bodies. By that time it was already hot. Our work tempo through the day was very slow. Most kids were emaciated, and sickly and moved like robots or zombies.

The Japanese did not have sufficient men to supervise us closely, so they patrolled the hills, observing our progress through their binoculars. The guards did their own cooking on charcoal *anglos* inside their bamboo headquarters, and of course we could smell their vegetables, rice, and chicken. The entrails of the chicken on a plate were visibly dumped through the window into a garbage can outside the window. A man in his fifties, who was assigned to special tasks, ran forward and grabbed the slithering entrails and slurped them as if they were a delicacy. The Japanese cook stuck his head out of the window and grinned from ear to ear, enjoying the man's maddening hunger.

One of the Japanese officers, perhaps the engineer, made a small model of the surrounding fields about two by three feet in size. For this model he used cooked rice, which sticks together and molds easily into shape. Once, when I had to deliver hot coffee through the window from a fire pit at our parade grounds, I got the chance to admire this art, but I would have preferred to eat the rice.

The swamps had been used as rice fields, but the Japanese wanted cabbage and *oebie*, a sweet-tasting root vegetable something like a sweet potato. The problem was that the climate, with temperatures between 80 and 105 degrees Fahrenheit, was too hot for cabbage. Further, oebie does not like to get soaked; it needs drainage. In order to correct this problem we were told to dig parallel ditches. The scooped-out mud formed long ridges that we had to fertilize with human manure. This cabbage and oebie project was doomed from the start. Everybody knew that, but the Japanese blamed us for the failure.

Downhill in the near distance we were able to see the Japanese barracks and training grounds of the officer training camp quartered in the old high school. Indeed we were awed by the persistence and stamina of the young trainees. All morning we could see them running back and forth over the extensive fields, singing most of the time, which we could hear clearly. Sometimes they would sing the "Kimigayo," their national anthem. On other occasions they would sing their notorious marching song, unpleasantly familiar ever since their campaign in China: "Aikoku Kyoshin Kyoku." When they would sing in Malay, "Antjur America," meaning "Chop up America," we certainly felt that it was meant to antagonize us. By the end of the morning, if the wind blew in our direction, we could smell their rancid sweat. We remarked among ourselves that they looked like walking showers, the sweat dripping off them. The Japanese were not adapting well to the heat and humidity of the tropics.

Before noon a group of older boys was selected, usually twelve older ones, cronies of the Dernier brothers, to pull three carts of cooked rice from Camp Bangkong to the fields. The carts were old ammunition transports, two-wheelers built of steel, including the wheels and rim, and designed for one horse. Now we were used as the horses. One boy was put between the shafts, and draped over his shoulder was a sling attached on either end to the shafts. Two Hei-Hos would be added to this caravan. The only advantage to this assignment was that it usually meant some extra nourishment. In the rainy season it was tough going through the mud, for a steel cart was heavy. The metal rims were at best two inches wide, and moving the carts over those coconut palm bridges was very difficult. Balancing the load was of the utmost importance, otherwise the cart would tip over backward and spill our food, an unforgivable mistake. Rice was placed in a large washing pail and cooked corn was carried in a crate. If there was soup it sloshed around in another pail.

If the accompanying Hei-Ho was not observant, the boys who pushed the cart used their spoon to scoop an extra bite of corn out of the crate. During the month of December one sergeant, Hashimoto, walked toward the hauling team and poked a stick in their stomachs. "You are fat," he said. He drove this group of perplexed boys off into the fields. Looking around, he picked a new nine-man team, which included me.

Unfortunately, Hashimoto was soon transferred and Johan Dernier, commandeered his favorites back on the job. The Dernier brothers and cohorts, we could see, had access to the fireplaces of the Japanese guards, and they profited by transactions carried out with natives and Hei-Hos halfway down the path. They wanted only particular boys to be aware of or participate in the bartering.

There was a break when the food carts arrived around one o'clock, then assembly and *bango*. If everything was found to be in order, we would get our ration of cooked rice, which we were told amounted to ninety grams, sometimes one or two tablespoons of cooked corn or cabbage soup, and rarely a banana.

A twelve-year-old was found standing for the second time in the food line, trying to obtain another scoop of rice. Charlie Dernier pushed the boy out of the line and felt that he had to show his authority and hit the kid's head with his cane. This boy tried to cover his head with both arms, than he ran away, keeping a safe distance from Charlie. Johan started to scream, "Charlie, don't hit him too hard, he will break in two." This stopped Charlie's violence. The kids in the lineup who had spotted this boy transferred their hostility to Charlie.

The two eighteen-year-olds, Pantas and Tegap, had become komichos to the brothers Dernier. They were openly allowed to get a second serving.

Most of us would find shade under banana trees after eating and lie down if time allowed. Soon after "lunch" it was back to work, in the oppressive heat of 100 to 110 degrees. Our Japanese captors ignored the unwritten law of the tropics and refused to allow us the traditional break during the hottest part of the afternoon.

On an evening in September 1944, not long after Bangkong had been filled with boys, two Dutch buddies, Piet and Penkie, both thirteen, went through the barbed wire near the back of the compound, just to eat at the *pasar*. Knowing that the local, who themselves were completely intimidated by the Japanese, could not keep them safe, the boys crawled back under the wire. Upon their return they were discovered by the Hei-Hos walking the perimeter. By this time it was two in the morning, but the Japanese rang the bell for tenko. Everybody, including the ill, had to attend. The hancho and komicho of the two boys' han had to take a position in front of us all. As we watched, the Japanese guard showed off his skill in an audible belting of these two, with such severity that the komicho lost consciousness. Due to the wartime blackout, the illumination of the sandy grounds was poor and made everything look even spookier. After this display of brutality, the two boys, also severely beaten, were pulled by a rope and paraded in front of all of us present at the tenko. While the guards screamed, we watched in deep silence, standing only in our shorts, while a cool night breeze surrounded us and made us shiver. There was nothing we could do. We had reached the point where we did not even cry anymore. We were finally released from the tenko after the Japanese felt they had provided a sufficient lesson. We returned to our mattresses, feeling mentally drained.

These two boys were locked up for about six weeks in the pigsty and received very little food. To make matters worse, the next day the Kempeitai, the Japanese secret police, marched in for further questioning, and both boys were whipped. Thank God another tenko was not called and we did not have to witness that. The Japanese could not accept the obvious explanation: the two boys were hungry. It was absurd to think of two thirteen-year-olds as a threat to the Japanese war machine.

We were always on the lookout for food, and in the early months at Bangkong the rainy season worked to our advantage, since there was more to forage for. If I was lucky I was able to find *kangkung*, a bluish-purple watery plant rich in iron and vitamin C. This plant was typically found in a swampy environment. The natives believed that *kangkung*, consumed in large quantities, could make a person loony or loco, but we felt lucky to find some.

The afternoon heat made most kids exhausted, and they just stood in the fields, leaning on their hoes. At four in the afternoon the gong would bang for another assembly and numbering, followed by the return march to camp. Upon arrival at Bangkong we were counted again. Sometimes, for no obvious reason, we were counted outside the gate while standing in the hot asphalt road. We were barefoot, and even though we had thickly calloused soles the heat made it hard to stand on the sticky surface. Many of us placed the metal part of the hoe under our feet to cool off. In camp we hoped that the water would have been turned on so we could at least drink and wash our feet, which were usually caked with mud, as if we were wearing mud socks.

The evening meal consisted of one slice of corn bread, at best one by four inches, two slices for the workers. A slice was no bigger than, half an inch thick. Afterward we would sit on the verandah's edge where it was cooler and talk until sunset, in an attempt to try to catch up with the latest events in camp. It was striking that very little laughter was heard, otherwise quite common among teenagers.

However the Japanese might have represented it, Bangkong was a labor camp. The one European nominally in charge was not a Dutchman but a Luxembourger; he was rarely visible around camp and never stood up for us boys in the face of Japanese tirades or beatings. He never even stood beside us during those brutal experiences. Deaths in the camp went unobserved by him, and we wondered what exactly he did to be in charge. Over time it became apparent that one of his primary roles was to sign for the food deliveries, and as long as there was a case of beer in each delivery for him, he would sign for food that was not supplied. The Japanese commandant pocketed the saved money. Both men seemed satisfied with this arrangement, but the boys held nothing but scorn for the Luxembourger.

All the Japanese did was give the orders; they did not want to be bothered by how the details worked, unless the arrangements clashed with their thinking. They left the organization up to the Dutch leaders. Several older men assisted the two Dernier brothers, who were in charge of the crews in the field. One of these men, Mr. Vetter, was a gentle person; he supervised the little kids in the field and really tried to protect them.

Johan Dernier was in charge, and he always yelled at his brother, Charlie. Charlie walked with a stick and assumed the right to beat us kids. He had an awkward walk; his trunk leaned back and he had a gait that was unforgettable. After he lifted his leg he would jerk the lower part out forward and sideways at a 45-degree angle. The other leg would follow the same spastic pattern, so his feet would land far apart.

I despised these brothers. Sometimes they made more noise than the guards.

chapter thirteen

HORSEPLAY

Tjiandi, with Camp Bangkong just below it, was a suburb in the foothills, which came down like a crescent on the swamps where the oebie fields were located. The marshlands ended at the only road, where the old high school was located. From there the city of Semarang sloped gently down to the harbor.

One blistering hot morning, after we had only been in Bangkong for two weeks, we had our routine tenko right after our meager breakfast of starch. While we were lined up in the usual pattern, three boys deep, a Korean guard, whom we had nicknamed the Bloodhound, suddenly appeared. Sergeant Hashimoto, the man with the voice of a castrate, accompanied him. Of course Hashimoto had an unkind nickname, but he never knew what our Dutch word meant, so we were safe in our ridicule of him. The Bloodhound pulled nine of us kids out of the ranks, including me. He herded us toward the back gate behind the kitchens.

Apparently the food-delivery system had not been sufficiently organized yet. Outside the gate, on the side of the road, were three old steel ammunition carts, very similar to the ones we used for hauling food to the fields, the posts connected by a noisy chain on either side. Here again we were made to be the horses. Three kids were assigned to a cart. Each of us was dressed only in a pair of shorts and we had no shoes. I was to become one of the horses, while two other boys pushed. The carts rattled terribly as we got underway, the chains connected to the metal posts on the sides clanging noisily. Everyone on the roadside stopped to look at our caravan. Going downhill toward town, the heavy metal cart accelerated, and I had to lean back on it constantly. The two boys in the rear had to lean and pull backward in order to slow the cart down further.

The two swaggering officers marched us off, assisted by three Hei-Hos as guards. The asphalt road sloped gently down, and my feet became warm from this sticky substance. Our destination was at first unknown to us, but it turned out to be a large warehouse at the harbor, quite a distance away. There, at the warehouse, Hashimoto made us load into our carts bags of tapioca weighing 220 pounds each, some salt, and unrefined sugar.

By the time the loading was completed it was noon and we were given some cooked rice in a banana leaf, which Hashimoto himself had purchased from the Indonesians. This was really special, for it came out of his pocket. A few times he showed human feelings, and for that he stood out from the others.

After this meal he ordered *yashime*, rest, for about one hour. The Japanese were really bothered by the heat and left the guard duty up to the Hei-Hos. The officers settled down in the shade and fell asleep. Some of us kids started to roam around in the storage building.

I found a sack filled with *dedek*, the husk collected after the Javanese women laboriously processed rice. In no time I could imagine myself back in that magical vacation spot on Mount Tampat, where we had watched the village women at work and heard their melodic songs in the evenings.

Each *kampong* had its own distinctive *loempang*, a hollowed-out tree used as the vessel for pounding rice grains to separate the husks. They were of different sizes in different areas of Java, and the type of tree used made the sound from each loempang distinctly different and unique to that village. In our area the loempang was shorter. After the rice stalks, averaging three feet in height, were harvested at the rice fields, they were bundled in *padis*, which were then beaten or raked in various ways to get all the kernels out. These were caught on an underlying *tikar*, a woven mat. Then, in the cooler evenings, the village women would pound in a rhythmic tempo, three working constantly together, and take turns at the loempang. This sound is very pleasant to listen to, like soft drumming. A woman, usually using a heavy blunt bamboo pole, would pound the rice once, then tick the edge of the log twice. When she ticked the edge once, she would tip the pole into her other hand. Then the woman standing opposite her lowered her bamboo, followed by the third in the group. This steady exchange created a sort of soft boom, followed by two quick bursts, bong-bong. The tempo was slower when older females pounded, the oldest woman controlling the tempo, and so the speed of the rhythm could change. A group of young women decidedly pounded in a faster rhythm. When two loempangs were in use, one by an older trio and one by a young team, it created a distinct musical rhythm. Small girls in the village would learn early how to participate.

This pounding music, often combined with songs, could go on for hours. The rice had been harvested, and now they could enjoy the fruit of their work. Singing often accompanied the processing, and even some distance away we could hear the rhythmic pounding and gentle songs. It was a beautiful sound. I loved to listen to this distant music, gently drifting up with the smoke through the coolness of the night and through the trees of a nearby kampong.

The Javanese wasted nothing. The leftover stalks from the rice harvest, *merang*, were used for many purposes. The merang was burned in a clay washbasin and mixed with water. After twenty-four hours the ash was sifted and prepared for use as shampoo. Another purpose for the merang fibers was to envelop bottles to protect them from breaking.

After all this effort the husked rice, *beras*, was placed on *tampahs*, large round woven bamboo trays, and the women shook these upward in the wind to separate the chaff, which I had discovered in the warehouse. This thought brought me abruptly back to reality. Mother had taught me that unrefined rice, slightly red in color, was especially nutritious, full of vitamin B1, and it was clear we needed anything nutritious we could get our hands on. Besides, I was always hungry, and even though dedek tasted like a mixture of house dust and talcum powder, I stuffed several handfuls into my mouth, choking on it. I tried to wash it down with water that I found in a barrel, not knowing how clean it was. Mosquito larvae were squiggling right under the water's surface.

I packed some more dedek in my handkerchief, flattened it, and carefully pushed it in my pocket so it would not be visible. In the corner of the warehouse another boy found sacks of moist brown sugar. We were always armed with a spoon, and we scraped the soggy substance out of the sacks, eating until we became nauseated. After all our roaming and scrounging, little time was left to rest.

Around two in the afternoon we were ordered to take the carts back to Bangkong. Our train moved slowly, for the route was uphill this time and the carts were heavy. Over my shoulder I had a strap that ran from the left to the right shaft, which made it easier to lift and balance the loaded cart. This strap started to cut into my skin as the trip went on. It was very hot, but in no way did we dare stop, for the asphalt would burn the calluses on our feet. Ahead of us I could see heat waves trembling above the road.

When I looked back and observed our lineup, we looked pitiful. Straining to pull the carts uphill, our breathing labored, we dripped with sweat, the drops evaporating after landing on the hot road, and advanced only slowly. We looked terrible, dressed in ragged shorts, emaciated, our bare feet leaving footprints in the hot tar and our stomachs protruding below skinny ribs, since we had stuffed ourselves.

The Bloodhound walked up front, one Hei-Ho alongside each cart, and the easygoing Hashimoto guarded the rear. The Bloodhound urged us to speed up, to no avail, as our miserable column marched through one busy downtown business street after another. I felt humiliated. Along the side of the road many Indonesians and Chinese lined up to see us pass. The Bloodhound, in a feisty mood, invited the crowd to cheer by turning around and making wild gestures with his arms. His left hand, with the palm upward, was pointed at the crowd, and he slowly raised that arm. The right hand made a sweeping motion over our lineup, clearly pointing in ridicule at us, the prisoners. One Chinese woman shook her head and placed her hand over her mouth. Whatever he hoped for did not happen. Instead, there was a deep silence all the way back.

chapter fourteen

THE DIARY

The guards at Bangkong exercised a great deal of sadistic control over our young lives. Besides the forty Hei-Hos in Japanese service, there were about eleven Japanese, although some of them in reality were Korean. These soldiers rotated through the various camps, especially after the female camps Karangpanas and Gedangan were emptied. We would have preferred to have only the more easygoing Hei-Hos around us.

The Hei-Hos were armed with bamboo poles topped off with bayonets. The Hei-Ho sergeant carried a parabellum, a heavy pistol. They walked around the camp perimeter hourly, in pairs, between two barbed-wire fences about fifteen feet high. The Hei-Hos had to exercise at times, running back and forth on the street. They were also forced to sing the Japanese national anthem, the "Kimigayo," and the song "Antjur America." We had heard this song several times from the Japanese officer trainees as they marched, out near the cabbage fields, and knew that the words were meant to instill hatred for America.

It didn't seem to be working with the Hei-Hos. Instead, by early 1945, several made it clear that they had developed a dislike for the Japanese.

They stood guard at the main gate and occupied a guardhouse adjacent to the main entrance, next door to the death room. They always walked with us to the fields or when we were assigned to other duties, especially any outside of camp. Although we had almost nothing of value left, several Hei-Hos still wanted to trade with us. They tried to maintain a form of barter, offering cigarettes, an item that upon detection the Japanese could not prove was smuggled. We spoke Malay with them, a fairly simple language but one the Japanese, on the whole, never took the trouble to learn.

It was in negotiating with the Hei-Hos that Pantas and the Dernier clique excelled, just as in Lampersari. Pantas spoke fluent Javanese, which was much harder than Malay, so he had a distinct advantage. Also typical of his ethics in Lampersari, he never shared the fruits of his barter with anyone but his friend Tegas. Both looked to be in robust good health, and although other boys would be severely punished if they were caught trading, neither Pantas nor Tegas was ever touched. If a Hei-Ho were caught trading with us, his punishment was also severe.

Some Hei-Hos were absolutely asinine; they would rat on us. We called them *klepon*, an Indonesian cookie, brown on the inside and army green on the outside. We warned each other which they were. My trusted companion was Anton, and I felt completely safe with only a few other boys from our Han, like Bob Tuizinga in our room, and Hans Doornebos from another han.

Communication with the Japanese was extremely poor, just as it had been between the women and their captors in Lampersari. Several of them seemed well suited to nicknames that gave us a bleak laugh now and then; of course, they did not speak Dutch, so they knew nothing about our names for them. One commandant who was in charge in Bangkong in the final months was called Beautiful Charles. Always spotlessly dressed, clean-shaven, with a clean white starched shirt and polished boots, he did not bother too much with us. Instead, he was known to spend his time chasing women. Then there was the Bloodhound, Zenyo, a Korean who had tried unsuccessfully to rally the locals against us as we pulled our carts through town. He always exhibited a sarcastic smile, like so many Japanese had when dealing with Hei-Hos or other Indonesians. Most of his mannerisms were like that of the Japanese. There is no question that he hated Caucasians. Others earned their names by appearance, like Easter Egg, or because of an oddity, like the castrate, Hashimoto, who had an abnormally high voice. The most telling nicknames were for those whose specialty was brutality, like Ian the Hitter.

In contrast with the Asian norm, which counseled not revealing much emotion, our Japanese and Korean guards were extremely explosive. We were told that in Japan itself the emphasis was on command of one's passions, especially in relation to others. Respect for their betters, which here in the Indies meant their superior officers, was an integral part of the soldiers' training. In contrast, no effort was given to self-control when dealing with prisoners.

If we were working in the fields, the Japanese guarded us from a distance. The Hei-Hos were always closer to us. Often, those Hei-Hos pretended that they did not see anything, like our little fires, for example, if they knew that the Japanese were not around. Typically the Japanese would sit at the top of the hill, observing us with field glasses, or at the window in their bamboo headquarters in the corner of the fields on top of the highest knoll. Whenever they drifted down the slopes toward us, we warned each other by calling, "Hot water." This was an excellent system, for so many of us would just stand there, half asleep in the heat, leaning on our hoes. I had never realized how much I treasured my freedom until these months in 1944, when I was used as slave labor.

Before 1944 I never had malaria, although Anton and Mother had suffered from it, and Dad had been deathly ill from tropical malaria when we were living in Surabaja. In mid-October, after we had been in Bangkong only one month, I was too ill with heavy chills to work in the fields. The doctor placed my blood under the microscope, which checked out positive for malaria. That afternoon my left groin swelled tremendously and made it painful to walk. The doctor at the clinic told me I had swollen glands, but I had no idea what that meant. I was prescribed three days of bed rest and given some quinine pills. I was very lucky that some pills were still available. Our camp ran out of that medicine shortly thereafter, for the Japanese soon refused to supply us with quinine. This widespread suffering of malaria was doubly ironic, since we all knew that Java was the source of 90 percent of the world's quinine production. The only time that the Japanese central office in Semarang was willing to send quinine was when an epidemic of tropical malaria took the lives of boys and adults in camp. Most requests for quinine or other medicines were countered by their standard answer: "The Japanese army does not have it, so you do not get it either."

Our pharmacist was ordered to falsify causes of death, so many infectious diseases went unmentioned. As a result, the hospital charts were inaccurate. Typhoid fever and dysentery were not allowed as causes of death, and they were changed on patient records to something like enteritis.

That first evening, after I had been diagnosed with malaria, when Anton returned from working in the fields, we were told suddenly at *tenko* that every boy had to be shaven bald. My brother had it done right away by somebody who owned a pair of hair clippers. He had to pay the boy a teaspoon of sugar, a high price. The big joke was to rub each other's scalps and announce that they felt like sugar. This rule of bald skulls was briefly and strictly enforced, then dropped after a few weeks.

On the Sunday following my first bout of malaria, we received some sugar and coffee early in the morning, which was so very unusual that I recorded it in my tiny diary. My brother and I mixed the sugar with the coffee extract and whipped it into a foam. That was a special treat indeed.

My diary consisted of a thin *Schrift*, a handwritten exercise schoolbook with a thin cover that I rolled up and inserted into my skinny bedroll. It was an excellent hiding place. Mother had brought a few writing supplies with us from Malang, perhaps thinking that she could keep us boys involved in some kind of studying, which of course was completely impossible. It was forbidden to have such an item in camp, but I found it immensely valuable; somehow it helped me keep my sense of identity in this mass of hungry and lonely boys. I eventually understood that it was also an act of defiance against the supposed superiority of the Japanese. I was determined to keep a record of what we endured, and in the first several weeks I was successful; I stopped keeping it, though, after about four months as my energy declined. Even at my age I could see that the Japanese were systematically destroying our hope for survival. Over the next months it would be a close race.

The Japanese gathered the small camp library, a remnant of the convent days, and burned it, though one of them selected two books from the flames and walked away with his treasure. None of the prisoners were allowed to possess a book. However, I did have one French study book, and this one survived all searches.

I tried to study during that first illness but was not successful; I fell asleep from chronic fatigue. One chapter was called "La Cigogne," the stork. At the time, while daydreaming, I chuckled at the realization that this bird certainly was not going to visit any of the camps in Semarang.

Only a few days after I had fallen ill with malaria, we were told that nobody was going to work in the fields because a group of very important people from Batavia was coming to inspect us. The anticipation of facing high-ranking Japanese leaders affected our guards much more than it did us, and they seemed relieved when, later on that day, the visit was cancelled. At a special tenko, the Half-breed, one of the Japanese guards, used a stick to strike every boy who still had hair on his scalp. The Half-breed, bowlegged, short, and slightly stooped, showed his teeth while he jumped and screamed while doing this, until I found myself mentally comparing him with a monkey. I laughed to myself; that was one way I dealt with my fear and disgust. Those boys whose scalps were injured faced a good deal of pain and possible infection because blood blisters would develop. Thank God by that time my scalp was also shaved.

Then that same evening we received a so-called tomato soup, made of very green and half-rotten tomatoes. The soup was so terribly filthy, full of sand, straw, and bugs, and so awfully bitter-tasting, that no matter how hungry we were we could not stomach it. The confusing events of this day were upsetting, especially the generalized beatings, but the loss of any kind of evening food was hardest of all.

Two days later the Japanese senior officers from Batavia finally arrived. All our rooms had to be spick-and-span, all mattresses rolled up against the wall. Even though I was sick I had to line up outside just the same. During that inspection the Bloodhound confiscated my two knives. That was terrible, for I used them for woodcarving, which is how I had managed to make myself some wooden clogs so that I did not have to stand barefooted in the filth in front of the urinals. That day, the nineteenth, the doctor told me that I still had malaria and gave me a note excusing me from work for another five days. Of the twenty-eight boys then in our room, seven had contracted malaria. Progressive malnutrition, of course, made us more susceptible to any type of illness.

Some other unusual things also happened during this time. My brother's birthday was on October 22, and as a special treat he was able to get a cup of warm water—yes, warm water. He mixed that with ground coffee and some milk powder that we had saved. The head cook, as well as some of the other adults, tried to acknowledge personal things like birthdays, but with fourteen hundred people in camp, they had an almost impossible job of it.

October was also the month that we started to detect lice in our mosquito nets. At first this created quite a bit of consternation, but like all other bad things, we learned to live and share our space with these fast-moving, bad-smelling, blood-sucking, fast-multiplying bandits. Disheartening as it was, whatever we tried, these lice outsmarted us at every turn. Killing them created a stink that I knew I could never forget; they smelled like *walang sangit*, a nocturnal insect that, when squashed, releases a most intense-smelling fluid. I did not believe anything could be worse. At night, when kids were bitten, they killed these lice, setting off this stench. Anytime I would enter a room that contained lice I was met by this odor. We tried to hang our mattresses in the sunshine, making the bugs desert us and bolt for shade. Armed with a large four-inch sewing needle, I was able to spear them, and I periodically cleaned the sleeping roll, but that same evening other lice reoccupied the same quarters. It could not have been more discouraging, trying to stay clean. Many kids just gave up.

Late in the month of October, during the afternoon of the twenty-fourth, a guard whom we called the Bolle, the Bread Roll, held tenko and gave us a speech while we, even the sick ones, stood in the hot sun. He told us in Japanese not to steal and said that we had to follow orders more precisely. There were parts stolen from a sewing machine. As the speech was being translated, he ordered us to turn in the missing parts by the next morning. This did not happen, although we chuckled at the idea of a disabled machine. Many of us had learned, without quite realizing it, that passivity was a form of defiance.

That day of the twenty-eighth, the Bolle came around and screamed that all the sick kids had to work. Several were assigned to the kitchen to stoke the fires, and others were to sweep the parade grounds. I ended up cleaning the drainage ditch by the bathrooms. At noon two trucks arrived, we had to unload eighty-pound sacks of rice. Afterward I was exhausted, and my knees buckled. After four o'clock I developed a chilling fever attack; my bout with malaria was not quite over. It never did become clear why our captors were suddenly so concerned about the appearance of the camp; perhaps the recent visit by their superior officers had reminded them of their duties. Again, whatever the reasons, their interest in camp conditions did not last long.

My little diary recorded that on the last night of October I was awakened by screams coming from one of the boys in Room 5. Leon van den Broeke, with whom I had played soccer many times in Malang, seemed to be having a nightmare, so I went to him and bent over him to calm him down. He struck out at me and foam showed at his mouth. He complained of pain in his hip and knee, apparently from an old ailment. His younger brother, Gerrie, ran for help, and a nun and another friend of Leon's showed up with a stretcher. Leon fought and screamed. The nun asked him, "Don't you want to come with us?" He answered, "Where to? To my grave?" And another sudden outburst. "Where is Gerrie? Is he still alongside me? Henkie, you get my tobacco. Tell Sipkes that I am not mad at him anymore! Ouch, my knee, ouch, my knee!" He rambled on. We succeeded with great difficulty in getting him to the improvised hospital. The rest of us were shaken by this episode, not knowing what we were dealing with. I heard Sipkes say, "Why did we have to have a fight?" After a few days Leon returned to our room, but we never figured out why this happened. Sipkes and Leon shook hands. So many dramas took place in our little camp, and often we did not know how to deal with them.

One day about this time I did not go out with the patjollers because I had severe diarrhea. I felt quite weak and made several trips to the bathroom. In the middle of the day, I was walking back in all that heat to the han. Suddenly I heard, *"Mari sini!"* Come here! The Bloodhound appeared and gestured to me to follow him. He walked to the small room adjacent to the guardhouse of the Hei-Hos. I knew that room all too well; I had been there before. Everyone who died ended up in the Roemah Mati, the death room. Inside was a murky darkness.

After we entered I saw on the table a dead man, very scrawny, in his late sixties. I had seen him always roaming around looking for food. He had had, years earlier, an amputation above the right wrist. The skin was withdrawn between the ulna and the radius bones, forming a marked slit between them. In our camp he had learned to make good use of the fork-shaped forearm by reaching the two bones over an item to be picked up, then twisting the radius over the ulna, and clamping the item so that he could lift it.

This was a painfully vivid image, for I had seen him dig with that arm through the garbage cans of the Japanese, scrounging for something to eat. I felt so sorry for the old man. He must have been hungrier even than I was to feel compelled to dig in the garbage. Often he would find the entrails of chickens and hold these guts in front of his face, then slurp them up like macaroni. As scrawny as the rest of him was, his ankles had become swollen as a result of beri-beri.

The Bloodhound said in Malay, "Here is an envelope. Place a lock of his hair and a fingernail clipping in it. Write his name on the envelope so we can mail it to his nearest relative." At first I was perplexed; I did not know what to make of this task. Slowly I realized that I had been picked for a terrible and dirty job. This was the first dead person I had to handle. He was followed later on by many more, including kids I knew in camp, and from Malang, such as Koos Spee, who suddenly died and left a brother behind.

I cut some of his nail, then a lock of hair, with a pair of dull scissors. I felt quite stupid stuffing these items in an envelope. With a big carpenter pencil I wrote down the man's name.

This was nothing in comparison with what I had to do next. Because the man had died more than twenty-four hours earlier, the corpse had become very rigid and was difficult to handle. I managed to close his eyes but was unable to do the same with his jaw. With an old, dirty cloth I tried to clean his skin. I left him in his shorts for lack of anything better. The old man then had to be wrapped in a thin woven mat called a *tiker*. In order to be able to push it underneath him, I had to roll him over on his left side. This caused body fluids to leak and drip through the bamboo board he was lying on. Then I wrapped the tiker over him and tucked it in on the other side. I had to ask for help to slide him into a bamboo crate, which was to be his coffin. On the front board I wrote the name of the deceased.

The temperature was high in that room, at noon easily 100 degrees, and the air was very still. The odor was not easy to ignore; it dominated everything in the room. Nobody acknowledged his death, so perhaps I was the only person who mourned him, even briefly. After accomplishing this task, I went to the bathroom, for the diarrhea came calling again, but I was unable to wash up. At that hour there was no running water, and in desperation I sat down at the edge of the ditch in front of our verandah. Next to me was the water tap, which I opened wide in order not to miss the first drop. A mixture of exhaustion and morbid feelings overwhelmed me; I wanted to cry but was not able to; I wanted to bury my face in my hands, but they were too dirty. Thank God nobody paid attention to a kid sitting for hours at the edge of the ditch with his feet dangling in it.

Occasionally it happened that women would show up to work in the fields adjacent to our area. At that distance we could recognize them as women from Lampersari, but we could not identify individuals. The first time this happened was during the month of November, in 1944. Then for several months no women were to be seen until April 1945, when they reappeared. No contact or conversation was allowed with these women. At best we dared to wave if we recognized somebody. Once I spotted my mother, and I was shocked at how frail and skinny she looked. Just seeing her there overwhelmed me, and I could not help wishing that she had stayed in Lampersari, for I thought that she would surely collapse doing that work. Then I realized that she had come out to try to see us! I was at that moment working at the manure pit, which was poorly supervised, and fortunately the location of the pit was close to the women. The small group that Mother belonged to started secretly to point at a grassy knoll close to a bush, and then they gestured to me to go over there as they wandered off. Slowly I approached this spot, to find a tin can containing four small animals made out of sugar.

Imagine, my mother, who was hungry herself, had smuggled these candies to the fields to give them to her boys! I did not want to take such a gift, really; I wanted her to have it. I could not leave it there, though; if the Japanese should discover the can, Mother would be in serious trouble. I picked it up and turned to thank her, but she had disappeared with the other women. My brother and I shared this special treat that we suspected Mother had traded for through the *gedek*.

Being hungry all the time made us always on the lookout for something to eat, and food became an obsession with us. When the rainy season arrived we found animals in the fields that we could eat. When we spotted a snake, we all ran after the fast-moving, slithering creature with our hoes. There was no escape for the brownish three-foot-long *sawah oeler*, abundant and harmless, in contrast with an extremely venomous two-foot long green snake with a fiery red tail. Then there was the python, rare in our area, and the small but extremely poisonous iron snake. This snake could be especially dangerous, for it looked like a night crawler and could easily be stepped on.

At the age of five we lived in Ungaran, and out of curiosity I frequently lifted the doormat by the front door to find these iron snakes hiding under the mat if the yard was inundated. This upset my mother no end, but she did not realize that I knew their danger and respected them accordingly. Our maid had warned me about their venom in very impressive words; she pointed at an iron snake, landed dramatically on her knees, and raised her hands in front of her face, declaring, "One bite and Allah can not save you."

So in the fields near Bangkong we were always on the lookout for snakes. We informed the Japanese guard that all snakes were poisonous to keep him at a distance so that we could catch them. I do not know if he believed us. Snake meat and frog legs tasted like chicken and provided a good source of protein, but unfortunately this menu was rather rare.

Usually I had more luck with frogs, catching them by hand, for they were often clustered in a hole. I would sever the body at the waist and strip the skin off.

Sometimes I could catch dark-tinted mud eels. They were at best ten inches long, and I found them in the muddy water of the ditches during the rainy season. In order to catch these cold slimy eels I would step up and down with my bare feet in the mud, and when I felt one crawl against my skin, I used my big and second toe to grab the slithering creature. I prepared these eels the same way as I would the frogs.

In the sides of the sawahs surrounding the rice fields were many small holes occupied by *kepiting*, small freshwater crabs. Only the little boys were able to stick their arms in the narrow holes, clear up to their elbows. When a crab pinched a finger with its claw, the boy withdrew his arm quickly, pulling the kepiting to the outside world. My arm was usually too thick for an average hole, but if I had been lucky, I would bash the main body of the crab with a rock; a small amount of meat was found in the upper legs.

The Japanese had ordered that we dig wells, four by four feet wide, usually eight to ten feet deep, to obtain murky water to be used in the dry season. We dipped water with a one-foot-long hollow bamboo cane. Attached to it was a skinny bamboo, stuck into the scoop at an angle, very primitive but effective. We filled buckets slung to a yoke as boys lifted the bucket between them. We had to walk in unequal steps so as not to spill the fluid.

I always skinned my catch and flamed the meat before eating it. Since we were not allowed to make fires, we would descend into one of the many wells we had been forced to dig. In the siding of the well, above the water-line, we had created small caves for dry wood storage. Then a quick fire was started to flame our prey. My frog legs were strung on a strong piece of yarn so I could run the meat quickly through the flames. I always tried to tell other kids to do the same, not to eat the meat raw, but they didn't pay much attention when they were so hungry. Afterward the hole was sealed. The Japanese watch on top of the hill would spot smoke and started his descent, but upon his arrival we were long gone.

When we had been in Bangkong for about three months, one of the youngest boys, an eleven-year-old, died. No one knew how to explain this to the other little boys. It seemed as if they were not really paying attention, since they were always so playful. Deaths were a daily occurrence, especially among the old men who came through camp, but this was the youngest one of our companions to die, and his death affected everyone deeply. When his little body was carried out in a small coffin, all the little guys lined up spontaneously to give the last salute, some with trembling lips, but silent and stalwart nevertheless.

The Japanese paid no attention to our attempts at a funeral observance. They were only concerned that the body be duly removed from camp. At least some of our middle-aged men, the leaders, such as Mr. Vetter, or Jacob the Jew, a kind man in his thirties, were present as we paid respects. Another one, Mr. Oelers, a middle-aged Ambonese, was a former chief of police who always tried to protect us kids. But at this and other funeral services, I never saw the Luxembourger, our so-called chief, who was obviously too cowardly or indifferent to attend.

I witnessed a rare event one day when Henk Voorstad, the only child of an important person in government in Malang, was suddenly called to report to the back gate. I used to play with him and compete against him in school; he was the one with the top score in my eighth grade in Malang. A Japanese in a sedan was at the back gate and told him to get in, and from there they drove to the Kobong Cemetery, where Europeans were buried. He was led to a fresh grave and told that his mother had died.

Upon his return Henk again entered through the back gate; it was after two o'clock and blistering hot. He acted dazed. Jacob put an arm around his shoulders, and they walked to his han. We all observed silently that Henk tried to control his crying, and he sat down on his mattress, holding his knees and resting his chin on them. Finally he burst out in a flood of tears. We could not help him. But grief visits everyone equally, and now he felt lost. We had no notion why he was singled out to visit his mother's grave. No others from camp were given similar opportunities, even though many around me lost mothers and sisters.

The ten-year-olds were achingly brave to manage in this crowded camp by themselves. During the day they would play some game while sitting between their mattresses; sometimes they were ordered out to work at the tables cleaning vegetables. One area where they liked to congregate was in front of the *goedang*, the storage area, looking over the vegetables being stored, while they evaluated the tasty vegetables, nodding at each other with very wise old faces.

As young as they were, some were still ordered to work in the fields. Mr. Vetter, their hancho, was kind to these kids and never drove them hard. As a result he received many a beating for work not accomplished. He was in his forties and had been heavy before the regimen of the camps took its toll. He always wore a straw hat as he stood in the fields, leaning on a stick, supervising these little ones. They had to pull weeds, and while working many were sunburned.

Skin problems always became less tolerable in the fatigue and hunger of the evenings. The little boys felt miserable, and they had nobody to console them. Sometimes at night we could hear them crying and calling for their mothers as they lay in their beds.

At night we older boys were not allowed to stay with the little ones, who were quartered in the church, even in the sacristy. Some were also in the aula, the gymnasium's hall, but none were in the *pendopo*, where the sick old men suffering from tuberculosis were housed.

During the daytime the nuns were truly helpful to the little boys. They hovered over the children when they were on their sleeping bags or working at the vegetable tables, but more importantly, they listened to their concerns. The nuns were available for the sick ones, and these children were quickly hospitalized.

We older boys had no choice but to accept these circumstances in silence. I wondered over and over again why this had to happen. How could the Japanese possibly consider ten- and eleven-year-olds to be a danger to Japanese imperialism? It seemed obvious that our captors did not care whether we teenagers died. A worse thought, as some other kids speculated, was the suggestion, "They are doing this on purpose."

Our camp lacked entertainment or healthy diversions of any sort. No musical instruments were in camp, and shows were not organized. From one day to the next we could fool ourselves, but what we missed as much as food was the nurturing touch of our mothers and families. In addition, the Japanese did not allow church services.

Two easygoing, elderly Indos in the camp managed to maintain a sense of joyfulness. One seemed to be older than the other. He dressed in a worn sarong made into a loincloth. His companion had just a pair of faded shorts. They could usually be found squatted down close to the vegetable tables, in hearing distance of the head cook in the kitchen. I was convinced that this close location served a purpose; the little boys would wander over after they finished their vegetable chores, and the cook could keep an eye on things. This cheerful duo always attracted a group of the younger kids. The skinny boys, dressed only in shorts, would sit or stretch out in a semicircle facing the two older men. Kake, whose name meant old man or grandpa, looked quite old indeed. He would entertain these kids by singing songs. One song began with the words, "*Kake soeda toea, gigi tingal doea,*" "Grandpa is already old and he has two teeth left." This was indeed the case, and the youngsters smiled and laughed, something they rarely did anymore.

The younger one, Pak, meaning dad or adopted dad, was quite good at telling folktales. He clearly added to his colorful stories for the benefit of the boys, and they cheered him on by shouting to him to tell more. The head cook was able to listen in and encouraged the storytelling, rewarding the older duo with some food.

One story I recall well was told on a day I was sick and thus not in the fields. It was about the moon, something the little boys paid a great deal of attention to. That was probably the only outside object they were able to see by gazing up between the church and our roof. Certainly I thought of freedom when I looked at the moon.

The Dajak legend, told by the indigenous peoples on the island of Borneo explained the origins of the blemishes on the moon. Two powerful ghosts, who had created the Dajak people, went underground and became feared by all. One time no sacrifice was made by the villagers, and angrily the ghosts sent four children to heaven, where they became the four phases of the moon. The girl, Kamat, was very beautiful, and her spotless round face shone brilliantly at night like polished silver. The other three children became jealous, especially Dom, the last quarter moon, the least shiny. One night when the four were cooking sticky rice porridge, Dom threw his hot porridge in Kamat's face. Her face was burned, and the scars are still visible.

Upon hearing this story, a skinny ten-year-old said, "I wish Dom would throw the porridge in my face." His tongue, full of desire, licked his upper and lower lips. The kid next to him retorted, "Who says you're beautiful?"

It was no wonder that these little ones were hanging on Pak's lips, as my Mother used to say. They did not want to miss a word.

Early in the morning on December 6, pandemonium broke out. We were told that no patjollers were going out to the fields. At seven o'clock, when everyone was moving about or heading for the toilets or showers, four hundred and fifty sick old men and boys arrived; two of their group had died on the train. As always, we had no early warning of their arrival. I happened to be standing next to the tables where vegetables were being cleaned, with a direct view of the gate. Suddenly the back gate opened and a procession of human misery passed through the open doors. Their transport had come all the way from Tjimahi, an old garrison town in western Java. The older brother of Karel Sipkes, who himself was with us in camp, was among these people, apparently to help with the many ill and dying men. We had adults admitted to our camp from all over, but this transport topped everything.

The poor old men, elderly, gray, some blind or limping, slowly dragged themselves through the back gate into our camp. Several had suffered strokes and used bamboo sticks for support so that they, too, could hobble into camp. There were crazy persons among them. All carried their meager belongings, usually a cup, a spoon, and a can to eat from and a towel wrapped around the waist or draped over the neck. These people still tried to show their pride and walk with dignity regardless of the Japanese, who were openly contemptuous.

These old folks were not to be given the opportunity to spend their last days in peace. Dressed in rags, they had not showered for days and were covered with lice. Many showed ulcers, especially on their legs. Among them were persons who were incontinent. When I watched this parade of walking skeletons I stared, horrified. As a result of all the commotion, our breakfast was not issued until eleven—a delay of which we hungry kids were keenly aware.

Some of the poor souls had died on the slow journey from Bandung in the railroad cars. Their corpses were brought into camp nevertheless. Many others of their group succumbed quickly in the succeeding days.

It was also at this time that the population in our room increased from twenty-seven to thirty-eight boys, and our camp had to accommodate the new influx of people. Many adults and boys were moved to other hans. The *pendopo*, the meeting hall, was given to these frail old men. This hall without four walls became a partial isolation area, the closest the camp could come to a sort of quarantine. There were many cases of open tuberculosis among the old men.

Worse than the further crowding and stretching of the meager food supply was the particular kind of suffering we witnessed among them. Within the group were at least a dozen men who were suffering from mental illness. They created a type of anxiety we had not asked for, and I wondered how much more we could cope with. One of these confused old men was assigned to cut vegetables. It happened that he felt threatened, so instead of cutting vegetables he tried to stab one of the Japanese guards. They overpowered him, tied him to a chair, and placed him in the hot sun. The next day he died. We tried not to imagine what had brought him to such a reduced mental state or what the Japanese had done to him during that last night.

One of the most brutal guards in the camp was a Korean by the name of Kimura, who, at the age of twenty, was not much older than many of us boys. He seemed to particularly enjoy tormenting his prisoners, and the crazy old men were easy victims for him. For no apparent reason Kimura stopped one of these men and held a bayonet in front of his face. Kimura knew that the man was crazy. When the Bloodhound also appeared, Kimura had an audience, and he proceeded to hit the old fellow with a stick. That was all the man could take; he grabbed the stick and counterattacked. The two guards retreated hastily to get help from the commandant. Together these three soldiers overwhelmed their victim. Kimura hit the man over the head repeatedly until he collapsed, unconscious. He bled plenty. After being dragged off the commons, he was locked up for three days in the pigsty, but he survived. The Japanese men declared openly: "Let these old men die."

It made no sense at all why sick people were moved so far to the east, since the trend was to move everybody west, away from the approaching Allies. With every group that had moved through the camp earlier, we heard new and different rumors, but we knew that no one had access to any kind of accurate information. The fact that we all, men and boys both, found some kind of hope to cling to was impossible to explain, but hope was the basis of those rumors.

Death visited the camp daily, and the death rate climbed with the arrival of so many older and starving men. Consequently, several of us boys in camp had to take our turns in the death room; it was a universally dreaded but unavoidable assignment. I was usually picked when I had to stay in camp, which was mostly when I was too ill for field duty. The other boys were usually in the same situation. This was another reason the hard labor in the hot sun was preferable to staying in camp.

I had to deal with the victims of dropsy, their bodies so swollen that the skin started to crack and ooze. Far worse cases were those bodies so swollen from beri-beri that they leaked on me when I lifted them. No matter how many times I was pushed into service in the death room, I never got used to it.

The Japanese always waited until they had four dead people, either all from our camp or in combination with the female camps, before removing the bodies to the European cemetery. An ox-drawn cart would arrive at the back gate, always at noon, to carry the four corpses. Sometimes there were already coffins in the *tjikar* from Lampersari or Halmaheira, and I am certain that everyone else wondered, as I did, when we might see a mother's or sister's name scraped on the flimsy wood. One of the more nimble little boys would scramble up on the driver's seat in an attempt to read the names on the headboards. We bigger boys tried to distract the driver's attention in the meantime, but found that some native drivers did not mind our attempt to see who the dead were. The makeshift coffins were so flimsy that often the bottom or a side would break and an arm or a leg would flop out. That had to be replaced, and not knowing what that individual had died from was as bad as pretending to be indifferent to death.

Our efforts at a callous attitude were shattered in a hurry if a boy died; we tried to understand the reason, and we talked a great deal about it whenever such an event occurred. These death carts carried four, but perhaps the outside world thought that only one person had died; it could be, though, that the Japanese were only trying to simplify their workload. We had to lift the coffins high to load them into the tjikars; as a result, fluids gushed over our own bodies. As always, I was dressed only in shorts. I felt terribly dirty after doing this type of job, but of course I had long since run out of soap. It would not have mattered in any case, since water was always shut off between nine in the morning and five o'clock, when the patjollers were due back. After working in the death room I longed for water. Nothing else mattered.

In December 1944, all of a sudden, we were given postcards and told to write to our mothers. The writing with pencil had to be in Malay, and we were allowed only to state that we were fine and to say hello. But at least we could inform our mothers that we were still alive. The same thing must have happened in Lampersari, because we got a postcard from Mother. Even though the words had been dictated, it was good to recognize her handwriting. We heard nothing from Dad, and we were thankful every time a group of sick men came through that he was not among them.

During the latter half of the month the quality of the food became poorer, and sometimes meals were omitted altogether, especially when the wood was so wet that no cooking could be accomplished. Our poor cook received a beating from the Japanese, since he could not deliver food to us, even though they probably did not really care whether we were fed or not.

The hours in the fields had been lengthened; as a result, we came home when it was getting dark. This was the first time that I noticed that Anton was getting weaker.

When Christmas came around we got the day off but no extra food. The Bloodhound observed a small Catholic service in church. Afterward he gave the priest some cigarettes and left. Officially no religious services were tolerated, and when the people in attendance started to sing, Kimura, the young Korean guard, stormed in and yelled that no service was allowed.

While I listened to the singing, it abruptly stopped, only to notice that boys were running out of church. Kimura had started to beat them up.

chapter fifteen

THE DISEASE OF DESPAIR

In the Indies there is a small and generally welcome nocturnal lizard, called a *tokè*, or gecko, a harmless tropical insectivore, six to ten inches long, with a beak reminiscent of a miniature crocodile. Its name describes its odd, croaking mating call, and if you hear this animal say *tokè* seven times, luck will drift your way. It attaches itself to the ceiling, hunting for mosquitoes. As kids we would feed these creatures tobacco attached to a stick in order to reach them on the walls or the high ten feet ceilings. The tokè's bite was firm and he would not let go; he would end up in a free fall and then walk like a drunk.

Many people in camp had nicknames. One of the three Dutch physicians allowed to practice in camp became known as the Tokè.

There were many more physicians, about sixteen in all, but most of them were assigned to work in the fields. Two who worked in the kitchen. Dr. Neuberger was the head of the hospital and made the rounds. Because he suffered from throat cancer, the Tokè, as we called him, could hardly speak. His voice sounded explosive, and he always looked exhausted. During the morning hours, he made his way daily throughout the camp, but it was impossible to see all boys. He was too weak to enter the individual rooms and bend over patients lying on the floor, so he would sit down behind a small portable table on the patio outside each han. The sick boys dragged themselves out of their rooms to stand in front of a doctor who had great difficulty speaking to them. Their trust in such a man was naturally low; many kids complained and scoffed about him openly, not realizing how unfair their treatment was. If he determined that a boy was sick enough, the child would be sent to the hospital, which was nothing more than a few empty classrooms with some steel beds and mattresses on the floor, supervised by several of the nuns. Some of these scenes, with a sick child and a sicker doctor, were unforgettable.

In the shade of the balcony was a simple four-legged-table. Behind it this skinny man, seated on a rickety chair, leaned on the tabletop. He supported his elongated head with his left arm, the left elbow resting on the table. His eyes were sunken, and his stubbly beard was colored like salt and pepper. In front of him stood a feeble boy, held up and supported by two other skinny kids. The patients waiting their turns were sitting or lying on thin mattresses spread out on the floor. When they were finished, the entire scene moved down a door or two, where the doctor evaluated the next sickly group. An assigned group of younger boys would carry the table and chair to the various locations where the doctor would hold "office hours." The European and Dutch doctors outclassed the Japanese ones by miles, especially in treating tropical diseases, but the Tokè could not combat the severe malnutrition and advancing starvation that was at the root of most ailments in camp.

When patients were dragged in front of this doctor to be examined, we all knew it was only to try to obtain a diagnosis, or to listen to the verdict, "You go to the hospital." As with our roommate, Leon van der Broeke, going to the hospital offered no comfort to most of us.

There were hardly any medicines available, although endless requests for medicines were put in to the Japanese. On top of the list was quinine. The typical answer of the commandant was, "The Japanese army has none, so you do not get it either." If we argued about it, we received a beating, or worse, everybody had to skip a meal. We reminded them about the fact that the island of Java produced 90 percent of the world production of quinine, but that infuriated the Japanese. They must have sensed that we were indirectly accusing them of lying.

I had found those medical texts fascinating not so very long ago when I was confined in Malang and worked to clean the doctor's office. Further, Mother's commonsense approach to dealing with parasites and tropical diseases had been ingrained in me, and so I always listened to try to understand the doctor's diagnosis when he saw my brother Anton or other boys of our han. Some of the diseases were worse than others, especially if they were contagious. We could not hope to contain spreading diseases when our bodies were depleted and there was such poor sanitation in camp.

One of the most persistent and debilitating problems in camp was diarrhea, but there were different causes and diagnoses. Two forms of diarrhea were not contagious. One kind, which caused the thin-wall condition of the bowel, was due to total emaciation. The second type was known as pellagra, from the Italian word for rough skin. The cause of this diarrhea was the deficiency of niacin, and was often combined with a lack of B2 and B6 vitamins. So, in essence, pellagra was a complex multideficiency ailment, and surely it was no surprise to the doctor to see it as often as he did. The onset was insidious, with a loss of energy, and photophobia, followed by diarrhea. Having pellagra and being forced to work in the hot sun created a discoloring dermatitis, which would itch horribly, usually our first alarming sign. Later symptoms were burning feet. The end stage was dementia and death.

When pellagra struck me in the later months in Bangkong, I stood in front of the doctor with dermatitis, which would itch incredibly in the sunshine, only to be told that there was no therapy available. He was kind enough to explain to me, however, what this ailment consisted of. My own simple treatment was to apply mud on the affected spots so the itch could be tolerated in the hot sunlight.

Other vitamin deficiencies clouded the differential diagnosis, and the continued efforts to make clear and accurate distinctions became increasingly ironic because the diagnosis did not matter when there were no remedies. I had the luck of some knowledge of the cause of the dermatitis and found *kangkung* in the fields that I ate; this created some small degree of control over my diet.

The most common vitamin deficiency, lack of vitamin B1, resulted in beriberi, what we called hunger edema. When protein deficiency was added, the heart would go into failure, and many of our companions would swell with fluid in the ankles and bellies. At tenko time I observed that many of my buddies in the lineup had swollen ankles, especially by 1945. This became so common that we tried to ignore the obvious implications.

Both deficiencies were common causes of death, especially among old men in camp, who had none of the resilience of youth to help their bodies fight back. Perhaps as important, they often gave up hope and instead would crawl on their mattresses and drift into a coma. Death by starvation in the final stage seemed to me a way to avoid any more suffering. The equally deadly and somewhat contagious disease of despair gradually spread through the camp in the advancing months of 1945.

Health and hygiene issues must have been a problem for our Indonesian neighbors outside the barbed wire as well. Like most Indonesian towns, Semarang was infested with flies, which visited us too. The Japanese, never at a loss for clever solutions, ordered that each boy had to turn in one hundred dead flies each week. As a reward each boy who did so got a tablespoon of sugar. Great! However, we soon found out that this sugar was taken out of our weekly rations.

Once I laid my hands on an empty can, eight inches in diameter with a low rim. I made a handle on it out of *kawat*, very sturdy wire. This device was handy to make a unique foodstuff whenever I could scrape together the ingredients. Some boys pushed some old bricks a few inches apart and placed stolen wood splinters in between. The wood was set afire by organizing a burning twig from the main kitchen. We took turns. I placed my pan on this illegal fire and rubbed a candle on the hot bottom of the pan so that it would grease up. Then I poured tapioca and water to form the "pancake." We needed the candle grease for its caloric value since we had gotten that year only one tablespoon of coconut oil. There was so little fat or meat in our diet. I had read, years before, how Robinson Crusoe made his candles from goat grease!

I was inventive, but I worried about how I could ever manage without my glasses. One lens had been cracked, and I had turned it in, hoping somehow for a repair. Several days later I was called to the main office, adjacent to the pharmacy, to receive my repaired glasses. The bill was not bad, only three and a half florins, but it might as well have been a hundred. Of course, I had no money, but somebody at the office helped me out. I never knew who, but I was very grateful.

There were many more transfers over the months, from other parts of Java.

In January a group of adult men *from* our camp was sent to the women's Camp Halmaheira. One man was dying, but even so, our doctors were not allowed to keep him in Bangkong. Worse yet, Halmaheira, which was still crowded with women, was not notified that these elderly and sick men were coming. With each move men were shuffled here and there between various camps, and many were moved multiple times. Nobody understood the reasoning. Shortly after their arrival in Halmaheira, some of the men were returned to Bangkong, while the rest were sent into the mountains. The Luxembourger got rid of those who had dared to speak up about the selfishness of our Dutch leaders in regard to food by including them in the latter group.

One late afternoon, when we were back from work in the fields, a small group of middle-aged men entered the camp. In contrast with the usual prisoner movements through the back way, they walked in through the front gate. They were engineers who had worked at the Tjepoe oil fields for the Batavian Oil Company. They were well dressed and looked well fed; obviously the occupying forces needed their expertise. They were kept away from us kids, and we could not learn anything about the progress of the war. It was quite apparent that several of them were horrified to see our poor condition. After a few days they were crammed in a small bus and taken away.

After several especially wet afternoons, I saw the head cook standing under a huge umbrella in front of the smoke-belching fires. The wet coconut wood was only glowing faintly, and the man was so desperate that he ordered, "Round up any type of fuel." It would not be the first time that he would receive a beating by the Japanese for not being able to deliver a meal. We went into the church, where the little boys were quartered. They slept on plank beds made out of teak. We ripped several apart, so a part of the church looked empty, and as we did we witnessed an exodus of lice that apparently had not volunteered to be cremated. Each of us cheered as we were ripping things apart. This was something different, and we were destroying something we hated! In triumph, a long line of kids carried the splintered wood to the kitchen. The fires that day were superb.

However, when the Japanese commandant found out, he first beat the hancho who was in charge of the little boys' han. He was told that he should have stopped this destruction. Then, as a further punishment, we were not allowed to have a meal that evening. This order was really tough. We were hungry, and the day ended with us boys talking uselessly about food.

On another occasion we did not get food all day, again as a penalty. Some kids had smuggled and were caught. The Japanese had an expression that translated to, "One does wrong, everyone does wrong!" By late afternoon my stomach was so obstinate that I resorted to eating raw ground coffee beans. By nighttime I was very nauseated and suffered from heart palpitations.

The three Jewish boys from Malang kept to themselves and huddled like scared little puppies. The eldest, just younger than Anton, was treated normally, and he had to work in the fields just like us. Everything changed after he became so obsessed with food, specifically how to digest rice. He would sit down on the floor of his han, his legs crossed, and use a large sewing needle to eat one grain of rice at a time. He claimed that it created better absorption. We tried to tell him how wrong he was, but to no avail.

When others started to eat slowly and with tiny bites, we told them that they were needle eaters like this boy.

As odd as this behavior was, we all knew how powerful a force hunger was. Eventually, however, this boy chose to increase his isolation and developed an indifferent attitude toward others, and then he became the butt of jokes. On every side, the courtesies and respect our parents had taught us were being sacrificed, for by now it was apparent only the very tough would survive. I felt very sorry for his two little brothers.

In early 1945, in another room of Han 1, three boys developed a fever for a week. That was not unusual in the least, but when they broke out in a rash over their trunks, it became clear that they had rat typhus, also known as flea typhus. Our camp doctors, in spite of adverse conditions, came up with the diagnosis in a hurry. Usually this ailment is miserable but not life-threatening; in this instance, however, emaciated boys were afflicted, making this disease more serious. The three sick ones were shipped to the hospital and their han quarantined for three weeks. The other boys in that room in their isolation suffered from excruciating boredom.

Whenever a severe illness occurred like this typhus, especially one that involved several boys, the Japanese guards would walk around with a white cloth mouthpiece to protect themselves. We found that hilarious, knowing very well that this cloth would not protect them, that this disease could not be inhaled. This was another reason that we considered them totally ignorant. They dared not walk into the typhus room. The Japanese relied completely on the Dutch doctors' judgment and order for quarantine.

The three boys survived. However, one of our frequent assignments was to be pallbearers, carrying so-called coffins made of flimsy bamboo. The kids who had to do this job were all around the age of fifteen. We brought the bodies from the death room, passing the kitchen area to the back gate, to be placed in an ox-drawn cart. We had no choice but to seem indifferent to this frequent parade; when a nun would call to one of us to move a body, we would shout to the others, "Corpses to haul!"

One event after another revealed the steadily worsening conditions that existed both inside and outside the camps. Daily for several months we *patjol* workers had made our way over the same route to and from the fields, and we knew every inch of the roadside. We once were approaching Djalan Siwilan when I spotted a real stir in the column ahead of me, like a spasm slowly moving down the line. Alongside the dirt road was a deep ditch, which we had dug, to deal with the heavy rains during the monsoon season. The column of tired boys swayed toward the ditch at a certain point, as if compelled to look into its depth. At the bottom, among the weeds, lay a dead infant of about five or six months, on its back. We could see its face, so still, as countless red ants swarmed over it; they went for the eyes first. When he noticed the commotion the Japanese in charge ran forward, kicked us back in line, and pushed us to speed up the tempo. The marching column slowly wound its way back to Bangkong, shrouded in deep silence. I despaired at the discarded infant. The Javanese were gentle and loving with their children, and they cherished them. What did this death say about the circumstances of those under Japanese rule outside the camps? Even though I had to deal many times with the deaths of those I knew in Bangkong and Lampersari, this picture of abandonment and death never left me.

The quantity and quality of our food supply deteriorated steadily in 1945, and I could track the results seemingly daily in my brother Anton. One day I brought him before the Tokè, who was seated at his portable table on the patio. The doctor tested Anton's blood and told him, "You have a fever from malaria, and the bloody diarrhea is a result of amebic dysentery. This combination makes you anemic." Anton received the last six green iron pills available.

The pills served only as a delaying action, however. Soon after, Anton developed pellagra. It was obvious he was suffering from a variety of vitamin deficiencies, all brought on by the starvation diet we were being given. His illness had progressed with severe episodes of diarrhea. He became extremely listless, and I began to feel increasingly desperate about how to help my brother overcome some of his symptoms. By this point, though, Anton was seldom well enough to work in the fields, and so he had fewer options.

After Christmas, on my return from the fields, Anton showed bluish bumps on both shins. He whimpered, unusual for him, since ordinarily he complained very little. He had leaned against the sink, next to where the food distribution took place. That was the place to rinse dishes, and it had a low rim, only knee high. After he washed his cups, he brushed his teeth and his gums started to bleed badly, which scared him. I checked his lower legs. Blue raised spots stood out from the shinbone, but worse, they were extremely painful. I had read plenty about *Scheurbuik* aboard historical Dutch sailing ships in the 1600s. This was scurvy, and the cure in those days was lemons or greens.

I realized that I had to do something. One time I managed to snatch a lettuce-like vegetable from the private garden of our commandant, adjacent to the guardhouse on the fields. Thank God I was also able to smuggle some greens and *kangkung* into camp. My secret method of smuggling was nothing more then a thin pliable iron wire, attached at each end to a tiny brass safety pin. I used to string these leaves and attach the pins to the inside of my three inch-wide belt.

I was also able to bring in some tiny shrimp that I had found in the standing water of a deep ditch, in the lower part of the fields close to the highway. As I often did, I had wandered off, searching for food. I used my old handkerchief like a dragnet in the shallow water, but these shrimp were less then one centimeter long and difficult to catch. I was so embarrassed about their small size that I kept this catch a secret. The tiny shrimp hidden under my belt would spoil fast, so Anton and I had to eat them almost upon my arrival, and raw. There was risk either way, for we knew that spoiled shrimp could make us very sick.

This smuggling supplied Anton with iron and vitamin C. His scurvy did clear up, but for the rest of his diseases it was an uphill fight. Some other teenagers, noticing that I carried leaves under my belt, teased me about smuggling wilted plants. They thought I should eat them on the spot. They had no insight at all as to why I was carrying anything, and they ridiculed me, but I did not care. I acted as though I did not hear them, for the less attention it got the better. In that heat I sweated like a horse and gave the leaves a good soaking. After arrival in camp I was not always able to wash the greens; again, I wanted no attention. As far as I knew, I was the only one to use the safety pin and wire method, and it kept me safe from discovery. This practice was strictly *dilarang keras*, forbidden, and if discovered a punishment was to be expected. Several kids who were caught smuggling food from the fields were severely beaten. However, I was never caught.

It was too bad that Anton also developed beriberi, the great killer in our camp. In the final stages of the disease the heart would go into failure, and the boys suffering from it would swell up like balloons from water retention. When I was picked to lift the beriberi corpses onto the funeral carts,

I figured that to be the worst experience I could ever encounter. Foul-smelling fluid would gush all over me. This was always my biggest agony, and now that Anton was showing early symptoms it became one of my biggest fears as well.

As bad as it was to come back from the fields muddy and exhausted, it was worse after some of the labors in camp. When entering the death room, I had a legitimate fear that I might encounter the corpses of kids who were well known to me. If there was no water to wash up after my work in the death room, I felt like crawling into a deep hole, never to surface again. I felt completely helpless, just sitting there, waiting for water, when hours felt like ages.

There were plenty of reasons to prefer the work in the open fields to the alternating horrors and boredom of camp. Of course, there was always the prospect of finding a bit of food in my foraging. Only one time was another of my wishes granted, when I was able to speak with my mother, who was working in the women's field. She and I managed to exchange some words as we walked slowly past one another. Her face was twisted by deep emotions, and I suppose mine was as well, but we both were so happy to see each other and to hear a familiar voice. By April 1945, when suddenly the women were back in the fields, I did not see her among them, and I became as fearful of losing her as I was of losing Anton. One tall Japanese soldier occasionally and very carefully allowed the smaller boys to talk to their mothers, but for me this one contact with my mother was just luck.

By the time 1945 was well along, the two barbed-wire fences surrounding the camp completely defined our world. Between them two guards walked hourly. In spite of their vigilance, smuggling was still attempted, although the spirits and energy of many boys were at such a low ebb that these adventures were becoming less and less frequent.

Two twelve-year-olds who had some Indonesian ancestry started to go out of the camp through the barbed wire rather regularly, about once a week. These boys would leave one day and come back the next. They visited Chinese or Indonesians at their homes, who would feed them. Upon their return they carried eggs for the hospital. While they were out they were reported ill during tenko. This smuggling team performed well for many weeks, until the Japanese decided one day to do a head count of the sickbay. "Two men short!" was the shouted response. This triggered an explosion! The Japanese guards, running around screaming, worked themselves into a rage.

This discovery happened just at the time that we had returned from working in the fields, close around five in the afternoon. We were tired, hungry, and thirsty, and dressed only in shorts. All four hundred of us stood lined up when, suddenly, the Bloodhound and Kimura stormed out of the building, the most horrible words rolling out of their mouths. Terribly agitated, they paced back and forth over the grounds as they tried to determine what to do next. Suddenly they grabbed the hancho of the han to which the two boys belonged and beat him unmercifully in front of us. Then they started to batter other leaders. Finally, with their rage only fired further, they began to strike boys at random.

The Bloodhound, a short, bow-legged, and extremely muscular sergeant, had a field hockey stick and started to hit bodies at random. The standard brown army cap was balanced on the back of his skull, and the soaked flaps rested on his neck. His shirt was wet with perspiration, front and back, as were his pants. His face was twisted from anger, and a waterfall of terrible words continued to come from his mouth. It seemed that his rage would never end, and indeed it lasted for hours. He demanded in Malay that we tell him where these two boys were. It became apparent that he felt he had been duped, and a good part of his rage was at the loss of face before his Japanese betters.

Nobody was willing to talk, and even our own leaders did not know where these two were. Somehow we enjoyed seeing the Bloodhound ready to explode. We knew it would not do any good to confess, so we might as well keep our mouths shut. On one hand, I was scared to death, not knowing what would happen next; on the other hand, I grinned inwardly at seeing these two guards losing total control.

Next to me stood fifteen-year-old Leo, who always became very nervous and scared under such stress, and he started to grin and smile. The Bloodhound noticed this and approached him singly, then took a pencil out of his pocket and tapped the boy on his forehead. The Bloodhound said, "Bodo-ka?" Bodo in Malay means stupid, and the Japanese always added the syllable ka to foreign words. This ridicule made the poor boy more nervous, and he grinned even more foolishly, as though he were tempting this arrogant and brutish guard. The Bloodhound stepped back, swung his hockey stick, and hit the kid close behind the left ear, fracturing his skull. The boy vomited, flipped over, and fell. Moments later he started to have convulsions. He lay on the ground, blood seeping from his left ear. Like a wild animal, the Bloodhound kicked him several times in the chest, screaming at him to get up. The boy did not move, and I noticed that he had wet his pants.

Finally the Bloodhound realized that his victim was unconscious. He walked over to the other guards and started to brag about how skilled he had been in this beating. Even though we did not understand Japanese, his wild gestures and motions mimicking his previous actions told us the story. Deep silence among our ranks followed this terrible event. We were stunned. Those of us around the injured boy moved to pick him up so we could take him to the hospital, but the Japanese guards barred us from helping and kicked us back in line. We had to stand at attention; we were not allowed to help. Kimura held a club in front of my face. Hatred boiled up in me, but I had to control myself, and I heard a great deal of grumbling from others who apparently felt the same emotions. We all realized that we were powerless. I was angry, and at the same time scared of this inhuman figure, but I had not lost my sense, and all my emotions remained bottled tightly inside me.

Leo lay there all night, dressed only in his shorts, with his face smeared by vomit. We had to remain standing, right there, wondering what was next. We were given no food. Many of us had to pee, and we did it right there, on the spot. That evening it started to rain. It became so cool that we skinny boys shivered, dressed as we were only in shorts. A cooling sea breeze touched our crew cuts. After the rain stopped, the usual nocturnal creatures started to announce their presence. There was chirping of the *djangkerik*, the cricket, and a few moths fluttered overhead. Swarms of mosquitoes started to dive-bomb us. We slapped the critters even as they were busy stealing our blood.

We also heard the distant nocturnal sounds of the city, gradually fading as the night progressed. That became a long night, trying to stand to attention, the sliver of a moon throwing long shadows off the ranks of boys and buildings. These reflected images were dark and savage. The faint light made our entire entourage very spooky. The church walls, supposedly white, looked in that light dingy and dirty. The dark roof of the church and its tall towers reaching for the sky looked grim and threatening. Surrounding us was total emptiness.

The Japanese stood there like phantoms in the darkened backgrounds. They, too, had grown silent. During the early morning hours a dead silence started to surround us, occasionally rudely interrupted by a kid coughing, or a mosquito being slapped. I was waiting for unexpected sounds to disrupt the fossilization of the deep quiet of our eerie surroundings. Yes, it happened, two boys passed out and laid motionless on the dirt. Any moment the guards might resume their screaming and hitting, but they remained motionless. Never was the absence of noise so unreal and deafening.

Finally daylight arrived, the sun's rays sparkling around the church tower. Carefully I dared to look around, and saw tired, sleepy faces, young faces that reflected the emotions of that night and the uncertainty of the oncoming morning. During the stillness of this sunrise we had lost the concept of time, and we were scared. I welcomed the warmth of the reaching rays hitting my dried lips, and I realized my extreme thirst.

The next day, the two boys returned to our camp. The Japanese immediately seized them and beat them terribly. "Where did you go? Where did you get the eggs?" Kimura yelled. We heard the screams and listened to the belt cutting into the skin of their backs. Then the Japanese placed hoses in the boys' mouths and filled them with water. Even so there was no confession. In the meantime we were still lined up. Kimura told us again to identify where these boys had gone, but we stood our ground and refused. The Kempeitai worked these two twelve-year-old boys over, to no avail, and then locked them up in the pigsty. The door was nailed shut and the window boarded with planks. Their tiny and dark cell was located very close to the kitchen, but food seemed completely out of reach to these boys.

Around two in the afternoon the Japanese finally dismissed us, and our lineup exploded into a run for the few bathrooms, only to discover that the spigots did not produce water. Our excessive thirst demanded water, but we were too exhausted to line up at the water taps. Instead, starting at the tap, we placed our personal cups in a long line to mark our places. Then, without a drop of water for nearly an entire day, we moved on to our mattresses to wait for the spigots to produce the desired liquid.

That night I happened to have the night patrol duty, *fushinban*, with another boy. We had to walk on the inside of the camp from midnight till two in the morning. If the Japanese guard came, we had to yell in Japanese that everything was in order: "*Shochi itashimashita.*"

As we walked slowly toward the pigsty, we talked briefly with one of the boys. His voice sounded weak and scared. We discovered a knot in one of the planks and we succeeded in pushing it inward. After this we rushed to the head cook and talked him into helping the two kids. With his aid, we successfully placed a hose through the opening and fed them porridge. We pushed the wood plug back in place to conceal our efforts, cleaning off any trace of food. The cook took over after our first night. I was so tired, for I still had not had any sleep, but the satisfaction of knowing that we could keep the boys alive compensated for this dreadful fatigue.

The guards suspected that we were able to feed the two boys but never figured out how. After three weeks the kids were released, without a confession. I felt that God had had mercy on them. The only result was an increase in our hatred toward the Japanese guards. This experience left us with a hopeless feeling; there was seemingly no end to all this suffering. All around us was only misery, illness, starvation, death, cruelty, beatings, and hard, heavy labor that we were barely able to perform anymore. We wondered how it all would end.

Late in the afternoon before that fushinban duty, the boy who slept next to my brother Anton developed an asthma attack. This asthma attack was so severe that he was unable to eat or speak. After sunset he squatted down on the edge of the verandah, trying to inhale the cool evening breeze. He supported himself by placing the dorsal tips of his fingers on the cool tiles like monkeys do, and struggled, gasping for air. His nostrils were flaring in a blue face, and he had an intense, audible wheeze. I sat down next to this twelve-year-old, wanting to help but not knowing what to do. I had never seen an asthma attack before, and this one obviously was a nasty one. Talking to him in a soft, encouraging tone seemed to help him. I told him that the night coolness was going to benefit him. I spoke about better times that were sure to happen. Slowly he began to improve. The next morning we found him on his mattress, exhausted but finally able to lie down.

I had to get up the next day, even though I had hardly slept that night and had had no sleep the night before that. During those forty-eight hours we had been shorted two meals.

Again that morning I marched through the gate with four hundred other boys to work in the fields. After arrival at the central field parade grounds, we went through the routine lineup and head count. I was assigned with a group of boys to dig out ditches and to raise the dikes at the far lower side of the fields. The rains had not yet let up and were creating a problem. I did not feel like mingling with the others, for I did not want to listen to idle talk. I was exhausted, physically and emotionally, and wandered off to stand far away in the ditch, with my ankles submerged in the muck. I leaned on my patjol and rested the blade on the dike. The tall coconut trees slightly uphill, beyond the cabin built for the Japanese, attracted my attention. A spectacle was taking place; several blekoks, white herons, were fighting over fish that they had brought into the crown of the tree. Making clattering noises, they flapped their wings and hovered a foot above the leaves. Some of the fish dropped, and the boys working at the manure pit who were the closest to the drop zone dashed for the delicacies. I was too tired even to consider running; besides, the distance was discouraging enough. Dreamily I looked at the distant road, the Deitjonghan, where traffic was light. The high school occupied by the Japanese officer training detachment stood out in the farther distance, quivering in the heat. South, I saw dark-green Mount Ungaran, where I used to live, its top crowned by a dark cloud.

I remembered stories that my parents had told us about the eight-thousand-foot-tall mountain. They had struggled to reach the densely forested summit. Mother had told us about the monkeys, who were upset and aggressive, throwing tree branches at them. Pictures taken at that time showed Mother with a walking cane, slacks, and puttees wrapped around her shins. My brother and I found that image quite hilarious. I closed my eyes to enjoy that mental picture and started to imagine other pleasant times. The sweat rolled down between my shoulder blades, and I embraced the sweltering heat, recalling the cold night from two days before. I tried to forget that horrible experience and started wishing for good times, such as to see my parents together again in our own home, to enjoy minor pleasures such as a card game, chess, a call for dinner, a book. I longed to work on my model railroad again.

I had fallen asleep standing while leaning on my patjol. I was rudely awakened by screams from others: "Hot water, Hot water!" Bewildered, I looked around and noticed Easter Egg approaching us. With his right arm swinging a bamboo stick, he spoke angrily in Japanese, which went straight over our heads. His cap was balanced on the back of his skull, and the flaps whipped up and down. His brown shirt, streaked by sweat, stuck to his chest. He waddled and swayed over the narrow dike, creating such a comical picture that we broke into laughter and were still grinning when we bowed at his approach. The terrible muggy heat affected his mood, and after he inspected our progress, he hit our komicho over the head, telling him that we had to work harder. In that rage he turned and, losing his balance, slithered off the narrow dike into the mud. His canvas boots soaked up the brown liquid, and with difficulty he drew them out of the mud, making sucking sounds. This exaggerated effort set off so much laughter that we could not suppress it. Easter Egg's embarrassment was so great that he just trotted off, beside himself in rage. Even our komicho forgot his sore head and smiled.

Leo survived.

Our house in Semarang. (See Chapter 2.)

The family Stutterheim at their home. Semarang, 1929. (See Chapter 2.)

In 1938 we sailed aboard the *Marnix van St. Aldegonde*, which was used as a large troop transport in "Operation Torch," the landing of U.S. troops in Oran, North Africa, in 1942. She was torpedoed by a German plane close to Gibraltar on her way home. (See Chapter 3.)

Author in native dress. Semarang, 1931. (See Chapter 2.)

Lampu lantern. (See Chapter 3.)

Native boy, a *katjong*, driving long-necked ducks home. (See Chapter 3.)

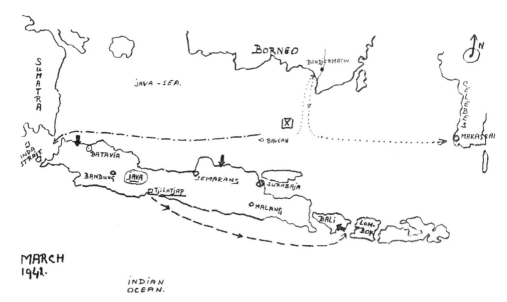

MARCH
1942.

INDIAN
OCEAN.

Allied navies around Java. (See Chapter 5.)

Key

— — —   Dutch flotilla and two U.S. fourstackers attempted to stop the Japanese landing at Bali.

⊠   The Battle of the Java Sea was lost by the combined forces of the British, Australian, Dutch, and U.S. navies.

....   After picking up survivors, the hospital ship *Plancius* set course for Makassar, where the Japanese navy boarded her and took over the ship. Captain Tuizinga protested in vain.

—·—·—   Escape of the cruisers *Houston* (U.S.) and *Perth* (Australian). The Japanese sank them in the Strait of Sunda. That same night three Dutch freighters tried to escape, and two were sunk. Several survivors swam ashore. Some were killed by the natives; the rest were taken prisoner by the Nippon.

➤   Areas where the Japanese landed.

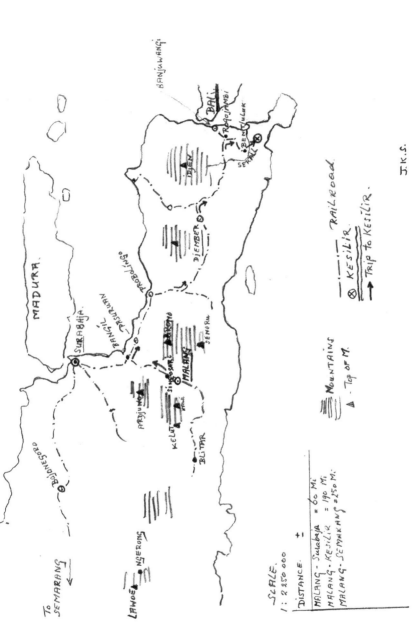

Trip to Kesilir through eastern Java. (See Chapter 7.)

This may look like an ordinary train station, but one has to realize the emotions of the women and children who passed through its gates during their deportations. (See Chapter 9.)

A native conductor providing coconut milk to thirsty toddlers on the railroad platform in Semarang, 1943. (See Chapter 9.)

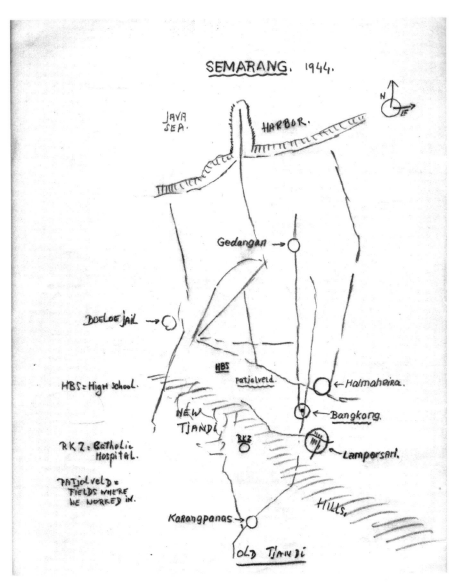

Semarang, 1944. (See Chapter 10.)

J.K.S.

THE TOKÈH

The *tokè*. (See Chapter 10.)

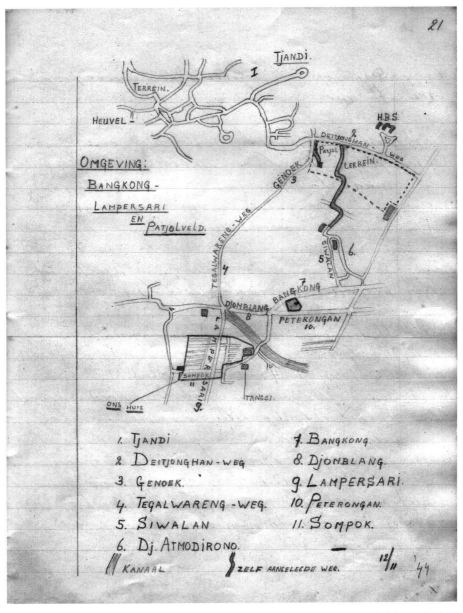

Page 21 of my diary, November 1944. The dashed line indicates the fields we had to work in, and the thick line extending downward from it is the road we constructed. It starts at Djalan Siwalan, named after the fruit of the lontar palm, shown on the cover of the book. No. 7 is Camp Bangkong and No. 9 is Lampersari. No. 10 is the ravine through which I escaped in September 1944, dodging bullets fired by the revolutionaries. I visited in 1993 and saw all that fields were built on, except Dj Siwalan, and part of Lampersari had been bulldozed. At the Cloister, Bangkong, I was shocked to learn that nobody in the local populace knew it had been a concentration camp. (See Chapter 12.)

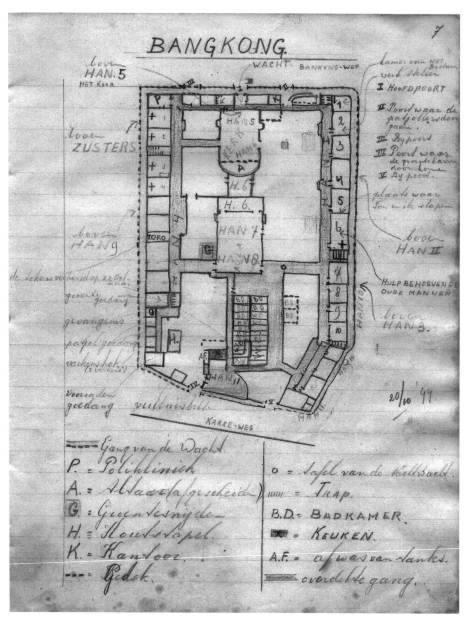

The plot of Bangkong. The 55 nuns lived at the hospital, marked as ++++. The church, in the top center, is where the 12-year-olds lived. The square: Aula, for the 10-year-olds. BD = 14 bathrooms for 1,400 people. On the right, the number of the classrooms we slept in with the commons in front. Room no. 5 was my brother's and mine with 38 boys. II is the gate we marched through. AF = lean-to over the kitchen wood fires. (See Chapter 12.)

Singing women, rhythmically pounding rice. (See Chapter 13.)

Hauling supplies. (See Chapter 13.)

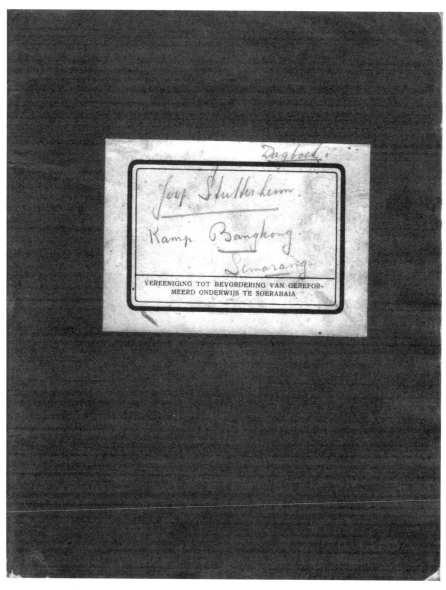

My secret rolled-up diary. (See Chapter 14.)

S.V.P. schrijf fouten laten zitten!

Zondag
15 October

De 13-14-15de Oct. heb ik moeten liggen voor Malaria. Voor het eerst had ik Malaria. 's morgens hebben we koffie en suiker gekregen. Ze zullen in het vervolg elke Zondag suiker uitdelen zolang de voorraad strekt. Ton moest 's morgens passtellen (op 't land werken). 's middags ben ik naar de Polikliniek geweest voor mijn lies want die was erg opgezet. De dokter gaf me 3 dagen vrij van alle diensten en appel. Toen Ton van het passtellen terug kwam werd bekend gemaakt dat alle jongens kaal moesten zijn. Toen was 's middags de eerste, die kaal was van onze zaal. Ik wachtte eerst maar af.

Het eten is voorlopig nog hetzelfde.

Menu: 's morgens — 's middags

1½ pollepel pap (350cc) (kedellie-pap) — rijst 300 cc
1 pollepel kedellie-soep 250cc
1 eetlepel sambal tonto of pak
1 theelepel gebrande kedellie

's avonds:
1½ pollepel pap (300cc)
1 eetlepel djagoeng en 1 pollepel hutspot 50cc
1 theelepel geraspte klapper met suiker

1 Liter = 1000 cc

Writing helped my anxiety. (See Chapter 14.)

While waiting for the water to be turned on, I felt depressed and dirty after cleansing the dead for burial during the noon temperature of over 100° F. Bangkong, 1944. (See Chapter 15.)

Bangkong. A *tjikar* had arrived to remove our dead. Coffins from the female camps were already stacked inside. A teenage boy is trying to read the names on the headboards of the coffins. (See Chapter 15.)

Outside kitchen facilities in Camp Bangkong. Notice boy with fan. We used oars for stirring. (See Chapter 15.)

Bangkong's gate, seen from the parade grounds. From left to right: Church, death room and guard house, gate, and the two-tiered classrooms. Above it all is the woven bamboo with barbed wire. Once we stood there for over 24 hours dressed only in shorts. That evening it rained and the mosquitos ate us alive. No wonder malaria was rampant. (See Chapter 15.)

The road we built. In May 1945, a blackboard reading "Germany surrendered" was hoisted into the banyan tree. (See Chapter 16.)

Guard of Bangkong's gate with Arisaka Rifle. (See Chapter 16.)

The 2,000-ton *General van Heutz*, smaller than a liberty ship, evacuated 2,000 women and children from Semarang, October 1945. (See Chapter 20.)

Surabaja, 1945. Sikh guard at the River Brantas Bridge. (See Chapter 23.)

Propaganda on a matchbook, 1942. The Japanese scissors are cutting the chain that holds the Allies together, and the Malaysian text reads, "The Strength of Asia." (See Chapter 24.)

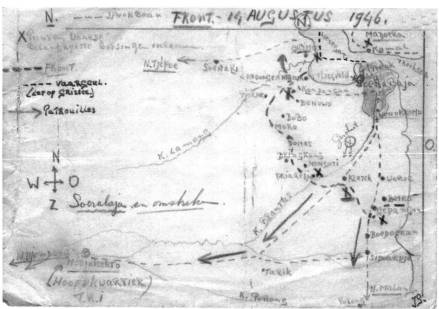

The area of Surabaja controlled by Dutch troops. The dotted line in the waterway shows the route our LCT used, cleared of mines. (See Chapter 24.)

Above: Brother students in medicine (John in the darker coat, next to Anton) at the Dam of Amsterdam, 1953. (See Epilogue.)
At left: Passport photo of the author upon his arrival in the United States in 1959 under the Pastore–Walter Act, an act specifically passed for former prisoners of Japan. (See Epilogue.)

This statue located in Bronbeek, Arnhem, The Netherlands, is a reminder of what we boys looked like in 1944–45. (See Epilogue.)

chapter sixteen

BLEAK PROSPECTS

My own brother was very ill by now and in bed most of the time, seldom getting up except to get food. He did take daily showers, which I considered a must. In the evenings we talked a little, but most of the time we listened to the conversations of all the other kids, in order to try to stay informed about developments in camp. Fortunately, during the day he was never alone, since several other kids in our room were sick as well. Anton simply lay on his mattress on the floor. I had made the skinny mattress myself so that it could be rolled up in case we had to be shipped out again. Taking a thin blanket, I folded it double and stitched it by hand in rows one inch wide, across the entire length of the blanket. Some kapok from an abandoned mattress on the other side of camp filled the empty tubes with the help of a bamboo stick. When all was filled I sewed the ends shut. Considering the tools, doing this work by hand was a major effort. There wasn't much to the mattress—the thickness was one inch at best—but it was better than seeing Anton sleep on the tile floor. I had left one tube open in order to be able to hide my rolled up diary, which was a forbidden item.

The lice were in total agreement with the comfort of this bedding, and they occupied it in no time. When I had a chance I would hang our mattresses in the tropical sunshine to drive the critters out, then spear them with a big needle. Killing them gives a special *wallang sangit* odor. Once a person smells it, the memory stays forever. Was I successful? Hardly. After another night new occupants joined us. Were the lice taunting me about my failure? Mother had always maintained such a clean home, and for months I had tried everything I could think of to keep us both clean and healthy, but the odds were mounting, especially against Anton. I knew Mother would understand the situation, for Lampersari had offered similar challenges, but still I was thankful she could not see Anton and me as we had become.

One time, as the dry season was approaching, one of the adults, known as Jacob the Jew, looked me up. In his thirties, he was clever in dealing with the Japanese. He knew that my mother was in Camp Lampersari. He told me to show up at the rear entrance of Bangkong at two in the afternoon for a work detail of fourteen boys, which would be heading there.

I was immensely pleased with the prospect of contact with her, and I wrote a brief message in minute script on a tiny piece of paper no bigger than two inches square. In case I could not see her, I could at least leave a message. I rolled it up tight and stuck it in the tiny hollow brass tube that functioned as a bar on which the pin of my belt buckle rested. After accomplishing that, I reported in at the rear gate in full anticipation about the possibility of seeing Mother.

We stood lined up when the Bloodhound arrived. His sweaty khaki uniform was wrinkled. His garrison cap had settled slightly over his right ear. On his belt he carried a bayonet and pistol. His right hand was placed defiantly on his right hip. His red face was heavy-jawed and puffy, and his eyes flashed angrily as he looked us over. He was in a terribly aggressive mood. The heat of the noon hour seemed to bother him immeasurably.

He inspected us extremely carefully; he even felt inside our belts, and when he checked me he shook my large buckle. Apparently the tip of the paper scroll started to slip down into sight, and he grabbed it. He became enraged; I knew what was going to happen, so I grabbed my glasses and held them in my hand behind my back. These soldiers were known to grab a prisoner's glasses, toss them on the ground and stomp on them.

He started to beat me. He alternated his two hands, hitting both sides of my face. The blows were severe; my ears started to buzz, and my face felt swollen. After his rage passed he turned to Jacob and, snarling, demanded that he translate the message.

Jacob looked at me and said, with an expressionless face, "He wrote to his mother that he is well and that the Japanese are treating us all right."

The Bloodhound swallowed this story and kicked me out of the lineup. The group marched off through the back gate with Jacob and the Bloodhound up front. When I came to the realization that I was left behind, I cried, not as a result of the beating, but because I could not go, and now no message would reach my mother. There was no way to correct it, and I felt I had failed miserably.

By this point, many boys were willing to give up, and depression set in. The presence of an underlying disease, as well as severe malnutrition, contributed to this willingness to simply lie down and let God take them.

Nothing much changed the deadening routine, but occasionally something would remind us of our lives before the war. There were occasions in peacetime, during the late afternoon, where several kids gathered on the back patio of our home in Malang and our cook offered us special treats such as roasted corn, *beras ketan*, sticky rice, fried strips of banana, *lontong* wrapped in banana leaf, and *kwe-kwe*, a native cake. Some kids would pout, not wanting this or that item. The memories of all that food made me drool, and I never understood why kids could become so picky about eating. This dreamy state of reviewing foods of the past became extremely popular among us teens, the more so as our meals were constantly reduced.

Life in the fields was full of surprises. One afternoon, right after our meal, a tall skinny thirteen-year-old started to scream. He stood a slight distance away, behind a cluster of banana trees, with his pants down and was gesturing toward his behind. What we saw immediately drew a crowd of snickering kids.

A half-inch-wide, long, pale, yellowish tapeworm strung out from this boy's anus, draped over the ground in the direction he had just covered by walking forward. The tapeworm originated at a heap of stool. The boy explained that for days he had passed short pieces of tapeworm with his stool, and had consulted the camp physician, because a tapeworm for this emaciated boy was like a death sentence. The medicine that was issued consisted of large doses of strong laxatives. The result was what we were witnessing. Normally the head of the worm is anchored in the stomach. The strips of tape are nothing more than clusters of eggs, high in protein, obtained from the host. By purging the patient, there is a good chance that the head will come loose; it is very small, so it is hard to spot. Several boys picked up bamboo sticks and unraveled the tape, hoping to identify the head of the worm. Some of them claimed that they found it. We measured the worm to be twelve yards. I wished then that we could have taken a picture of this bizarre trophy, for it seemed incredible even to us who had seen it.

Moeder Overste, the head nun, died of starvation on March 19, 1945. This was a painful death to all of us, especially to the smaller boys, who had benefited so much from her caring presence. Her funeral was very special indeed by the standards of Bangkong.

Her coffin was of better quality than the usual flimsy bamboo boxes, and a priest recited a special prayer. He opened the procession, walking with the cross, and all Dutch camp leaders were present. Some had white shirts on. A big surprise was that the Japanese commandant showed up. At no other funeral did he ever show his face. Even the Luxembourger attended, the only death observance we knew him to make throughout the life of camp. The casket was carried between a double line-up of boys. The other nuns carried the coffin to the gate of Bangkong, singing "In Paradisum," and from there one Japanese officer took her remains to the cemetery.

The same day two old men died, and their bodies, covered only in dirty shorts, lay unattended in the death room. They must have been taken to the cemetery a day or so later, when there was a regular shipment from the various camps nearby.

One Sunday in April 1945 was unusual for two reasons. We had not been sent out to work in the fields, and that was a rare event in itself. This meant that around four hundred boys could rest for one day, albeit with one slice of bread less in their rations. The second event affected only a few of us, and it was so surreal that it seemed to be fantasy.

Hasegawa, commonly known as Beautiful Charles, was the camp commandant at that time. Many stories circulated through camp about Beautiful Charles. He was tall and spotlessly dressed; that morning he was wearing a white shirt and a clean brown cap with the traditional flaps hanging down on his neck. His uniform was the typical drab brown. He was clean-shaven, and even we boys had to admit that he had a friendly face. On a sturdy belt he carried his splendidly polished scabbard. His boots were so well rubbed that they could have been mirrors. His manner was smooth, and he clearly had an eye for the ladies.

We rarely had contact with him, but on this particular Sunday morning he walked toward us and selected himself fifteen of the older boys, including me. There were no Hei-Hos present. He marched us through the front gate to where a Japanese army truck was parked, and he ordered us all to climb aboard for a special job. A sack of tapioca suddenly appeared and was placed on the floor of the truck. The commandant grinned from ear to ear and sat down next to the driver.

Soon we found ourselves driving through the hills of Tjiandi, up the Gombel Pass, toward Ungaran. The ride, although bumpy, was pleasant and relaxing for us, for we were able to see the lush green vegetation and hills on either side of this winding road. Striking was that life seen from our truck appeared so normal. I was hoping to see Ungaran again, where I had spent good years of my childhood. At last, after half an hour or so, the truck branched off east onto a dirt road that led to a farm.

A woman, apparently the owner of the place, came out to welcome us and spoke in Dutch, informing our group that she was of Portuguese-Malay ancestry. She was young and very attractive, with long raven-black hair and a friendly open face. Her dark red *kabaja*, a long shirtlike garment falling down over her hips, was open in front and held together by a dainty golden brooch. To this ornament was attached a long thin golden chain reaching toward her navel. The long sleeves of her kabaja were folded back to display a rich fabric embroidered with silver thread. Underneath the kabaja was her sarong, also dark red with flowers. All fabrics were in traditional batik. On her small feet she wore brown sandals.

The commandant placed his arm around the woman. His hand ended up on her derriere, and they both went inside the house, giggling. We started to realize why he was so spotlessly dressed.

After descending from the truck, we looked at our surroundings. We were on a small farm but it had a good-sized barn. Some cows roamed in a pasture, and a few goats with marble-size bells around their necks were staked out on ropes. A large flock of geese, which must have been excellent guards, welcomed us with outstretched necks, threatening us by making horrendous honking noises, only to calm down as they got used to us. Our appreciation of all these animals was summed up with the comment, "They would taste great as a meal!"

A cow outside the stable was in labor, trying to deliver a calf. A long leg protruded, and a veterinarian was trying to turn the calf around by placing his arm up to the shoulder inside the animal. It was our assignment to clean the manure out of the stable and move an outside manure pile farther out to the fields. The commandant had told us that after the job was finished we could make a fire and cook our tapioca. That would be a real treat.

Firewood was easily rounded up. We found a kerosene can of eighteen liter totally cut open on top, ready for our cooking. After we washed the container we boiled water and added the tapioca. We ate so much that our stomachs protruded between our skinny ribs. I filled an old gallon butter can, with tapioca to take back for Anton. When we had finished our meal we noticed that the veterinarian had succeeded in delivering the calf and was leaving.

Our work finished and the tapioca gone, we lay down under a big shade tree. Suddenly one of the boys realized that it was a mango tree and that the fruit was gorgeously ripe. But at the same time we also discovered it was infested with red ants, and their nests, built by pulling together the hand-sized leaves, were the size of a football. Red ants are slightly larger than carpenter ants, and their bite stings and burns plenty.

Nobody dared to climb the tree. After quite a bit of hesitation, I decided to get those mangos. I figured if I climbed very slowly the branches would not move and I might be safe. After selecting a good supporting branch, I moved cautiously toward its end. I started to grab fruits, but it was slow picking. By then the ants had sensed an intruder and they started to swarm out of their nests. Noticing this danger, I quickly stood up, grabbed a branch with each arm, and started to shake vigorously. The mangos rained down like hail, but so did the ants.

When I figured we had plenty of fruit, I tried to move back to the trunk of the tree for the return trip. The branch that I occupied had turned completely red with angry insects. Some ants started to get in my short pants and proceeded to bite me on the buttocks. There was no choice, so I dropped from a fair height to the ground. I was not hurt, but I started to shake and dance and got busy knocking off ants. The others had already scrambled for the mangos. The ripe fruits that I got tasted delicious! They were juicy and sticky and stained our shorts, but we cared not a bit about that detail. We washed up at the tap in the yard, than rested in the grass for at least an hour.

Suddenly the farmhouse door opened and the woman and her guest appeared. She smiled, and he was in a jolly, relaxed mood. His clothes were quite disorganized. He told us as we climbed in the truck that he was satisfied because our labor had paid for the woman.

On the trip back to camp our stomachs were filled, and the commandant's visit to this woman did not bother any of us. But we understood why he had not wanted any Hei-Hos along.

That visit to the farm, with fresh fruit and relaxation in the shade, seemed like nothing more than a dream within days, since the harsh daily routine had not changed. During April 1945, when it seemed our bodies and souls could not endure much more, the camp sustained an epidemic of the feared blackwater fever. Two adults and four boys died. Our medical staff pleaded with the commandant, but he refused to provide quinine, even though it was abundant, Java producing 90 percent of the world's supply of it. We explained that the same mosquito that had infected these boys would stick him and give him the same illness. The next day, a miracle happened: a small quantity of quinine pills arrived.

Other things, however, did not change at all. The Japanese continued to mete out punishments; the only surprise was in their inventiveness. Two boys were harvesting *oebie*, the sweet potatoes. The guard in charge discovered that they had stolen a potato each. He gave them a solid beating and made them stand in the full sunshine, each with an arm raised above his head and the stolen tuber held high. Every time their tired arms would come down, they received another beating. This went on for three hours, stopped only for roll call.

Our hancho said, "Those damned Japs are going to pay for it. We'll get them."

Another episode occurred when the ten- and eleven-year-olds under the supervision of Mr. Vetter were caught not doing their work. The older man, always leaning on a stick, was their hancho and was supposed to spur the little kids on to pull weeds in the vegetable beds. He yelled constantly, "*Met wortel en al,*" meaning "with root and all," but most of them would just sit there. Suddenly the warning went out: "Hot water!" A Japanese guard was approaching. He went into a rage when he discovered that nothing had been accomplished. Taking the stick away from Mr. Vetter, the guard, in a fury, started to hit him on the back with all the force he could muster, and he did not stop until the hancho fell to the ground. This scared the little boys so much that they started to work, and they continued at it for about an hour, only to slacken again from exhaustion. Their supervisor had a hard time recovering.

One guard, the young Korean named Kimura, stood out especially for his brutal nature. He passed on his enjoyment of torture to twenty-year-old Fukuyo, another Korean, who, using a lit cigarette, took pleasure in burning off the eyebrows of young kids at the slightest provocation. Many times over it happened that a minor infraction ended up with a punishment that was completely barbaric, almost beyond belief. These troops were out to show their disdain for us, who were to them nothing more than defeated people.

I was determined not to give up. I came close to it, but what kept me going was my belief that God had not abandoned us. Although I did not fold my hands to pray, I had the conviction that it was a fact. I also had a strong conviction that our side was going to win the war. Mother had told me that evil was going to lose eventually, and I wanted to believe that. It seemed foolhardy to remain so hopeful, though, without us knowing anything. We had a complete news blackout, no inkling of what was happening even just outside our camp. We heard only stupid and unbelievable rumors such as, "The Americans just landed in Surabaja and will liberate us in two days!" Some thrived on these rumors even though they realized there could be no truth in them. The belief gave them some way of maintaining hope.

By May, I often felt shrouded by feelings of hopelessness, loneliness, weakness, hunger, and desperation, as if there were no end in sight. People around me were dying one after another. Evenings, while resting on my primitive mattress, negative thoughts would storm through my mind. I tried to push those grim ideas aside, struggling to create an image of what my possible future might be after the war. Hope. That was all that was left, hope, only hope.

One of these many old men who arrived in camp was a celebrity of sorts, Pa Van der Steur, who came to us in early May of 1945. He was a very popular Dutchman from Magelang, in the highlands of central Java. He had come to the Indies as a young man and had started to care for orphans, especially those children of military people. He had a small church and always managed to get funds from private resources. Generations of boys, who came to be known as *Steurtjes*, owed him their existence.

At first the Japanese left him alone; then they hunted him down in the belief that he had hidden funds, which was not true. On numerous occasions, he was arrested and dragged into the Kempeitai headquarters, but he was never jailed for long. He stood up to them quite convincingly, saying the Lord was with him. Finally, when he was in his nineties, he was brought into Bangkong. He was a skinny, gray-haired old man, easygoing and very kind. To many of us he seemed invincible, but we knew that he had no defense against his tormentors, and this only added to our depression.

In May 1945, right after lunch, when we were back at work in the fields, the Japanese suddenly became very agitated. Obviously they had received a communication from a truck that had just arrived. They shouted immediately for the Hei-Hos. We had to line up, *tenko*, *bango*, in a great hurry, and we were told to return to camp. As we walked close to Djalan Siwilan, I could see that all heads in front of us looked up. A big blackboard had been hoisted in a large *waringin*, or banyan tree. Written on it in Dutch were the words, "Germany surrendered!" At first the message did not sink in.

Then, all of a sudden, a joy that was difficult to suppress rippled through the long column of boys. Under no circumstances did we want the Japanese guard to notice the message in the tree, and lucky for us, as well for the individuals who had hung it there, he did not see it. We gradually realized the importance of that piece of news. It meant we were a step closer to our liberation, and that possibility gave us renewed hope.

Even though the Japanese never let on that their ally had been defeated, after this news everything changed in the camp. We older boys had to stay on the premises, and the younger boys, the thirteen- and fourteen-year-olds, were put to work harvesting the *patjol* fields. At first we thought that the Japanese distrusted the older group and were anticipating possible sabotage. But this misconception was suddenly cleared when an Indonesian carpenter entered the camp, and under his supervision we were put to work to construct an old-fashioned three-piece sawmill. It was erected directly inside the main gate and took less than a month to put together. Once it was built, the heavy labor began.

A log was hoisted up into a horizontal position at a height of about twelve feet. A nail was placed on each end of the log and an ink line was strung under tension between them. When we lifted the line and let it snap, a marking line would show up on the bark. When sawing, we had to follow this ink line. We were given large, long saw blades with a handle on each end; the tall kids stood on top, pulling that dull, rusty, heavy saw up through the wood. Our progress seemed infinitesimal.

Quite often I felt very weak, from hunger as well as fatigue, and I felt my strength ebbing away, especially since we sawyers did not get the extra slice of bread anymore. I started to have blackout spells. I became too weak to pull the blade up, and I was deathly afraid that I would fall the twelve feet to the hard-packed ground. Most of the time I tried to hang on to the frame of the mill. There was no way anymore to obtain even small bits of extra food, as had been possible when we were working in the fields. I was sixteen at this point, and it became clear that if this situation continued, neither my comrades nor I would survive.

Still, the will to live endures. Hopes that Allied advances were taking place in the Pacific and the knowledge of Germany's defeat explained exciting and desperately needed deliveries. On May 16, we received our first Red Cross packet.

This was such a landmark in Bangkong that I recorded the contents in my second diary. At the time of the first distribution the Japanese commandant gave a speech saying that the Japanese were so kind as to allow the Red Cross to provide us with food parcels. Each parcel was sixteen by sixteen inches square and four inches tall. The contents were wonderful, items we scarcely remembered as having really existed. Among the treasures were the following items: one can of Spam, which was totally unfamiliar to us; one block of cheese; four small cans of cheese spread; one can of jam; one can of corned beef; a tin of butter; graham crackers; forty sugar lumps; coffee; powdered milk; powdered eggs; two bars of chocolate; liver sausage; dried prunes; raisins; five packs of Chesterfield cigarettes containing five cigarettes each; two packs of chewing gum; two pieces of toilet soap; and a can opener.

We received one packet for five boys. We were thrilled to open this packet, but we found it difficult to divide the contents evenly. Still, we were very careful to portion this food as fairly as we could. We used a metric ruler to divide items such as the chocolate bars by five. A thimble was used to measure out the powdered milk and eggs. The biggest problem was the butter, almost melted in that heat, but the fat was so needed and the taste so welcome. How do you divide a prune? My share of cigarettes I swapped for food, since many of the older men apparently wanted to smoke more than anything. Even the empty cans were in demand for storage, so we arranged a lottery.

The order was issued that all empty cans had to be turned in. In July 1945, superior officers in Semarang made an inspection, and some Japanese walked through sickbay. When they saw an empty Red Cross can beside a sick boy, the Japanese officers went into a rage, beating three physicians and forcing them to stand at attention for two hours in the hot sun. Some of our camp dwellers spotted Japanese officers smoking Chesterfields, so they obviously had confiscated some of our Red Cross packets. We hoped to receive medicines, but never saw any.

There were kids so addicted to smoking that they picked up discarded cigarette butts, no matter who had smoked them. The art of their game was to find fine paper so they could roll their own. One young boy, who was quite an entrepreneur, possessed a Bible whose pages were of very fine paper, ideal for cigarette wrapping, and he traded pages away. Some miserable jokes were cracked about rolling these cigarettes in Bible paper. A callous thirteen-year-old made statements such as, "Thou shall not steal has been printed here on this page. I will inhale the Ten Commandments rather than read this Bible!" Another more sincere boy commented angrily, "You pharisaical hypocrite, you're *pienter boesoek*." This meant smart-mouthed and rotten.

Another sudden change made for wild rumors in camp. In the late part of May 1945, the Bloodhound and several other Koreans disappeared, and we learned that their status as Koreans in Japanese service had not protected them at all. Slowly bits of news filtered into camp, whispered to us by the Hei-Hos, that the Koreans on the islands had staged an uprising around the time they learned that Germany had been defeated. The Japanese killed them, and most likely this included the Bloodhound.

An Indonesian division in Japanese service, called the Sukarillas, also mutinied around that time in the vicinity of Madioen in eastern Java. The Japanese cruelly suppressed the rebellion. We heard this story as well from the Hei-Hos, who did not dare to speak openly. They were visibly scared by this time, which was no wonder, and it became clearer than ever that they did not sympathize with the Japanese.

In spite of growing indications that the Japanese were beleaguered, they continued to come up with new projects for work parties. On June 12, 1945, there was a sudden tenko for all the older boys in the camp. It was a bit after six o'clock in the evening, and it was already getting dark.

The Japanese in charge, the castrate, strode up and down and told us in his effeminate voice that he needed one hundred boys. The plan was to move them out of Bangkong on June 14, which happened to be my seventeenth birthday. He told us that the selected group was going into the mountains to cut wood in the forests. All the camps were desperately in need of firewood to keep the ovens going. I was in the lineup because of my age and height. The kids who did not look fit enough were thrown out of the lineup, but the castrate left me in the ranks. I was not eager to go, since it sounded like only more exhausting work.

The castrate turned in annoyance when he heard crying in the dark on the patio in front of our sleeping room. The sobbing came from my brother, who sat at the edge of the patio, with his feet dangling over the edge of the deep gutter. As always, Jacob was there too, helping us communicate with the Japanese. The castrate asked Jacob, "Why is he crying?" Jacob checked and reported, "The boy who is crying is very sick, and you are taking away his older brother, who normally cares for him." The castrate's response was, "Who is this older brother?" They pointed at me, and I was pushed rudely out of the row. So I stayed to work on the logs in the sawmill and tried to care for Anton.

My brother was very sick with a variety of ailments, all resulting from slow starvation. While we were still working in the fields, I had heard from the women across the barrier that Mother was too ill to work, so I could not see her anymore. On top of all that, I had not heard from Dad for almost three years, and I had no idea where he was or if he was alive. There were times that I was full of despair.

We were hungrier than ever. Some kids broke into the soldiers' quarters to look for food, which infuriated the Japanese, and since they were unable to find the ones who did it, we received no food at all for a day and a half. This had disastrous results. At evening tenko several kids fainted, and seven died that week alone. The Japanese killed three kids I knew in this slow way: J. Vos, sixteen, H. Doornberg, seventeen, and Koos Spee, fourteen.

The months of May, June, and July were horrible, with starvation the worst problem. So many kids were sick, and the death rate rose steadily.

We always seemed to talk about recipes, especially in the evenings. Foods we used to despise were given special placement on our imaginary dinner plates. I had never been fond of cooked liver, but at that time I went almost nuts thinking about it.

Our days continued to be less predictable than in all the prior months in camp, but we were almost too far gone to understand that the Japanese were finally in a defensive and reactionary posture. In late June a second Red Cross pack arrived, shipped from South Africa. In spite of the shrinking population in camp, we had to divide this package among nine boys. The contents consisted of one chocolate bar, one piece of toilet soap, and several small tins of cheese, bacon, margarine, a beef roll, meat, tomatoes, condensed milk, and apple pudding. There was even one can with rice and cream, along with a few cookies, and we found a packet of tea, one can of syrup, and two sugar bars. I again listed this in my diary, for it was to us like manna from heaven. It is impossible to describe how we nine kids sat around that packet when we opened it. Each item, as it was lifted out of the box, was announced aloud, triggering screams of joy.

There was more to this than the presence of decent food. The package and its contents told us that we were not forgotten. It had often seemed that we were totally abandoned in that small, miserable camp, enclosed by that high wire and bamboo fence.

Yet again, a few weeks later, a third round of packages was delivered, and this made us begin to wonder if the Japanese had not held back these packages all along. This time, each Red Cross package was divided among twenty boys, a near impossibility. Yet our method of meeting the challenge told me that we had not lost our senses or our humanity. One boy stood in the corner and faced the wall. Another boy held an item or an imaginary item up in the air and asked loudly, "Who is this one for?" It worked something like a lottery. In this package was one bar of soap, one box of tooth powder, one comb, one toothbrush, one pair of underpants, and a pair of shoes. Whoever could fit into those shoes kept them. There was also one box of shoe polish, which triggered lots of laughter, it was so meaningless to us by now, and another item, which was just the opposite, a handkerchief. The kid who drew the handkerchief clowned, waving it in the air, then acted like he was sobbing, pushing his face into this piece of cotton. It triggered smiles. But what crowned it all was an etui, a small case with sewing materials. At the time we thought this was hilarious, a pointless luxury, but it turned out to be quite practical. It contained a pair of small scissors, a card of buttons, yarn and thread, three needles, and three safety pins.

Even though the contents of a Red Cross packet when divided by twenty amounted to very little, again the realization that the outside world seemed aware that we existed was enough to cheer us up, it meant that much to us. Afterward we sat together and talked about the Red Cross for hours.

By this time it was August, and we were well into the dry season. One evening dark clouds crowded together in the sky, drawing over the camp and making the full moon disappear. Several of the smaller boys suddenly went into panic, a kind of hysteria, and cried out, "This is the end of the world; the moon has disappeared already!" It took a great deal of convincing to settle them down. I never thought anyone could have such a stupid idea, but it showed how desperate their state of mind was.

With no news from the outside, and always the same routine, some boys' minds started to get muddled. The only persistent thoughts were about how to obtain food. Nobody played any games; we were too weak and listless to display any eagerness or to accomplish anything at all. If we did not have any duties to perform, we would lie on our skinny mattresses. Sometimes I would pull myself together and look at my only book, the French lesson book that I had hidden. Just doing that bit of study exhausted me and I would fall asleep.

Have there ever been teenage boys who would not talk about girls and sexual attraction? Well, by now this was not heard in our group anymore; the advancing starvation knocked out any desire. This was the reality. No one seemed to care about anything much at all. I wondered every night if Anton would be alive in the morning.

chapter seventeen

DEATH AND UNEXPECTED

FREEDOM

At the end of the first week of August, an air raid alarm went off while the evening was still young. The alarm was shocking enough, but we had had some insignificant air raid alarms before. This one, however, was real and electrifying. At first there was a deep stillness. Nobody was allowed to go outside. Suddenly we heard the drone of airplane engines. Then multiple explosions came from the direction of the harbor, and we soon realized bombs were falling in that area. That could only mean that Allied planes were raiding the harbor and that finally the war was coming our way again after years without any apparent action. Every time we heard an explosion, the entire camp population started to scream, "Hurrah!" The Japanese began to run up and down through the inner camp, yelling at us, "*Diam!*" "Be quiet!" Remarkably, their threats did not frighten us any more, and the cheering continued. After all the noise both inside and outside the camp finally subsided, I could not sleep for hours. At last we saw something to show that liberation was ahead for us. It reaffirmed my belief that the Allies were going to win the war. This belief gave me an inner peace, but no rest came that night.

On August 15, 1945, the behavior of the Japanese suddenly deteriorated yet further; arrogance and brutishness were replaced by volatility and an immeasurable nervousness. They hit us at the slightest provocation and seemed always to be looking over their shoulders. We were ordered to dismantle the sawmills, which we accomplished in three days, a record time. We were happy to be able to use the wood of the dismantled mill in the kitchen, where we desperately needed dry fuel. It never occurred to me that by destroying those mills we were eradicating the evidence of teenage hard labor. Nobody was called upon anymore to work in the fields. There was a change in the air, and we could only guess why. Hope became almost tangible.

On August 16, some adult male prisoners were brought in. They spread the rumor that American troops had landed in western Java. I did not believe them.

On August 18, ten Japanese soldiers replaced the Javanese Hei-Hos. On the following two days we were sent to the *patjol* fields, but only to harvest vegetables, and they were all for our own use. As a further treat, we received a double ration of food. A bigger miracle came yet, when two days later 180 pounds of meat was carried through the gate, together with twenty pounds of bones. We were so surprised and elated that we could not believe our eyes. Good food! The realization started to hit home that something really had changed.

Then, at noon on August 23, two aircraft flew over Semarang. I happened to be in our room when I heard excited boys screaming, "Planes, planes!" I ran outside to look, and in no time hundreds of us were crowding the parade grounds. Two bombers were circling over our city, flying lower and lower. It became apparent that they were looking for something. Then it dawned on us that they were looking for our camp! Finally these planes flew so low that they thundered right over us. They were so close that we could see the head of the pilot, and the tail gunner wiggling his two machine guns in a salute. The planes were B-25s, Mitchells, with red, white, and blue markings. Leaflets separated from these aircraft and fluttered and sailed through the air slowly, passing the camp, and missing us totally. I wondered how they knew about our camp's location, or its existence, for that matter. The Japanese just stood there silently and did nothing. For once they were as helpless as we had been for so long.

The two Mitchells circled over us three times. Later we found out that they were flying in a triangle over the three camps in Semarang: Halma-heira, Lampersari, and Bangkong. They apparently knew the locations of each camp. After a moment of deep silence and admiration for the passing aircraft, we understood. "The war is over!" The entire group of boys went uncontrollably wild. We danced, jumped, and screamed until we became hoarse. We climbed on each other's shoulders to wave at the planes. Sick kids had crawled onto the verandah in order not to miss anything, some with tears in their eyes. Still, there were some who were deathly ill and they remained inside, unable to witness this exhilarating event.

All the nuns came outside, and for the first time we saw them all together. They started to sing the Dutch national anthem. This solemn ceremony quieted the boys down.

Then reality set in again. The planes were gone. There was a sinister quiet, followed by a grumbling. We wanted more than this ending; we needed food, medicines, and much more. We demanded for the gates to be opened. The Japanese refused, but this time they did not beat anyone to show their superiority. We could not understand why.

That afternoon, in the dry, blistering 100-degree heat, the guards herded us together. This turned out to be the last time they forced us to obey. We had to face the camp commandant, Beautiful Charles, as he stood before us on a three-foot-high platform. He told us that a terrible bomb had been dropped on Japan, which had surrendered on August 15. "*Senzo owari*," he said. The war is over. We looked at each other, shocked, for it was now August 23. However, Beautiful Charles continued, the Japanese were already preparing for the next war, which they would certainly win. Was this the seed of revenge, or was it more of the old arrogant *bushido* attitude? We were confounded and could not absorb what we had just heard. The commandant bowed and descended. All the Japanese left together and went inside their quarters, not to appear again inside the camp.

Crowds of Javanese and Chinese gathered outside the barbed wire. Without interference from the Japanese guards, who apparently intended to remain outside the gates, we pulled the *bilik*, the woven bamboo, out of the barbed-wire fences in order to communicate with the other world. Some persons on the outside started to throw *djeroeks*, orangelike fruits, over and through the barriers. They looked so good, and they were so welcome! We had not tasted such food for two years. To me the juice was a delicacy. I saved some for Anton, who was lying on his mat, too weak to take in the scene.

I stood fairly close to the front main gate and looked at the people outside. They were normal human beings, people who were not sick, not emaciated, but properly dressed, with shoes or slippers on their feet. I could not feel a part of them. Emotions bubbled up, and tears came to my eyes. Was it possible that the war was truly over? Had the end of this terrible, deadly camp finally come? Could we start to live a normal life again?

The thought of any normality seemed absurd when I turned to look around me in camp. There were countless sick kids, many of whom were so severely malnourished that other diseases like malaria had laid them motionless on their cots or on the floors.

Hundreds of other boys had only minor ailments, but even so, they were still barely able to function. Nearly all of us needed medical attention, and some of the boys needed long-term care.

That first afternoon of quasi-freedom I spent with my brother, who was still so terribly ill that he was scarcely aware of the events of the past days. He was emaciated, and bedridden, and harbored symptoms of malaria, amebic dysentery, anemia, beriberi, pellagra, and scurvy. I wondered if the war had ended too late for Anton.

Later that same afternoon, when it was time to get in line for food, I walked under the long overhang of the school. A few doors down from our room I spotted an easy chair, one of the few we had in camp. The chair was pushed into a corner where a flight of stairs led to the second floor. On that chair, on his back, lay my former neighbor from Malang, Dutrie van Haeften, who was just a year older than I. I stopped and noticed how beriberi had made his body so swollen that the skin on his legs had cracked and body fluids oozed out. The sudden realization that he was not breathing, that he had died, brought tears to my eyes. In anguish I asked other kids when this happened, but they shrugged their shoulders and kept moving. He must have died there in the corner, alone. No one knew how long Dutrie had been dead. I wondered if he had seen the planes and if at least he had experienced the joy of knowing the war had ended, but I realized as I stood there that I would never know.

chapter eighteen

HIDDEN DANGERS

When we got up on the morning of August 24, we found the main gate open and no guards in sight. The atmosphere in the camp was eerie. Many of us walked to the gaping opening in that high fence, which now allowed us a view of the outside world. We were all very cautious, and many boys appeared hesitant and afraid. It seemed that this was a dream and the gate might slam in our faces at any time, for its open state felt unnatural. Was this gate really open? No more guard to stop us? After three years of yelling from the guards and the required bowing to the Japanese and their flag, there was instead a deep silence. It was too much to comprehend.

Many boys, I among them, approached the gate slowly but stopped short of leaving camp. Still, I felt a desperate need to see the outside world again. The realization that I was free came slowly. I took a deep breath and pinched myself. I felt so grateful to be able to experience that moment. God had been good to me, to let me stand there and be well enough to take in all the proof of a world still functioning. What a sight, to see people on the road capable of making their own decisions, talking and laughing with one another and among their own families.

Beyond the gate, the Indonesian world went on about its business. There were vendors with *pikolans* over their shoulder and a large basket of woven bamboo on either end. Some of these baskets carried a charcoal oven, burning to be on the ready for stir-frying. One of the favored items was *bah-mi*, a Chinese dish that consisted of noodles with vegetables and bits of meat. Some boys flagged the Chinese vendor down and clamored for a meal, paying with a handkerchief.

Tjikars passed by at a very slow pace, big two wheeled ox-drawn carts used to haul everything. Trotting horses pulled dogcarts. Young persons passed by on bicycles, passengers astride the *gontjeng*, the luggage carrier. What I really saw were people on the move, and their energy and sense of purpose was overwhelming at first. Many of these people stared at us, and suddenly I became awkwardly aware of my own appearance; as usual, I was barefoot and shirtless, and only a pair of faded, half-worn shorts covered my skinny frame.

I turned and fled into the camp again. There several Indo boys stood together, were saying farewell to many of their *sobats*, friends. They were so young, and they seemed quite agitated and somewhat fearful about accomplishing their plan to leave the camp and go east. They preferred to travel as a group, since most of them were heading for Surabaja. I watched these skinny barefoot kids, their belongings on their backs, walk through the gate, heading for the downtown railroad station.

Several others also witnessed this exodus in silence, everybody with his own feelings. Indeed, I felt for a moment the pull to join them, to get away from this camp, but I knew that I had to find Mother first. Besides, Anton needed help.

When I returned to the classroom I found my brother lying on his bedroll, warm and increasingly listless. He had not been eating or hardly drinking. It was a struggle for him to take sips of fluid, and he was so weak that he had trouble swallowing. I knew something needed to be done for my brother quickly if he was to survive, but all resources seemed impossibly out of reach. Luckily, the kitchen provided me with bouillon that Anton was able to drink while sitting up.

Even as the gates stood open, I began to feel more desperate and alone than a day earlier, because now there was suddenly no camp structure. I could rely only on myself. After all the emotions and turmoil I felt exhausted and rested next to my brother. Several of the boys in our room did just the same, taking siestas. After eating better and starting to get more food, we had to regain our strength. Others also expressed the uncertainty of what to do next and many ideas were brought forward and discussed, only to be rejected, for everybody realized the uncertainty.

On August 26, the boys who had been sent to the mountains as loggers returned. This group of one hundred laborers came back after Japan surrendered. They, too, had heard the news days after the surrender. It was not easy to get stories pried out of them, for by that time they were elated about the surrender of Japan and far more interested in what to do next. We did learn bits of their experiences, however. When they left in June, they traveled by train to Kedoengdjati in the mountains, located on the road that connects Semarang with Soerakarta.

Upon their arrival in Kedoengdjati, they found another hundred boys who had been scavenged from the Ambarawa boys' camp. During their stay of over two months at the logging camp, they had all slept in an old wooden church. Their biggest problem was to get water, because this was the dry season. There was no water for bathing or washing clothes. They even had to scrounge for water for cooking. Often the well, which was their only source of water, was not more than a pool of mud. Once in a while they were allowed to go to a nearby river, the Kali Tjeret—a name that says it all, for it means "squirt river." The name clearly illustrated their water problem. Sometimes, to their joy, there was water in the river; sometimes there was close to none. One result was that their skin became crusted with dirt, especially between the shoulder blades. A sour note, just as in Camp Bangkong, was that the dirtiest kid was called King Daki, having a skin crusted with dirt.

A Japanese soldier, Sergeant Kadowaki, was in charge of the boys. They had been pushed relentlessly at hard work with extremely poor tools. The quality of the axes was inferior, and the saw blades, made from poor material, were nothing more than metal strips into which teeth were filed.

Neither the boys nor the sergeant knew how to cut a tree properly. One story they told us was how they selected a big mahogany tree and cut it on all sides, like a circle. All of a sudden the tree fell, right in the direction of Kadowaki, who had to run to escape. After the tree had fallen, no one was able to spot Kadowaki. Then someone noticed a helmet pop up in all that green toward the crown of the tree. Kadowaki was barely hurt.

Food in the mountain camp was not much better than that in Bangkong, even though they had to do exceedingly heavy labor. Production was limited as a result. The camp was quite isolated, and the boys there were ignorant of world events. Our only contact with these boys had been at the end of July, when our head cook in Camp Bangkong received a truckload of wood. He became excited, for he discovered some of their names written on the surfaces of a few pieces of wood.

When the boys came back, we looked at each other and realized how skinny we all were. At the urging of a camp doctor, who examined some of the returnees, we weighed ourselves on the kitchen meat scales. I weighed approximately ninety-five pounds, and most of them did not weigh much more. A few boys loaded their pockets to appear heavier, since we were all afraid of being hospitalized for malnourishment, but nobody qualified.

Among these filthy returnees, we elected the one who had really a crust between his shoulder blades as King Daki. He was placed on a table and stood there, grinning sheepishly. Then a garden hose of the kitchen was opened up on him. He accepted the stream of water with joy. Most of them drank lots of fluids first and then headed for the showers, where they scrubbed each other's backs. They had a ball, enjoying the sensations and throwing buckets of clean water at each other.

We were unspeakably happy that we had survived, and it felt so good to see each other again. Each one of us was looking forward to the possibility of getting away from Bangkong, although it was impossible to imagine where we might go or what we would find at our destination. Some kindly Indos came to help us after the Japanese left, and they remarked that our chests looked like birdcages, ribs sticking out. They advised us about conditions in town, but more important was information about the tough circumstances in other parts of Java. They cautioned us about the Merdeka, the newly proclaimed Indonesian independence movement. We ignored their warnings, for there were so many other things on our minds.

The Luxembourger, our alcoholic leader, was just as invisible now with the Japanese gone as he had been before, when his presence during the many speeches and beatings would have been at least a morale boost to us boys. We intensely hated this fellow, and we blamed him for the death of many teens. We considered him a traitor and profiteer, and to us nothing could be worse. At dusk a few days after the surrender of Japan, a large group of older kids went to his quarters and dragged him into the assembly area, where he was pushed and pummeled. The mob of boys, in an ironic twist, then made the Luxembourger—who, by the way, was not skinny like us—a prisoner himself. Some kids wanted to kill him. Enough of us had not lost our own humanity to prevent that, but we had no objections to treating him roughly.

It seemed that hanging him would be too kind, and so we decided to let him do some of the camp's dirtiest work. On the evening after the planes had come over, some people on the outside threw oranges over the barbed wire and handed us pig's feet through the fence. That evening we had a feast, but it turned out to be too rich for our guts and caused severe diarrhea. There were not enough bathrooms to accommodate all of us, so we all squatted over the ditch. Later on, the Luxembourger was forced to clean up this mess. It gave each one of us satisfaction to see him having to perform manual labor of the lowest type after he had been a lazy parasite for the last year.

The next day the Luxembourger disappeared. The rumor went around that he had fallen into the hands of the revolutionaries beginning to roam the countryside, and we assumed that he had been killed. None of us shed a tear, and his rumored death earned no sympathy from us, though I was glad that it was not at our hands.

Finally, on August 27, I felt confident and strong enough to head for Lampersari to see if I could find my mother. Anton appeared more stable, and I thought he could be left to himself for a few hours. The conditions in our room and the camp as a whole were chaotic, and I had to see to it that Anton was protected. The boy in our room who suffered from asthma promised to keep an eye on him. Of course I had wondered about Mother daily, but no news had come from Lampersari. I had to confront the real fear that if I managed to reach Lampersari I would only learn about her death.

The walk to the women's camp did not take long, but I felt awkward and conspicuous, barefoot and shirtless, and tried to ignore the people staring at me. One of them was selling tomatoes, and I offered her my hankie for several of the fruits. She packed them on a small bamboo tray, and when handing it to me she gently said, "*Sinjo*, boy, eat and get strong again."

This open awareness of my situation made me quicken my pace. When I walked through the open gate of the *benteng* in Lampersari, I noticed all these very skinny women, who themselves hardly took notice of strangers walking in. I looked first for the home at Sompok, at the very end of the camp. As I covered this distance I noticed the appalling deterioration of the camp, which had become far more crowded. I grew hesitant, not know-ing what to expect. There, next to the barbed wire, was that plain little brick home, sitting on a rise. Alongside the worn steps leading from the road was the oven I had made in 1943, and it looked as though it was still being used. Annie Bruinvis was outside, and my arrival surprised her. In amazement, she called me by my nickname, "Jopie." I stopped and said hello, noticing how skinny and slovenly she looked. She hugged me and nodded toward the familiar room, saying, "Your Mother is there."

All the doors had been removed, perhaps for firewood, but a door re-quires space to open that they did not have. I entered quietly and saw Mother, sitting on a trunk, alive, but very sick and emaciated. She cried when we hugged each other, but I was shocked to discover how weak she was. She could hardly stand.

On my knees, I pulled at her left hand and tried to talk with her, asking her how she felt. Her right hand brushed my scalp and she whispered, "I am fine." Tears wriggled down her cheeks. Then she asked, "Where is Ton?" Carefully I explained that he was alive, but very ill, and still on his mattress in Bangkong. "Why didn't he come?" she asked.

It dawned on me that she did not, in fact could not, comprehend his situation. Dickie Berendsen put her hand on my shoulder and said to my mother, "We will see him later on." Mother nodded in agreement. By now I realized how sick and confused she really was, and I felt helpless.

After I got up, I embraced Mother's two girlfriends. They were only a shade better off than she was, but I was most deeply shocked by the appearance of their three little daughters. Each girl was incredibly skinny, weak, and hollow-eyed. They reminded me of puppets, without a spark of life sitting on the floor against the wall, while staring at me, with recognition but without animation or much response, even in their eyes. Although I was relieved to see them alive, their condition was deeply disturbing me. How terribly this little group of our friends must have suffered in the preceding months.

I shared the tomatoes I had brought. Mother tried to eat some bits of fruit, but it made her sick, and she vomited several times. Malaria and food deficiencies had dragged her endurance to the breaking point. Shaken badly, I did not know what to do. At the same time, it was a relief to be among our old group again.

All six women and children were still in the same nine-by-twelve-foot room that I remembered; it had no furniture and was filled with cabin trunks stretched out along the walls and covered by rolled-up mattresses. The chalk on the walls was blistering and flaking, exposing the red brick. The nails used to suspend the heavy mosquito nets from the ceiling had been pulled out several times, leaving tears and cracks. The tile floors were chipped, cracked, and discolored. The few cooking utensils were stacked in a corner. The sole window revealed panes that were stained and fissured, allowing rainwater to enter. As a result, the sill was warped and rotted at the rim. It was inside this depressing drab, dirty room that the three mothers and three little girls had tried to find reasons to fight for their lives.

After sitting there and trying to talk with them, it became apparent that we all had too much to tell, and it was too crushing. I felt tears welling up, but I contained them with the realization that I had to get busy. Nobody had any concept of what to expect or what to do. I wanted to help each person, but was not sure how. I had just turned seventeen and was not sure that I could handle such responsibility. Yet there was no one else able to tackle the problems surrounding us.

Aunt Annie and Aunt Dickie were bartering for food, but they had to walk to the main gate, for the Javanese were not allowed yet to enter camp. They were scarcely in shape to walk any distance themselves, and they hated to leave their frail daughters behind. Getting our hands on nourishing foods had to be one of my jobs, at least for the short term.

Late that afternoon I left reluctantly. I told Mother that I was going to bring Anton over the very next day if at all possible. I realized that I could not take care of them both at two different locations. On the way back I realized how exhausted I was. The distance was not great at all, but my emotions and my attempts to plan everything for the next day caught up with me. When I saw Anton again, my determination grew that I had to pull it off. I just had to succeed. When I went to bed, the emotional events of the day caught up with me, and I lay awake for a long while, doubting that I could handle it all.

The Japanese had abandoned some food supplies when they left, and our kitchen in Bangkong used them up. This kitchen, to my surprise was still functioning, however poorly. Very few people were helping out with the cooking. Early that morning, after getting food from our kitchen and helping Anton, it struck me how everything had become chaotic at our camp. I looked around and noticed the changes. Many kids, especially the little ones, had left for Halmaheira and Lampersari to join their mothers. The church and aula were almost empty. The *pendopo* still had some old sick men, apparently attended by the nuns. The hospital still functioned under the care of a few nuns. The second floor above our room lost a great many of its occupants. That morning I went upstairs to see for myself what was going on. The rumor was that the upstairs was going to be fumigated. Under the supervision of one of the physicians, people I had never seen before were indeed getting ready to seal off the windows and doors.

I found several thirteen- and fourteen-year-olds on the second floor playing games on the verandah. Their yelling and screaming echoed and vibrated through the almost empty upper story. They jumped constantly, and the noisemaking was so unusual, for none of us had been capable of that amount of activity for a long time. Their actions were a form of desperation. They had gone to visit the women's camps to find their mothers, only to discover that they had died, leaving them orphans. They had no idea what to do or what would happen to them next. They clustered to get a sense of safety and support, and to keep themselves from falling apart. I did not see them cry, but their bizarre behavior was more upsetting than tears would have been. Their fear and frustration somehow kept them together. Each boy could not face being alone, and they were all looking to each other for support. As a group, they moved downstairs with all their belongings, where they gradually calmed down.

At noon the fumigation process began, and we could smell the sulfurous gases. While I was feeding Anton, I happened to look at the ceiling. To my astonishment, I saw long lines of lice tracking down the walls, like an army on the move.

Cracks and fissures enabled these bedbugs to escape. In horror, some kids grabbed brooms to kill the pests, but it was no use, they kept coming. The odor of killed lice mixed with the smell of gas.

The assault stiffened my resolve to move Anton to Lampersari. That afternoon I brought our simple belongings to the Sompok house.

The following day I loaded my brother piggyback with the help of another boy. The mosquito net and eating utensils were the only items I had not yet taken over. The mosquito net I tied to Anton's back and the utensils to his belt. The effort became quite an ordeal, even though the distance was not great, for although Anton weighed very little I did not have my strength back yet. Carrying Anton was exhausting. In the daytime heat I had to make several stops. Fortunately, another boy heading in the same direction stayed with me to help hoist Anton back on my back after each rest. Many Javanese passersby stared at us, but nobody offered any help.

In this halting manner I carried Anton to Lampersari. Upon arrival, I collapsed with Anton at the steps leading to the house. Several women came to help, which I considered an embarrassment, even though I needed the extra hands. Mother welcomed him, sobbing, but again without any real comprehension of the situation. Anton was then lowered to the floor, where he soon fell asleep. The trip over had not been easy for him either. Aunt Annie Bruinvis shook her head and realized very well that the tough circumstances they had been coping with were compounded by Anton's arrival.

The first order of the day, every day, was to get food. Since the Japanese had left, no more supplies were being delivered. The group of women shouldering the leadership of this large camp estimated a population of close to ten thousand people in the postwar days. These numbers, of course, exhausted all supplies remaining in the warehouse in no time. The leaders ordered that those in the hospital be fed first. As a result, we were on our own, and many women were compelled to try to barter for food outside the camp.

We had no money, but I grabbed some handkerchiefs out of Mother's trunk. She was too weak to question me, and besides, I got the feeling that she approved. I was after foods that were highly nutritious, such as tomatoes, bananas, coconuts, carrots, and roasted meats. So many women were out there as well, some poorly clad in contrast with others, who were wearing sunny prewar dresses, bartering for food. Our cooking still took place in my old oven, but now we were able to use charcoal instead of wood. I surprised Mother and the other women once with coffee for their breakfast, an old tradition in our families they had sorely missed.

We eventually learned from the camp leaders that at the time of surrender, our island, Java, was originally to be included in the American zone of liberation, but at the last minute the Indies were transferred to the British zone. The British were originally told that they could expect to find ten thousand women and children in the entire former Dutch East Indies. The British officer in charge of the region was Lord Mountbatten, the viceroy of India, whose base of operations was there. All sorts of news like this trickled in and, once in camp, traveled faster than it could have by telephone. We were so keen to get any information that false rumors started circulating just as readily.

As an unofficial representative of her government and her husband, Lady Mountbatten flew in to the Indies three weeks after Japan's surrender. That was a gutsy move, since the Indonesian revolution was causing turmoil. She toured all the major camps and took many photos. She also visited Semarang and spent time in Lampersari, where she met with Mrs. Van der Poel, who briefed us all on any progress in our situation. So many of us were desperately hungry for any type of news, for our future depended on it, in relation where to go, or to hear where relatives were found and whether help was on the way for the severely ill. For them it meant their very survival.

Lady Mountbatten discovered that instead of the ten thousand anticipated prisoners, there were at least 102,000 surviving civilian prisoners out of the 125,000 original count, besides the military, scattered over multiple islands, over a distance from northern Sumatra to Celebes. During the last days of fighting, the British troops had just taken Rangoon in Burma, and it was their closest base. They hurried to Singapore and from there tried to deal with the liberated POWs from the death railway in Siam. With British civilians in desperate need as well, and scattered over a huge geographical area, efforts to reach and care for so many civilian survivors, not to mention the military prisoners of the Japanese, became a monumental challenge. The British supply chain became so overburdened that it took three weeks for relief to reach Java, entering Batavia first and eventually reaching Semarang by ship.

Anton was dehydrated. He still did not respond adequately and did not take much nourishment, in contrast with Mother, who at least was eating and able to get around. She really started to improve, and her mind was clear again, but that meant she had to acknowledge our precarious situation. It was obvious Anton needed medical care and immediately. Both he and Mother had malaria, and we still had no quinine. Annie Bruinvis and I had known how life-threatening Anton's situation was, and Mother started to comprehend this as well. Then luck visited us.

Dr. Berendsen, the veterinarian and the husband of mother's friend Dickie, arrived from the vicinity of Batavia shortly after the liberation. One afternoon he walked into our room, unannounced, ending his determined search for his family. He had been told that the women from Malang had been moved to Semarang and Ambarawa. We had never met him, and I liked him immediately. He seemed a nice man, and very quiet. Tall and skinny, dressed in army shorts and a white civilian shirt and native slippers, he looked to us as a visitor from another world. His reunification with his wife Dickie and his little daughter Jettie was an unforgettable scene. They held each other quietly for hours, sitting motionless on the floor.

Annie Bruinvis had a hard time with this picture of joy. She was not jealous, but wondered openly what had happened to her husband. She heard rumors that his unit had been sent to the Thailand railroad.

Dr. Berendsen then started to look over the little girls, and eventually the other children. It was apparent that seeing his daughter and the two Bruinvis children in such emaciated condition was hard on him. He encouraged all of us with his presence. To my relief, his attention turned to Anton, and he made it clear that we had to rehydrate him.

When he had been in the Dutch army during 1941, he had been in charge of the cavalry horses. He still carried long needles and tubing with him in a medical bag. With these simple tools he took aggressive steps on Anton's behalf. I was lucky, for he explained every step he took and why he did it. He asked for my help, and we boiled water, than added some salt. Needles, tubing, and bottle were boiled. He created a slow drip system, inserting the eight-inch needles subcutaneously in both of Anton's thighs. This system was extremely primitive and probably not completely sterile, but it worked. After two days of this treatment my brother woke up and started to drink, slowly at first, but his recovery accelerated as time passed. My mother's spontaneous and warm acceptance of his wife in our home in Malang after she fled from the island of Madoera was more than repaid by her husband's lifesaving care of my brother.

Dr. Berendsen then recommended coconut milk for Anton, containing certain salts necessary for the body to function normally. So we gave Anton coconut milk and followed up with *nasi tim*, a mixture of cooked rice, broth, spinach, and soybeans or carrots. Extremely nutritious, it was fed to infants in the prewar days. For all its homely appearance, it even sounded good to me. As I watched and helped Dr. Berendsen over several days, I came to understand that he had arrived just in time and had saved my brother's life.

I kept wondering about the orphans in Bangkong that no one was looking after, so I decided to walk over there to try to help them. As I was on my way that day, dressed only in shorts and without shoes, a young Indonesian woman came out of her home and asked, in Dutch, "Boy, don't you have a shirt?" I answered, "No ma'am, I don't," and I again became very aware of my ribs sticking out under my bare skin. She went into the house and got me a Dutch green army shirt and made me put it on. I was so embarrassed that at first I just stood there with a red face. Then, abruptly, I thanked her and rushed off.

In Bangkong I found chaos. The boys did only what they wanted, and the place had become dirty. It appeared that no leadership of any sort existed. Smelly garbage had accumulated at the back gate. I was shocked, but there was nothing I could do, so I decided to leave. Before I left, I heard that Dutrie van Haeften had not died, as I had thought, in camp but was transferred to the hospital in Semarang, where he did die a few weeks later.

That afternoon, on the way back to Lampersari, I noticed in the distance a roadblock manned by Pemudas, young Indonesian revolutionaries. On the roadside a simple table was visible, covered with papers and weapons.

Across the road was a barrier, made of barbed wire preventing any through traffic. I stopped to appraise the situation. The Pemudas noticed my hesitation and pointed a rifle at me, then gestured at me to join several boys who were standing there at the side of the table, captured.

I had no intention of being captured again, so I turned and ran. The Pemudas took potshots at me, but thank God, they were inexperienced with their weapons. When I heard bullets whistle I ran into a small, shallow, mostly dry canal and escaped. The floor of the canal was rough on my feet, but that did not slow me down.

When I arrived in Lampersari, covered with sweat and out of breath, I thought I should tell the women gathered there what had just happened. The women looked at me in disbelief, and then they shrugged their shoulders. They were not ready to accept this type of bad news that boys were taken prisoner and that as a result we might be restricted to our camp again. I felt exasperated and could only shake my head in discouragement. Here I had just told them what I had seen and experienced, and they acted as if I was making up a story.

I headed for my family. When she realized what I just had gone through, Mother only hugged me without a word said. Gradually the women in the camp started to realize that the circumstances had dramatically changed. It became dangerous to go outside the fences.

Although we were no longer prisoners of the Japanese, we were trapped to a great degree by the developing revolution, and most of the women and children remained where they were in the camps, only venturing out to trade for food. The absence of any kind of stable governmental authority and the constantly swirling rumors of deaths at the hands of the revolutionaries made most of us even more fearful and illustrated how helpless we were in the face of these monumental events. It appeared that, after a struggle to survive the camps, we were being confronted with a new threat to our survival.

While the former prisoners in our camps were struggling with their freedom and were trying to overcome their diseases, hunger, and orientation toward the outside world, the noise and agitation of the Merdeka movement suddenly hit our gates. There was hostility in the air, and the people selling food to the camp dwellers were driven off by the *pelopors*, the youthful arm of the revolution. Just as the women thought that they were regaining some control over their own circumstances, the doors of opportunity slammed hard in their faces.

In the meantime, unrest and violence around us on Java became a real problem. We heard about the jailing of the feared Japanese Kempeitai, the secret police, in Semarang by the Indonesian revolutionaries. Several days later, these feared Japanese were machine gunned through the bars of their cells. The revolutionaries were too afraid to line them up against the wall for execution, for the Japanese had been known to attack with their bare hands. The Kempeitai had a horrendous reputation for their aggressiveness, and too many Indonesians had suffered at their hands.

Lord Mountbatten, in command of the advancing British forces, had ordered General Terauchi, the Japanese commander of forces in Southeast Asia, not to turn over any weapons to the Indonesian revolutionaries. This order was obviously ignored; all the proof anyone needed was visible in the streets of Semarang.

Another rumor, later proven to be true, explained how the Indonesian rebels suddenly were so well armed. The Japanese troops in the islands, in defiance, had handed many of their weapons over to the Indonesians in certain areas, as in Semarang and Surabaja. It appeared that although Japan had conceded defeat in the greater war, the broken nation was still pursuing its declared goal of "Asia for the Asians." This time they were using more devious means.

It was three weeks before any British troops began to arrive. In the meantime, every Caucasian citizen in the islands was threatened, for the revolution of the Indonesians against the Dutch government exploded. Rumors ran wild, but there was a great deal of truth attached to some of them. We heard of countless Indos who became the first victims of the revolution. Many Javanese and Indos who did not want to side with the revolution were killed or imprisoned.

During those first weeks in Lampersari I heard one part of the story explaining why my Mother's health had deteriorated so severely over the last year, but Mother said not a single word to me about these events herself. I learned from other people that she and her two girlfriends, Annie and Dickie, were determined to get extra food for the three little girls. They went out at night to trade through the barbed wire, linen for food, especially eggs. My mother was usually the one who did the actual trading, but one day she developed severe diarrhea, so she asked Annie to take her place.

Everything apparently went well. However, the next day one of the Japanese officers discovered that trading had taken place, but he did not know who had done it. He threatened to punish the entire camp if the real offenders did not come forward. Mother's intention was to remain quiet, for she had no trust in the commandant, Yamamoto. Annie, however, insisted that they come forward, so as not to cause even more suffering, especially for the children, and they went to report.

Their punishment, after the routine beatings, was severe. For one week, each day at sunrise they were made to kneel in an open field, dressed only in shorts and bras. A long bamboo stick was placed in the crooks of each of the women's knees. They had to rest on their calves, with their hands tied behind their backs, while a Japanese soldier jumped on this thick bamboo. This caused excruciating pain, for by jumping on the bamboo the knee joints were stretched apart. All three women also had to endure the hot sun, without food or drink, until sunset. Other women had to carry them off, for their knees would not bear their weight. The circulation in their lower legs was restrained, further disabling them and keeping them from walking. Mother and Dickie had constant diarrhea, aggravating their dehydration.

The next morning the entire process was repeated. Dickie Berendsen, the younger woman, wore thin crepe rubber slippers on the first day. The crude rubber soles melted in the noon heat and burned into the skin of her feet. Perhaps luckily, at the time she was unable to sense that, since her lower legs had gone numb. The bottoms of her feet became scarred, impaired her walk from then on. This terrible episode never affected the close friendship between these women, but rather deepened it. There was never any question about their loyalty to one another, and they continued to try to look after each member of this unique family. Soon after this brutal treatment, my mother contracted malaria and started to suffer from vitamin deficiencies. This combination left her in a deplorable condition, and her recovery from this emaciation was painfully slow. This feeling of anger and helplessness about this torture never left me.

I saw again the two women who had shared our home in Malang, Mrs. Malu and Greta, the good-looking newlywed. Both women survived Camp Lampersari, but what a difference there was between the two. When I saw Mrs. Malu in August, she was extremely skinny and far more stooped, but mentally sharp, with bright compassionate eyes. When she spotted me, she grabbed my hands in a firm grip and said, with tears in her eyes, "I always prayed that I would see you boys again." She had remained the shy and gentle woman whom I had first met.

In contrast, Greta was hardly recognizable at first. Her hair was cut short, her face was wrinkled, and her body was skeletal. She was clothed in torn and dirty shorts and a blouse and was barefoot. It was obvious she did not care at all about her appearance or condition. I was shocked. Mother said, "It is a miracle she survived her illnesses." Mother clearly knew that Greta's spirit was broken, but she refused to criticize the poor woman.

Greta's husband showed up some weeks after our liberation. He was spotless in full white navy dress and had advanced in rank. When he found Greta, she was barely able to get up from her bed, which was a mattress spread out over her cabin trunk. He just stood there, and in his surprise said, "Greta, is that you?" He could not bring himself to touch her, when a warm embrace was what she desperately needed. Two days later he left. Greta sank into a deep depression. She told Mother that he had found himself an Australian woman and had asked for a divorce. When I heard this news I felt a cold rage come over me. He was abandoning his wife, who needed him now more than ever. In the following weeks, though, Mrs. Malu hovered over Greta, and I began to realize that Greta was in good hands and might survive after all.

Soon after my near escape from the Pemudas at the roadblock we experienced a thoroughly frightening situation. Our home in our little peninsula at one corner of the camp was located in a precarious situation. We were more exposed to a possible attack from the outside than anywhere else in camp. That night a full moon showed, and menace was in the air.

Around midnight we heard thousands of voices singing rhythmically, "*Rampas-rampas,*" plunder and kill, while the mob shook countless pieces of hollow bamboo, half-filled with water. The relentless sloshing sound carried very far, drifting down from the hills, and it was unbearably intimidating. The women in our overcrowded home could only listen to this cadence of rhythmic sounds in frightened silence. Each woman was suddenly faced with a different kind of fear than she had endured daily in the Japanese prison camp. Dickie started to pray. The three little girls huddled together, wide-awake. They were shrouded in deep silence as well. They had learned all about fear in Lampersari, and they understood.

This frenzied crowd came streaming out of the hills, thousands of them, many armed with bamboo *runchings*, sharpened bamboo spears, and machetes. Then suddenly, and dramatically, a Japanese officer with eleven soldiers appeared, apparently to defend the camp. They spread out along the inside of the barbed wires. This was a shocking surprise, and we did not understand their presence, especially as our guardians. Our world seemed suddenly turned on end, again, and we could not identify our friends or enemies, it appeared, from one day to the next.

That night, the entire camp became deadly quiet, in contrast with the distant sounds as each person listened to surges of water and pounding of footsteps steadily coming closer. Reflexively we held our breath, out of fear of being heard.

I found a machete and settled down on the steps of our porch. I was determined to fight in our defense. Suddenly a Japanese soldier appeared with an Arisaka rifle and only eleven bullets. He brought up a wicker chair, placed this in front of him on the lawn, and settled down in its shadow. This gave him a vantage point four feet above the road, and he was able to look out over the Sompok road and the school. Since it was a full moon, the light was bright and the shadows were deep. I picked up another chair and followed his example. I tucked myself into the shade of the wicker chair and tightened my grip on the machete. I felt extremely tense, but concentrated my senses on the approaching sounds. The soldier and I never exchanged a word. I was certain he knew what I was doing, but he did not blink. I could not think of a more awkward situation. It felt like eternity that the noises were thundering in our direction, and not before long we saw the danger in front of us.

Finally, then, it happened. In the moonlight this dark, heaving mass of noisy people rolled down in front of the Sompok School toward us like an unopposed flood. The barbed wire was all that was left between them and us. At that moment, to my own surprise, my fear left me. I tried to concentrate on what to do next. Out of nowhere a Japanese officer appeared, armed with only a large-caliber pistol. He stood in the middle of the road, all by himself, and faced the screaming crowd. Then he raised his left hand and aimed the pistol with his right. In Malay he ordered them to stop. One man stormed forward and was killed at point-blank range. The crowd stopped. Silence descended on the entire mob like a cloak. When the officer fired a second shot over their heads, they turned and ran. We could hear that the crowd resumed all their yelling and bamboo sloshing, but these sounds slowly faded away into the distance.

At daybreak, the real attack took place on the other side of the camp, at the main gate, after that same hostile crowd had made a semicircle around the camp. The Indonesians had brought two machine guns that chattered away at the main entrance of Lampersari. To our amazement, the few Japanese remaining attacked the mob, took the machine guns, and turned them on the attackers, routing the mob.

This experience was so bizarre that it seemed like a dream, but it really happened, and the Japanese soldiers had saved us. What a strange result after a startling night of intimidation. At daybreak I was exhausted but unable to sleep. Many of the women tried to resume their normal activities, but everyone sensed the uncertainty of what to expect next.

That morning, the Japanese army started to clean up the town. They surrounded district after district, set fire to the compounds, and shot anybody coming out. In twenty-four hours the city of Semarang was empty. Everybody living outside the camps had fled. The cruelty of battle raised its ugly head again in these mass killings, where so many innocent women and children were massacred. However, it could have been us instead, so I was thankful to be on my side of the barbed wire.

That day, billowing black and gray smoke pulled up and drifted over town like a thick blanket. I was awed by all this and wondered what had happened to our liberation.

The Japanese were the topic of conversation in every dwelling in Lampersari that next day. Soon after, Mrs. Van Der Poel shared her speculations, which turned out to be correct. She suspected that we were pawns in a blinking contest at the highest level.

In camp, a persistent rumor circulated that General Terauchi had initially given the order that all civilian and military prisoners were to be killed. Such an order would have meant the deaths of close to 450,000 people. This order was given after Japan had surrendered.

The rumor continued that, in response, General MacArthur had commanded that Japan's Emperor Hirohito was to be killed if Terauchi's order were carried out. A cousin of Hirohito, Prince Chichibu, flew in a special plane directly to Bangkok, Siam, and was able to convince General Terauchi about the seriousness of the threat to the emperor. As a result, Terauchi cancelled the planned mass executions.

Later on, I learned what seems to be the truth: that General Terauchi had moved his headquarters from Singapore to Saigon. There he sustained a stroke on April 10, 1945, two days before President Roosevelt died. Prince Kan'in Haruhito brought him the imperial edict to lay down his arms. Terauchi had already heard on the radio about the capitulation speech of Emperor Hirohito. On August 16, Terauchi held a debate with his commanders, some of whom wanted to keep on fighting.

The debate was inconclusive, and in the end Terauchi made his position clear: "I received with respect the order from Imperial General Headquarters. I want the Imperial Army to end its days with honor. The forces under my command are not my forces; they belong to His Majesty. You all received the order just as I did. I am anxious that you do your utmost to send back to Japan, with honor, the officers and men of the Japanese forces. Does anyone have objections?"

Everyone stood up when he had finished. There were no objections.

Hirohito, whose voice was never heard by the common man until he announced Japan's surrender over the radio, was considered by the Japanese to be a half-god. His death would have represented the true collapse of their civilization.

Our fear of becoming killed by the Japanese was not totally without merit. After they invaded Luzon, the Americans made every effort to liberate POWs and civilians with remarkable success. It was suspected that the Japanese would execute all of them, just as happened on the island of Palawan, where few POWs escaped.

On the island of Dutch Borneo were two hundred civilian prisoners living in Samarinda, a mining town. They were fairly decently treated at first, and the families kept together.

According to historian James MacKay, on July 30, 1945, two weeks before the official surrender, the Japanese moved their prisoners to Loa Kulu. All women were separated from their husbands and children and were slashed and bayoneted. The Japanese seized the screaming children one by one and hurled them down a mineshaft six hundred feet deep. The men were compelled to watch the execution, which must have been an indescribable mental torture. They, too, were executed, their bodies dropped into the mineshaft.

It is my suspicion that this barbaric episode was in response to the loss of Balikpapan, where oil was extracted. Balikpapan's location was north of

Samarinda. Australian troops on their way home from Europe after so many years, were diverted to land in Balikpapan with the help of the U.S. Navy. It was here that many Japanese troops surrendered, which seemed to have been a first. The Australians were from the area of Perth, in cattle country, and they resented being assigned another job.

An eyewitness from Washington State informed me that, as a sailor aboard a PT boat, he saw two Australians in a jeep driving a herd of Japanese POWs in front of their jeep. Another cowboy soldier sat on the hood of the jeep, cracking a bullwhip to urge on the stragglers.

chapter nineteen

THE BRITISH

Finally, after many weeks, the British landed in significant numbers. Immediately it became clear that they were there to protect the camps and disarm the Japanese, but they disassociated themselves completely from taking sides between the Dutch and the Indonesians in the growing revolution. The British troops were mainly Gurkhas, soldiers from Nepal, and some Sikhs, all under the leadership of British officers. Within a week all the Indonesians were back in the town of Semarang, and conditions appeared to be peaceful. We did not see any armed Indonesians or Pelopors, the young insurrectionists.

Some food and medical supplies started to trickle into the camp, delivered by the typical British lorries. These rations had arrived by ships, which were lying in the roads and were unloaded onto landing craft that delivered their cargo at the major wharf. At first the British Indian troops handled the transportation at a cumbersome pace. This improved as time went on and they got a better handle on the shipments. The provisions were welcome, for among other things they meant antimalarial medicines for Mother and Anton.

Mother started to regain her strength, but to my joy, she also regained her mental judgment, and for the first time I did not mind that she had started telling us what to do. Anton slowly started to participate in all activities, but he tired out easily.

The other ladies in our home became more interested again in cleaning and cooking. Many women throughout the camp started to pay attention to their appearance, some in anticipation of the return of their husbands. They had very few sewing facilities but managed to put garments together.

Bad tidings, such as the death of a husband, trickled into our camp and were visibly devastating. The widows became totally lost, especially those with children, and they wondered what to do next.

In the midst of all the turmoil in our camp, still people in the hospital were quietly dying. The medicines had arrived too late, and for them the war and their suffering had finally ended.

Javanese women showed up at the Lampersari road to sell their products. They were still not allowed to enter Camp Lampersari, but with their baskets they lined the street leading to the main gate. We were able to barter for food. After my brother recovered enough strength to move about he became a real expert in barter. The two of us would dig through Mother's steel trunk and find items to trade away, usually linen, which was in great demand outside the camp. Ordinarily we walked through the main gate to enter the extension of the road that cut Camp Lampersari in two. Javanese women lined it on both sides. Many squatted, but others had a wooden stool, very much like a small box, to sit on behind their merchandise in the shade of large trees. The items we looked for were foods such as tomatoes, bananas, coconuts, or *pateh* beans; a single bean's aroma would penetrate and dominate any kitchen, especially when stir-fried. Chicken or duck eggs were a good source of protein that we needed so badly. Bean sprouts were good too, if we were able to get them, or in different forms such as *katjang idjoe*, the unsprouted form, *or tahoe*, bean curds.

My brother was so slick in trading. He would squat down opposite the women and start a brief conversation, making so many jokes that the women would roar with laughter. The result was that their prices dropped substantially. After watching him in action a time or two, I encouraged him to do all the trading. After we had concluded our purchases we would treat ourselves to *sate babi*, pieces of pork stuck on a fine stick of bamboo and roasted over a coal fire. Those morsels were absolutely delicious. Other available meats were chicken or goat. Upon our return to Mother's room, we did our own cooking on a coal fire that someone had to fan constantly, in order to keep the heat under the pan. We were very willing to perform all these tasks, for we ended up filling our stomachs.

A small Dutch cruiser, the *Tromp*, came into the harbor one day. This was a lucky ship, for it had survived the European theater of war and the Battle of the Java Sea and was used for the rest of the war escorting troop transports around the New Guinea and Papua coastlines. The crew baked bread for the women and children in the camps. It was so well received that they ran out of flour in no time. Imagine, we had not seen white bread for more than three years. Mother reminded me that we had seen this light cruiser in Lisbon with its bow bashed in on our return trip from Holland in 1938, and I began to understand how much history I had been witnessing even at my age.

The only surgeon aboard ship tried to help us, but after he came ashore he found himself completely unprepared for the level of medical care needed. The demand for his services was overwhelming, and in no time he became overworked and grumpy. The doctor was a tall man, with long arms. His face and blue eyes looked tired, and stubble showed on his chin.

I had an abscess in each armpit as a result of a bad case of scabies, for I was constantly scratching myself, so I ended up standing in line for help. Actually, the contagious skin problem of scabies had occurred after we were liberated, when no one had the motivation or energy to keep the camp clean anymore. There was no more discipline, and a chaotic mess developed, turning Camp Lampersari into a dirty disaster. For a time, while the revolution exploded, garbage had no way of getting to the outside, no pickups at all were made. This contributed to the hygiene-related health problems.

As I waited in the lineup for medical help, in front of me stood a fourteen-year-old who had a huge bulge in his left flank, a perirenal abscess. A pillow was thrown on the tile floor, and the doctor ordered the boy to lie prone on it. The surgeon, out of anesthetic, had a knife and tubing in his hand. He said to his patient, "Here, bite on this piece of rubber." The doctor then kneeled so he could stab the boy's left flank. The kid screamed and passed out. The pus from the abscess spouted out several feet high. The surgeon jammed tubing into the hole for proper drainage. When he got up, his white shirt was soaked from perspiration. It appeared that he was not accustomed to the afternoon heat of the tropics. Several days of overwhelming work under very primitive circumstances had started to take their toll. Abruptly he turned to me and asked, "What is your problem?" By that time I was not so sure that I needed help. I stood there in my shorts and pointed to my abscesses. He ordered, "Place your hands on top of your head." He looked disapprovingly at my frame and said, "Kid, if I hold a burning candle behind your back, I can see the light." Then, without further discussion, he made quick cross incisions in both my armpits, and I felt immediate relief of the pressure but, to my surprise, very little pain. He wiped my armpits and seemed satisfied. Then he said, "No work and no sweating." It was 104 degrees, and I belonged to a small group of kids that was able to work. We had to do the work in this camp, for there was no one else. Thus his order struck me so funny that I started to laugh. That made him mad. He said, "Stand at attention and obey!" I shrugged my shoulders, thanked him, and walked off. I kept my upper arms away from my torso, walking like a gorilla, for bloody drainage seeped over my skin.

I realized as I walked back to the Sompok house that the doctor would never understand the circumstances of our lives in our camp. Over the next several months I learned that lesson again countless times. No one who had not been in a Japanese prison camp could understand.

Our small group of boys was needed to unload the landing craft that had arrived in the harbor. This was the first time I saw an LCT, as these little vehicles were called, and I was fascinated by the simple practical construction. An LCT was powered by two diesel engines whose propellers turned opposite each other for better steering control. The bow was nothing more than a large flap that was lowered upon arrival at the quay, for easier unloading. Trucks were thus able to drive off the ship.

Our job was to load supplies from the LCTs onto the lorries so that food could reach the two women's camps. One item supplied in abundance turned out to be corned beef from Argentina. It came in large tin containers. In some camps it became the daily food. A British lieutenant was in charge, and Sikh troops were also doing the same work.

We considered our assignment a form of competition, for we disliked the tall, slick Sikh troops, who were from northwest India. On the other hand, we admired the Gurkhas, a totally different people, short, easygoing, and stoic. A Gurkha man shaved his entire skull except for a small hair lock over the back of his head. The Gurkhas believed that when they died God would pull them up by this strand of hair. The Gurkhas were a proud, fierce tribe, out of Nepal in the Himalayas, and they were respected as excellent soldiers. Each was armed with a razor-sharp knife, called a *kukri*, whose blade, curved slightly, was over a foot long. These were lethal, and a Gurkha could easily split a hair with this weapon.

In the mountains of central Java were several camps, among them Ambarawa and Banju-Biru (Blue Water). Soon after their arrival, a troop of Gurkhas was assigned to go over the passes in trucks, returning with more than two thousand women and children. On the way back, the road through Ungaran, where we used to live, was blocked owing to the surging and shifting actions of the revolutionaries. Heavy fighting took place, and the Gurkhas launched an aggressive attack after one of them was wounded. A British cruiser off the coast was given the location and shelled the roadblock to pieces. This enabled the column of refugees in their trucks to descend to Semarang, over a stretch of road less than fifteen miles long.

Semarang had by now many thousands of former prisoners from numerous camps, and each new group of women and children had to be housed in the camps in town where they were closer to the British supply lines. Lampersari was the most crowded, with close to ten thousand civilians. Halmaheira had more than five thousand, and it took in the two thousand evacuated women and children from Ambarawa. Bangkong still housed about nine hundred, mostly boys, many of them orphaned by the war and the camps or separated from their families.

The British in India set up a unit called RAPWI, Recovery of Allied Prisoners of War and Internees. Representatives of RAPWI arrived in Semarang and started to arrange for a train transport to Surabaja for families that had been reunited. So many were just happy to get out of Semarang, which held only miserable memories. An entire trainload of these families departed, the only one to make it safely to Surabaja.

The Red Cross was attached to RAPWI and handled information and letters from prisoners. There were many young nurses with that organization from the Netherlands. The southern part of Holland had been free since September 1944, and many young people volunteered for the Red Cross and the Dutch marines. These nurses were especially resented, for they acted in many cases as if they had all the answers. They were stylishly dressed, their caps coquettishly perched on their hair, and they had makeup and nail polish. They provided a stark contrast to the women prison survivors, and further had little understanding of what those women had endured.

These girls were totally ignorant about the tropics. This became apparent when they moved through camp and had to deal with sick kids and women in the various homes. But most of all, they were appalled by the sight and stench of the ill in the hospital. Some were hesitant to roll up their sleeves and help with the problems. The women in camp still did the real dirty work. In the evenings we spotted these girls flirting and drinking with the officers, creating further hostility among the survivors, who considered them useless. When these nurses tried to encourage stories from the women in camp, of course they failed. Some women started to open up, but as soon as they told part of their experiences, these nurses would interrupt and stated how rough it had been under the Germans. Such responses made the women in camp feel even more isolated.

chapter twenty

ESCAPE FROM HELL

What was once a very peaceful country had erupted into a lawless land. The revolution made even routine activities dangerous for anybody suspected of not supporting the uprising. Many Indos, or Eurasians, were arrested and jailed or, worse, killed. This happened over the entire island of Java.

As always, rumors about atrocities committed by the revolutionaries descended upon us, and if only half of them were true, they made me realize how lucky we had been not to have left, for at least we had a measure of protection in the camp. In any case, even in September Anton and Mother were really not capable of the physical demands of traveling. We continued to wait for news about Dad. It seemed better to stay in one location, so we hadn't left right away for Surabaja; besides, that might have been in the wrong direction. For some reason, I felt even then that Dad was alive, somewhere.

As we entered the month of October, still with no idea where Dad was or if he was alive, the situation became a real worry for Mother. Our three families discussed at length what the options were, but making plans seemed hopeless. We dropped the subject, for it was no use to keep on guessing.

Under the British forces, we boys, as volunteers, performed our daily duties, hauling goods and unloading trucks and working at the harbor under the protection of the soldiers. When we were not at the harbor, my brother and I spent our time trying to barter for food for the eight of us. We became even more closely connected with each woman and child in our small home.

So many women did not know what was going to happen next, like Annie Bruinvis, who had not heard from her husband either. Just before Java surrendered, her husband told her to stay put until he could return. At first, since communications were extremely poor, she learned that her husband's unit had been sent to Siam, to work on the Burma Death Railroad. What a discouraging information that was.

Our resources for barter almost ran out. By this time, several weeks after the departure of the Japanese forces, Indonesian and Chinese traders were free to walk through our camp, for the British had become much more lenient, and only at night was the gate closed.

One morning a lady in her late fifties appeared with a bar of gold nearly four inches long and one inch wide. Living in Mother's home, this woman, who even now was still stocky, had clearly been heavy in her prewar days. At one time she had been very wealthy. She was still domineering, in a friendly sort of way, and as far as I knew, she was without family in Lampersari. Without any explanation she displayed this gold bar. Everybody gasped and wanted to hold it in their hands. When this forceful woman realized that some mothers of the smallest and sickest kids had no more supplies to barter for food, she pushed herself forward and cheerfully announced, "This is the time we were waiting for. We have a need for it now." I stood gaping as she held court on the front steps, displaying this small bar to the Chinese salesmen. The Chinese merchants literally pushed each other aside, bid against each other, and lowered their prices to obtain gold. The lady stood there and asked the mothers what they needed for their youngsters, and then she paid by slicing off thin slivers of the bar. She really helped everybody, especially the little kids, making possible the purchase of nutritious foods such as fruit, milk, carrots, and soybeans. All the mothers knew that soybeans were high in protein, which was particularly necessary to rebuild their babies' sickly, starved bodies. The mothers had other fears for their children as well, about invisible damage.

Through conversations I heard among our friends and neighbors, I began to understand the worries many of the mothers had been harboring for years now, about the long-term development of their small children. Several of these emaciated little kids had some developmental problems. Their motor response to eye contact was tardy and clumsy, while others had trouble walking or just trying to get up. We had gotten so used to these problems that at that time very little special attention was given. Nevertheless, several mothers constantly worried about these symptoms, asking themselves, "Is this going to be permanent?" For example, some toddlers who were over two years old were so behind in growth that they appeared barely the age of a year. Their cry was nothing more than a whimper as their frail mothers tried to comfort them.

I was as impressed as everyone else with the generosity of the woman who was paying for vegetables with gold, but as a teenager I had another burning question. I could not figure out where this woman had hidden that bar of gold during all the searches the Japanese had made. I was about to ask her directly, but my mother stopped me. "Do not embarrass her," she said. With difficulty, Mother told me that the woman had held the gold in her vagina during the searches.

The British were deliberately nonpartisan during this time, called the Bersiap, the Indonesian term for their drive toward independence. They allowed the young rebels, the Pemudas, to come back into town. British troops patrolled only our camps, the harbor, and the road connecting these parts of town. Apparently their policy was to remain neutral in the face of the revolution against the Dutch colonial leaders. The result was that we were again surrounded by unrest, just as we had been before the Japanese troops cleaned out the town. There were many fights and killings when the revolutionaries went on rampages, trying to force people to join the uprising at the threat of death. Many Indos and certain groups of Indonesians sided with the Dutch, especially Menadonese and Ambonese natives, who were predominantly Christian and from the Eastern Spice Islands. Throughout the previous two centuries they had served in the Dutch East Indian army.

There were about 125,000 Indos living in the islands. In general these citizens were hardworking, well-educated, and peaceful people who themselves had suffered a great deal under the Japanese. They spoke Dutch and Malay, and often were able to speak additional languages such as English, German, and sometimes French. They had lost homes, jobs, businesses, and other property under the Japanese occupation, and like us they were bewildered by the swift changes of power. Not many chose the Indonesian identity, even when threatened by the Pemudas.

With the violence in town and on neighboring islands for a backdrop, we attempted to reestablish some dignity to our lives in the camps. Slowly news about relatives dribbled in. Death announcements were heartbreaking. News that husbands or sons were alive left women shaking with relief, but to their surprise many of their husbands were far away, in Burma, Formosa, or even Japan, and no one knew how long it might be before their families might be reunited. Other women tried to console those who had received bad tidings, but they could in reality do very little. A widowed mother's despair was complete, especially if she were alone with sick little ones and had no idea what to do or expect from the future.

Two months had passed since our liberation before we learned that our own father was still alive. Finally, in late October, we received a postcard from Dad, forwarded through the RAPWI offices, saying that he was all right. He was working at the airport at Andir, just outside Bandung, a town located in the mountains of west Java. He said nothing about where he had been or what his physical condition was. Mother just sat there on her trunk and held the postcard in her hands while tears trickled slowly down her cheeks as she read to us the content of the postcard. Her hands shook when she looked up and said, " He is alive." We were so excited and suddenly restless when we learned that Dad was alive and well enough to work.

Mother wanted to go to Bandung immediately, for she understood that Dad had a job that he did not want to give up. The dilemma was how to get there. I had no idea, but I knew we did not dare travel overland. We had heard about what happened to many of the people who had left for Surabaja immediately after liberation: the Pemudas had captured them. They wanted *merdeka*, freedom, for Indonesia. The word *Merdeka* was painted on walls, trucks, cars, railway coaches, and buildings. The red and white flag of Indonesia became visible all around us.

We were not able to telephone Dad, and thus we assumed that he did not know of our survival or situation. No immediate solution was at hand. Then, as had so often happened during other trials, when our desperation reached its peak, a solution presented itself.

Near the end of October a British lieutenant approached our group of teenage workers and said, "We need your help. A small Dutch troop transport is riding at anchor at entrance to the harbor. This ship arrived yesterday, and this morning its native crew abandoned ship." As soon as they sighted Semarang the crewmen decided to go home, for they had been at sea for at least four years. The Dutch officers could not move the ship by themselves.

This old coaster, built in 1926 with a shallow draft to travel near the coast and up some of the rivers, had been refitted as a troop transport. It was the 4,000-ton *Generaal van Heutz,* and it became my symbol of freedom. Here was the *Van Heutz* in Semarang to rescue us and to show us again what civilized life was all about. When her presence was announced, we felt anxiety and fear, as well as the wonderful anticipation of boarding her and leaving Semarang.

The British lieutenant asked for volunteers to work as a crew aboard the *Van Heutz*. This ship was to carry two thousand women and children to Batavia. The group of women and children selected to go first were the weakest and sickest ones, but they had to be at least ambulatory. Fourteen of us boys and several Indo boys jumped at the opportunity. However, I was determined to bargain with this officer. I told him, "I will go only if my mother and brother can join us." He had no problem with that. "Be ready tomorrow morning." I was lucky that I had dared to ask, and I was extremely grateful.

The next morning British lorries were waiting for us. We faced an extremely emotional moment, saying farewell to Mother's two girlfriends. They had spent over three years living so closely together that Mother had a hard time dealing with the reality that we actually were separating. Kneeling down, I received warm hugs from the three little girls and fought off tears. One last time Mother thanked Dr. Berendsen, the veterinarian, for his lifesaving treatment of Anton. Again I admitted to myself how skinny and frail-looking my mother was, but I also saw in her a determination to succeed in this latest step. We headed for the trucks and Anton and I loaded our trunk. Every woman had to be helped to climb aboard, for they uniformly lacked physical strength. Two boys stood at the tailgate, pulling them aboard by grabbing their outstretched hands. After boarding the lorries we drove under guard to the harbor to board an LCT, a landing craft tanker. An LCT is flat-bottomed and rides only two feet deep; it is driven by two propellers, which turn toward each other, making steering possible by speeding one up.

Two thousand women and children arrived at the quay that morning. Under the hot sun these people were slowly divided into groups in order to be loaded into the LCTs, and every step contributed to an extremely slow process. The parade included so many sickly perspiring women, with little kids clinging to them as they tried to handle their meager belongings at the same time. Fortunately, there was help from the soldiers. We volunteer crew members went in the first LCT. I spotted Mother and Anton farther down the line. Anton gestured that they were going to be okay. Mother sat down on a suitcase. After we got under way, I looked back to see the long line of small ships heading for the *Van Heutz* lying in the roads, then I turned toward the transport ship, its silhouette clear in the distance. The sea was quiet and brownish colored from recent heavy rain runoffs, and each boat created a small white bow wave. We passed a great quantity of floating debris, coconut husks, bamboo, and even whole banana trees. A *blekok* sitting on a partially submerged and rotting coconut tree watched us as his perch bobbed over our bow wave. I listened to the humming sounds of all those engines, and we boys felt pleased and excited that we were finally leaving Semarang, a place of such suffering. I watched as the harbor became steadily smaller, finally appearing as only a dark scab in the distance. Dark monsoon clouds began to stack up over the coastline and against Mount Ungaran. I felt a cool breeze in my face, and I wondered what kind of trip we were in for.

Our LCT came alongside the *Van Heutz*. As always, these Dutch ships were taken care of, and no rust showed through the camouflage colors. Even though the sea was calm there was a continuous bobbing of our smaller craft. Full of emotion and expectation, I looked up and saw the steep gangplank secured to the hull. In order to stabilize it, two sailors from the LCT grabbed the bottom platform railing of this movable bridge. Other sailors helped the women and children make the awkward first step onto the vestibule.

We boys went up the gangplank first and asked permission to come aboard. The boatswain, rather stocky and thoroughly intimidating, stood at the railing. With his hands planted on his hips, he demanded of our group, "Who are you?" Our proud answer: "We are the crew!" We were full of expectations. For his part, however, what he saw were scrawny boys, very poorly dressed, most barefoot. My sore armpits did not allow me to put my shirt on; the cotton rubbed too much, even though it had been several days since the abscesses had been lanced. My shirt hung loosely over my shoulders. We must have looked like mismatched scarecrows.

The boatswain's face showed his bewilderment. Then he looked skyward and said, "God help us!" We took that as an okay and proceeded aboard. This deck smelled like hot tar, which had been applied between the wooden deck planks earlier.

We asked for our assignments. He systematically divided us into work details. Most of the Indo boys, who were in better physical condition, were assigned to work in the engine room. I was not assigned there, since I was still bothered by the armpit sores, and the heat would have only aggravated them. As tough he seemed, the officer mellowed at the sight of all those sickly women and children. They came in an endless stream, stumbling up the narrow gangplank, helping each other, some falling to their knees even as they were carrying a toddler. Each woman who stumbled was only holding up the advance of human misery. Slowly all these people were quartered in the various holds, where going below decks created further difficulties. This ship was a troop transport, so steel bunk beds had been built, stacked three high, in the holds. The sickest people were given the bottom bunks.

I worked in the aft hold, helping the mothers and kids find bunk beds. So many women were still in deplorable condition, so weak and easily distressed that they vomited often and without warning. But nobody gave up, for they realized they had to make it. Some were hardly able to care for their little kids. After the long journey from the camps, many toddlers fell asleep right away. It soon became surprisingly quiet, considering so many people in a rather small area.

I helped carry many children as their mothers struggled over the deck and into the holds, but one child I knew I could never forget. She was a little girl of five years old, a victim of polio, unable to walk. I had noticed that her mother was exhausted after trying to carry her up the gangplank,

Halfway up she fell on her knees, holding up the flow of people. I went down, grabbed the youngster, and pulled the mother upward. This little one hardly weighed anything. I carried her over the deck and down into the hold. I did not know her name, and I never saw her again after that day. We had learned that polio had been rampant in the camps, especially in Camp Karangpanas.

Our youthful crew did all kinds of odd jobs on this ship, doling out food, helping people with diarrhea to the bathroom, cleaning up dirty messes, talking to toddlers and drying their tears. The time raced on. Late that afternoon the *Van Heutz* blew her horn three times as a sign of departure and then raised her anchor. She slowly came into motion, then turned and headed west. There was no time to watch the coast pass by. After a meal of white bread, which was to my taste exquisite, most of the kids and mothers fell asleep and a peaceful deep quiet set in. The lights in the aft hold went dim, and I decided to go topside. It was approaching evening by now, and there were twinkling lights along the coast as we moved west. I experienced a fascinating beautiful tropical evening in which the moon reflected itself on the surface of the Java Sea emphasizing the foam of the crest of the bow wave. The unforgettable surrealistic moonlight had its silvery grip on the sharply outlined coast. The night was cool, and a soft breeze calmed my strong and churning emotions.

Thank God, it had finally happened. We had left Semarang.

While leaning over the railing, I suddenly sensed another person standing next to me. The boatswain stood quietly, and when he noticed that I was aware of his presence, he asked if I was all right and not too tired. He mentioned that he was so pleased with our help, for our presence enabled his ship to get under way. Later on he admitted that he had first thought we would break easily, the way we looked. I smiled and informed him that we had faced tougher assignments under more dreadful circumstances. He asked many intelligent questions about our time under the Japanese; some I was unable to answer. I asked him about the *Van Heutz*. He pointed out that the *Van Heutz* was small by contrast with the 6,000-ton Liberty ships that he assured me I would see in Batavia. In disbelief I heard him tell how the United States shipyards had built some 2,700 such vessels, under the motto, "A ship a day." The boatswain turned out not to be so tough, and he was eager to tell what happened aboard the *Van Heutz* during the war. He filled his pipe with tobacco and quietly lit the meerschaum, deep in thought. Slowly and haltingly at first, he started to recall that part of its history. What a thrill, to hear her exploits. I was all ears and listened closely.

The *Van Heutz* belonged to the KPM steamship company and was named after a general of the Dutch East Indies Army, who subdued Atjeh at the northern tip of Sumatra in a thirty-year guerrilla war from 1873 through 1903. The Dutch were forced into this action by the British, who were annoyed by the piracy of the Atjeh people in the Strait of Malacca.

After the *Van Heutz* fled the Dutch East Indies like so many other freighters at the arrival of the Japanese, they spent the war sailing between Australia and eastern New Guinea. Those KPM merchantmen brought American and Australian troops around the eastern tip of New Guinea into the Coral Sea, using Port Moresby as a base. These ships were small and built for the tropics so they could enter the shallow waters of Papua, Milne Bay, Oro Bay, and Goodenough Island. The mighty 80,000-ton *Queen Elizabeth* transferred three thousand American troops to three smaller Dutch ships, the *Cremer*, the *Maetsuyker*, and the *Van Heutz*. Their destination was Eastern Papua.

The boatswain took a deep breath and continued his story. He said that more KPM ships were to follow under British command, following orders from Commander Branson in Milne Bay. His voice trailed off, clouded by his memories of all those ships and men. He turned to me and said, "So many ships were lost." The *Heemskerk* sank in Milne Bay, the *Bantam* in Oro Bay, and the *Jacob* was abandoned at sea. The *Outhoorn* and the *Balik-papan* were severely damaged, trying to supply American troops. The Japanese bombers continually caused heavy damage to those ships, for they were accustomed to the dangerous waters and were repeatedly sent out, often without protection.

He said, his voice markedly affected by the recall of events, "I lost many good friends on those and other ships that were attacked and sunk."

Here my raconteur took a deep draw on his pipe and continued his description of the *Van Heutz*. In 1943 the ship cashed in on a bomb from a Japanese plane, taking a direct hit in the forward hold, which also destroyed the bridge. The narrator continued his story, "Our crippled vessel limped into Milne Bay. Our captain, who had survived the bombing of the bridge, calmly and cheerfully invited Commander Branson of the Royal Navy for lunch."

The boatswain, with emotion thickening his voice, quoted Branson's words in a speech at that lunch. "I cannot find the words to praise these captains. They did not worry, they did not ask questions. They accepted their instructions and left to carry them out."

I could hear the pride in my storyteller's words. Here again he paused, and raised his head in reflection. "You know," he said, "we were ordered to proceed to Australia on our own, without escort. Our ship was repaired, and now we are here."

We stood there in silence, slightly illuminated by the light of a bulkhead, otherwise shrouded by the dark tropical night. He turned to me with sadness in his face and said, "I never expected to see what I witnessed this afternoon." After some time, when the boatswain's pipe had burned out, he wished me good night and left. It was difficult for me to do the same. While leaning on the railing, I was trying to digest all those stories. At the same time I was enjoying the night air, and was mesmerized by the view and sound of the repetitive action of the bow wave rolling over while forming fluorescent foam, slowly stretching itself for hundreds of yards off the side of the ship, to disappear in the night. When looking back to observe this fascinating fluorescent effect, I noticed the whirling action of the water behind the stern, leaving a long trail of white foam behind us. This peaceful observance gave me a sensation to place trust in the future and hope that the worst part of the camps and the revolution was left behind in Semarang.

I had no idea what was going to happen the next day, but I was willing to accept just about anything. By midnight I was so exhausted that I fell asleep sprawled on deck, to be awakened by the morning sunshine. It had taken overnight to reach the harbor of Batavia, Tandjung Priok.

That remarkable view of the harbor was what I woke up to. Before me was a clear picture of the devastation that had taken place there. Slowly steaming into the harbor, we passed a partially sunken rusty hull, some of the decks visible above water. Cranes were wrecked, and warehouses were bombed out. When we were finally alongside the quay the ship's engines came to rest. I hung over the railing, watching the activities. My eyes started to drift farther down the quay and it was then that I spotted a passenger train resting on its tracks alongside the warehouse. A conductor sat on the steps of the platform, smoking a cigarette. The engine driver walked alongside the impressive wheels of the steam engine, oiling vital parts. What a difference the activities in the port area here were, when compared with those in Semarang. Here many Dutch were in charge. We spotted British and Dutch naval ships and uniforms. Apparently there were no revolutionaries in this harbor, so we were coming into a comparatively safer environment.

The women started to crowd the decks. Kids were running in various directions. Nobody knew what to expect.

The moment the gangplank was down, curiosity drove me toward the waiting train. I approached some people standing next to the steam engine and asked them, "Why is this train here?" To my surprise they said, "We are waiting for the people to go to Bandung." I felt as if I had been struck by lightning. This was it! This was our chance to reach Dad! Then I realized that I did not know where my mother and brother were berthed aboard the ship. I had taken my work so seriously that I had not even seen in which hold they had been quartered. I felt quite guilty about that. I decided that I had fulfilled my obligations and considered myself relieved of duty.

I rushed back to the ship but had a hard time finding Mother and Anton among all those people milling around. Finally I spotted Mother down on the lower deck. When I told her that a train to Bandung was loading she was so happy that tears showed in her eyes. Defying her own frailty, she

190 : *Escape from Hell*

stubbornly straightened her shoulders and took charge again. She told me to get our belongings together so we could disembark this ship. Anton was caught up in the excitement and helped carry our belongings down the gangplank.

The three of us, after slowly maneuvering our way across the quay, boarded the long train, pulled by an immense steam engine. The passenger cars were the old type, open, but did have compartments and the traditional platform on either end. This time the windows were not covered. We boarded as free people, and we had decent seats. Surely Mother and Anton were comparing this trip with our transport from Malang to Semarang in 1943, just as I was. A detachment of British Punjabi soldiers from western India arrived, armed with Lee-Enfield rifles. They divided themselves among the railroad cars, one soldier per balcony.

The train was soon full, mostly with women and children, and departed around noon. We heard the steam whistle as the cars slowly came into motion. Our train rattled over switches and started to pass the outskirts of town. Many times we heard her whistle at rail crossings and could see that she was picking up speed as we passed between *kampongs*, clickety-clacking over the tracks. A steady stream of air cooled us, for the humidity and heat was substantial. Soon the train was in the country, and we snaked along past numerous rice paddies. Mother and Anton settled down comfortably.

The journey was uneventful until we started to approach the mountains.

As always, I preferred to sit outside. On the porch of the following passenger car was a soldier who had just dozed off. I was watching him as he stirred, and all of a sudden his rifle fell overboard. The soldier on my platform got up with a start. He yelled out in his native tongue. The awakening army man was so startled when he realized what had happened that he jumped inside the carriage and pulled the emergency cord. The train came to a screeching halt. The British lieutenant in charge strode down the tracks to see what was going on. When he learned what had happened he became furious. He went back to the engine and ordered the engineer to back up the train slowly to look for the soldier's weapon. They found it back a few miles beside the tracks. The terrible part of this tense delay was that we were sitting right in the middle of enemy revolutionary territory. We had no appreciation for this kind of military discipline, and we wondered, as we crept backward, how vulnerable we were. However, in the army, a soldier is inseparable from his rifle.

This was the first and the last train to come into Bandung for some time. At first we did not realize how lucky we were to get through. After that day Bandung was encircled and isolated by revolutionary forces, and it sustained many nighttime attacks by the Indonesian revolutionaries.

To our profound surprise, Dad welcomed us. He had come down to the station to see if he would recognize anyone aboard the train. There had been no way that we could send a message to tell him that we were coming.

Dad appeared to be in good spirits, but he was skinny-looking in his shorts, and his legs revealed many healed ulcers. He helped Mother, who was weak and very tired, but she was overcome with joy. They held each other what seemed to be a long time without saying much. It had been over three years since they had seen each other. Then he turned to Anton and me and gave us each a tight hug, but still did not say anything. His feelings must have stuck the words in his throat.

Our family was reunited at last. We had no idea what to expect of the future, but at the moment that didn't matter.

We walked to an office at the camp, called Tjihapit, to secure family quarters. It took some doing at the administrative office to obtain housing and mattresses. No beds were available, so we slept on the floor again. It took further days to organize some kitchen utensils and necessary house-hold goods. After all those years of primitive living we were grateful for any item we could get—even a *sapoe* so we could sweep the floor. More importantly, Dad was able to have us assigned to a small bamboo home for our family alone. It consisted of three rooms and a bathroom, all roofed over by clay tiles. The floors were concrete. The house was located very close to the border of the protected camp, which itself was surrounded by barbed wire. This time the aim was to keep the revolutionaries out. The British were in charge of the camp. Just like us, they were completely cut off from the rest of the world, here in the mountains of Java.

chapter twenty-one

A FAMILY AGAIN

During the war the Europeans in Bandung had been imprisoned in Camp Tjihapit, located on the outskirts of the city. After their liberation the Europeans, for their protection, remained restricted to that camp, which was still encircled by barbed wire. The railroad tracks going through this town determined the division between Dutch- and Indonesian-controlled terrain.

As in Semarang, the British arrived many weeks after Japan's surrender and took over the protection of the camp and the airport at Andir, some distance away from the camp itself. Tjimahi, close on the west side of Bandung, had been a garrison town before the war. The Japanese had imprisoned a large contingent of former KNIL troops, including Dutch and Ambonese, in the old army barracks of Tjimahi. They came over to join the European community in Tjihapit, but the British refused their request for arms to defend themselves against the young revolutionaries, the Pelopors.

For political reasons the British restricted their defense of this district of Bandung to the bare minimum. For instance, when the *pemudas*, the guerrillas, would fire at us, the British kept their distance.

In the evenings, the pemudas often shelled our camp with mortars, which were quite intimidating. The noise of the explosions was sudden and startling. Most of the time the incoming projectiles hit either the barbed wire or the homes close to the border, and as a result fires repeatedly broke out, and some dwellings burned to the ground. When things got desperate enough, the British responded with a counterattack, but many Dutch felt that the British response was halfhearted and ineffective. There was a great deal of grumbling about the British position, and our leaders protested, but to no avail.

Fortunately the house Dad had found for us was some distance away from the worst shelling and fires. We even had running water, a distinct improvement over conditions in Lampersari and Bangkong. Water flowed into the *mandibak*, which was a concrete container, usually one cubic yard in capacity. If we wanted to take a bath, as we did twice a day, we had to dip a *gajong* and pour the water over our heads. At first there was no soap available, but this lack was remedied as time went on. We were chronically short of many items that we had considered essential a few years earlier. Mother lacked even the most basic kitchen utensils, and of course there were no curtains, pillows, or even a tub to handle the wash. We ate out of army-issue aluminum containers.

Although Dad was the same in some ways, his manner had changed over these harsh years. Anton and I had trouble understanding that at first. He dressed more simply, in shorts, and had become skinny and mellow, not the stern individual he had been before the war. These days he would listen to our concerns and help us plan in a constructive way. Before the war he would have told us, "Do it this way or else." In total he had endured more than three years of imprisonment, and apparently ulcers and malaria had plagued him during that time. He was so happy to have his family back together, that nothing else seemed to matter to him anymore. He became very protective of Mother and frequently asked us to help her.

One afternoon, Anton and I suddenly stopped what we were doing, startled because Dad was singing while taking a bath. Mother raised her head, smiled, and whispered, "Listen to that." So often before the war Dad would do exactly that, but it seemed that he had lost the spirit for singing.

Dad never wanted to discuss what had happened to him. All we knew was that after being confined in Kesilir at the easternmost point of Java, he was moved to Ambarawa in the mountains of central Java, most likely in late 1943. I tried to find out how long they stayed there and to get some idea of what had happened. All he would say was that they were moved to Bandung in 1944. When we boys asked Dad about his camp experiences, he would stare at us, then shake his head, and tears of sadness would appear in his eyes. It was too difficult for him to discuss any of it. It became evident that he hated the Japanese, but he never said so.

Mother acted as if nothing we faced could be bad, so happy was she that we were together. Sometimes she just stood there motionless, observing her family with a faint smile. She cooked over a hot anglo in a primitive kitchen adjacent to the bathroom and tried her best to cook up tasty meals. This kitchen was nothing more than an elevated stand for the anglo and a concrete sink under a water tap, next to a board to handle food. Traditionally one wall of this cook room was absent in order to vent smoke and hot air. We boys had to haul charcoal from the central depot, and sometimes it was difficult to get. Most of the food came out of cans, such as Argentine corned beef or military rations, since there was no market to make purchases.

As did many other women, Mother made an effort to bring the right spirit among us by serving tea during the quiet, even dull evenings. There was no radio or newspaper, although after some time Dad brought back from the airport so-called news bulletins. In those first weeks we sat on the floor eating or drinking our tea under the single bare light bulb. We had discussions about what the future would bring, for there was still a myriad of uncertainties. The most noticeable was our encirclement by revolutionary forces. For this there was no immediate answer, and Mother said, "Let us take one step at a time." Sometimes we tried to play canasta or bridge. Usually all four of us went to bed quite early, and Dad awakened Anton and me a little after five o'clock. Mother, whose strength was returning only very slowly, welcomed the afternoon siestas and tried to convince us boys to rest also. We slept on our mattresses on the floor during our entire stay in Tjihapit.

Anton really needed his siestas; his health was not at all restored, and he had markedly swollen ankles. Mother's entire shins were swollen and puffy, even this many weeks after our food supply became stable, but gradually they improved over a long period, and she never complained.

At this late stage, along with many others in Tjihapit, I started to develop swollen ankles, too. It was apparently a late occurrence of malnutrition, for in the camps I had had no swelling. There was no medical explanation, and it took Anton and me deep into 1947, almost two years, to overcome this nuisance.

Tjihapit, a huge camp, was not so bad, even in its isolation. The nights could be cool, and in the afternoons we got seasonal rains. Truck convoys moved anything and anyone between Tjihapit and Andir. There were times when food was rationed, especially if we were cut off from Andir, our only connection with the outside world. Dad commuted daily back and forth to Andir in the convoy, which was sometimes obstructed by revolutionary activity. When that happened, Dad could not come home from his accounting job there. Once no transport came through for five days in a row. As a result, Dad had to stay at Andir under the most primitive circumstances. Many in camp strongly voiced the sentiment that the British could do more than simply try to keep the road open.

Late in November 1945 the situation got worse, with night attacks galore. We boys would rest on our mattresses and listen to the noises coming to us through the darkness. In desperation the Dutch and Ambonese troops broke into the British warehouses, stocked with arms, and took the needed weapons that had earlier been denied them. The next day they counterattacked, to the surprise of the pemudas, who fled in a hurry. The British were pushed aside and showed very little inclination to interfere as the old KNIL troops worked like a steamroller through the adjacent kampongs. The result was that all the natives fled, and for several days, peace returned.

My brother, a friend, and I took advantage of that first quiet day and went through the barbed wire to enter the kampongs. We never saw any of the residents. The only thing we were met with was an eerie quiet. We looked around, expecting something startling. Even the usual roaming chickens were not there. An occasional scrawny dog was spotted but took off at our approach. Every indication suggested that people had left in a hurry; we noticed many useful items that had been discarded.

My friend led the way into the largest home, obviously a dwelling belonging to a Chinese. There were statues of Buddha and several expensive-looking traditional lacquered beauty cases. Chinese lanterns hung from the ceiling. On the wall was a classic Chinese dragon's head. On a small table to one side were dishes with smoldering incense sticks. Inside the large main room we found stacks of books rising from the packed dirt floor to the height of our belts. I started to browse through these books. They were Dutch, probably stolen, the names of the previous owners still written on the inside covers. We scanned these piles and took several atlases and a beautiful book about the construction of the dike that sealed off the Zuiderzee in the Netherlands. We had mixed feelings about taking these books. They did not belong to the Chinese family, or so we reasoned. In Camp Tjihapit very few books were available, and I was desperate to have something to read and study again. Anton and the other boy also found books to their liking.

It was so quiet, so deserted and so hot, and we could hear a slight wind rustle the bamboo walls and bamboo awnings, and watch it stirring up dust on the dirt road. A few pigeons in their cages high up on the bamboo poles started to coo, which startled us at first. We sensed danger lurking even though we could not see anything. We decided to hurry back. Instead of returning to the main gate, the three of us went through the barbed wire to cut the trip short.

Mother was not very happy with our unannounced expedition. She knew better than to punish us, though, and instead just looked at us and shook her head in disapproval. She liked the idea of the atlas to help us with studying, but under no circumstances did she allow another trip to the outside. We were surprised that Dad did not react to our foolish excursion as he would have before the war. The book about the Zuiderzee dike I read from start to finish, I was so eager to learn how it was done.

Several teachers tried to organize a high school in a large building within the barbed wire. It was tough going. Everything was in short supply: teachers, books, paper to write on, even ink.

I went into the eighth grade and had a very difficult time. I had trouble keeping my mind on school and was easily distracted. I had a constant feeling that other momentous things were about to happen. The first hour of school, held at a roundabout in front of the building, was given over to gymnastics to get us all in better physical condition. The exertion was demanding, considering the heat and my state of health, and often, as a result, I would find myself dozing off in a large classroom crowded with students. This attempt at school was a fiasco.

During the worst period of isolation and attacks we were unable to get rid of the garbage. All the debris was dumped in a park about the size of a city block, soon piling up to five feet. The stench in that heat was quite overwhelming. When the KNIL broke out, several large trucks arrived, and we schoolkids were put to work loading the garbage onto the vehicles. It took quite an effort to clear most of the park. Several of us boys hung onto the outside of the truck's sideboards as the loads were driven away from the camp. What an experience it was to get that far outside the camp, even under military escort. The debris was dumped at an old garbage belt at the edge of a hill. From that vantage point I could see for miles over the surrounding highlands. On those faraway hills I spotted armed Javanese, who stayed at rifle-fire distance.

It took an entire week to clean up this stinking mess. Every day after work Mother sent us stinkies, as she called us, straight to the bathroom. Like so many of the other teens, regardless of our attempts to stay clean, Anton and I picked up scabies during this cleanup. Again we itched terribly and scratched constantly; the armpits were the worst. Mother would not even hug us during this period of infection. Sleep was hard to come by with that relentless itch. Dad brought in sheets of thin rubber to spread over the mattresses in efforts to contain the pests. The mattresses were easily cleaned, placed in the sunshine to disinfect them, but we had to haul them in early, for the rains came daily at around four o'clock. We received sulfur ointment, which indeed helped after about a week. The treatment was quite effective, but slow. The steady joke then was that we smelled like a volcano.

Times were not easy, but we were relatively free and among family. We tried to make the best of our situation. Mother was so frighteningly frail. In a manner she was mellow, unlike her former very stern self, and to such a degree that I had a hard time getting used to the change. She was so happy to have the family together that nothing disturbed her anymore. As postwar humanitarian aid improved, she learned that she was qualified to go to Australia for recuperation. She turned that offer down, for after being separated from Dad for three and a half years, she did not want to leave him anymore. When she reached that decision she placed her arms around all of us and said, "We are going to make the best of it, together." Nobody could convince her otherwise.

December arrived. Nothing much changed. I did poorly in school. I found it difficult to concentrate, and I could not take these efforts seriously. Anton did a great deal better, but even our teachers were in not much better shape.

Christmas Eve came. Dad was at work. That late afternoon Mother decided to go to the evening church services. She put her arms around our shoulders and told us to wash up, dress, and join her. At first we were reluctant to go, but staying home was boring and we wanted to help Mother, just in case.

At the edge of the camp was an old white wooden church. Wide worn-out wooden steps led up to the entrance. The large front door arched upward underneath a droopy fascia, and a tall narrow steeple, leaning slightly, draped this structure. The saddle roof sagged in the center, showing its age. The peeling walls were in need of a paint job. The side windows were cracked and weathered. Still, small as it was, it was a church, and it was ours at Christmas Eve. Most people tried to dress up a bit that evening to go to the service. Mother put on her only dress, and we boys put on the shirts and shoes that we had all just received a few days earlier. Mother walked between us, determined to get there.

It was dark when we arrived at the church, which was already full. Droves of people stood outside, on the front steps, on the neglected front lawn, and on the sidewalk. Mother insisted that she was comfortable enough to stand there between us on the sidewalk. We listened to the preacher's voice, relayed by a speaker attached to the outside wall. This metallic call reached us through the otherwise quiet night, interrupted only by the occasional shuffle of a foot or a suppressed cough. I thought I could hear people take single deep breath.

All of a sudden all hell broke loose. We were being shelled! The target was the church, but the shells were landing away from us. The missiles exploded in the surrounding homes, both inside and outside the barbed wire, just far enough away that the exploding fragments did not hurt the crowd. These houses were built of bamboo and burst into flames. The scene before us became an inferno.

The white church was soon illuminated by the flames. Its walls and windows changed color, first white, then yellow, orange and red, reflecting the fluctuating intensity of the fire. There was quite a stir among the people around us, but nobody moved away, nobody ran. I tried to pull Mother away to a safer area, but she would not budge. The preacher prayed as though nothing had happened. We continued to stand there on the sidewalk in front of the church, listening, while the crackling fire tried to interrupt. Mother squeezed our hands, as if she were saying, perhaps to herself, "Don't be scared."

I knew then I would never forget the sight of the crowd, encircling that church in a crescent. These people, their faces lit by the fires, solemnly kept their places. The church, its steeple rising high, stood out starkly against the flaming red sky, beyond which was the intense dark of night. The shelling had been brief, and thank God it was not repeated. I was no longer frightened; a tremendous feeling of peace came over me, inspired by Mother's steadfastness.

The preacher ended the sermon with a prayer, followed by the unexpected sound of music. Oh, what beautiful music it was: Schubert's "Ave Maria." The gathering settled into an intense quiet as every soul listened to those tranquil, melodious sounds, played against the background of the crackling fire.

For most of us it was the first time in three years that we had heard quality music and had been able to attend church as a free people. We had experienced a service that excelled in its simplicity, and, perhaps for that reason, was deeply meaningful.

After the service was over we turned our backs to the hot fire and walked home slowly, as if nothing unusual had happened. Not a word was exchanged between us. I could see that Mother was struggling to suppress her emotions, and I thought it better to stay quiet.

When we arrived home, Dad had just returned from the Andir airport with big news. The British had mailed him a telegram with a request: "We need your help to set up the accounting department for the city of Surabaja. Come as soon as possible." In Dad's hands was our Christmas present. Mother sat down and at first looked at him in disbelief, then responded a moment later with a big smile on her face. "Oh, Jo, we are going back to Surabaja. What an honor! The British really seem to mean business, and they called you!" She hugged him, and for a time she didn't even look so tired.

Apparently Batavia had recommended Dad when a search was instigated. We boys did not know what to think of this whole affair. But we adjusted fast, for, as it turned out, Dad already had accepted the invitation for this position. At least it meant we were leaving the beleaguered town of Bandung.

chapter twenty-two

TIME TO FLY

After all this time in November and December without any sense of progress, suddenly the pace of our family's life picked up with Dad's call to Surabaja. We needed no time to reflect on the sudden change facing us, and as little to prepare for the journey. Dad was told that we had to be ready, with all our things, at five in the morning at the entrance of Camp Tjihapit. It would still be plenty dark, and we faced running the gauntlet between camp and the airport, as the truck drivers called the trip.

Mother was in charge of packing our meager belongings. She seemed happy and was looking forward to a better and more normal situation for the family. That goal was a strong impetus to get organized, and in any case there were few items worth taking with us. Anton and I were excited about this new adventure.

As we left early that morning, Dad, Anton, and I made certain that Mother had an easy load to carry. Full of anticipation, we walked together to the departure area, close to the main gate where the British soldiers stood guard. We did not look back.

Under the cloudy sky by the light of a slow daybreak, we could just make out the outline of approaching trucks. Each truck was equipped with mattresses that had been stood up straight, tied to the railings of the truck beds, and topped off with a canvas cover. No more than ten other people gathered around the lorries. They, too, were heading for Batavia. It was soon time to climb aboard. Mother was given a hand as she climbed the wooden steps placed behind the vehicle. We were told to sit down with our backs to the mattresses, and we packed ourselves in, shoulder to shoulder, on the truck bed. The mattresses gave us "bulletproof" protection.

Mother figured that the six-inch-thick, kapok-filled mattresses were flimsy, and she became uncomfortable and reacted nervously, for Dad hadn't told her that this was the customary transportation to the airfield. Right away, Anton started to search for bullet holes and claimed to have found several. Mother really let Dad know what she thought of his earlier silence, but his response was a nothing more than an understanding smile. After a while, he pointed out that the bedding gave fairly good protection.

It had rained in Bandung plenty the night before. Since this was the rainy season, it made sense that it must have rained at Kemajoran airfield, in Batavia, as well. Airfields in Asia, like those in Andir and Kemajoran, were nothing more than grass mats.

Throughout the entire war, both American and Japanese forces had struggled every rainy season with soggy airfields. The Allies, however, soon, improved the flight conditions dramatically for their pilots when they brought in perforated steel strips, which could be laid out like mats for takeoff and landing.

At Andir we waited until noon for a sight of the incoming planes. Their journey was to start at Kemajoran, which we were told had been delayed by the weather. The grassy fields there were as soft and soggy as a swamp, and no planes could take off until the fields dried out.

We waited in a very primitive hanger. Most of us stood, but Mother was provided with a simple seat. At about two in the afternoon, we started to prepare for boarding. In the meantime, Anton and I had been roaming around. While surveying the austere surroundings, we noticed heavily armed guards at the periphery. Sandbags protected machine gun emplacements. Jeeps with machine guns patrolled the area constantly. There was no food, but the soldiers offered water.

The first plane to land was a Mitchell bomber, a B-25. The grass in the field was two to three feet tall. As it touched down, the plane's left tire blew, the plane made a ninety-degree left turn, and the wing mowed the grass. The B-25 itself sustained no damage. Mother blanched and said, "I will not go." People around us were clearly relieved to see the plane come to a safe stop.

The second plane to arrive was a DC-3, nicknamed a Gooney Bird by the casual Americans. The British called her a Dakota. This time the plane made a safe landing, but I saw how the grass was laid low under the force of the engines. We were told, "That is your plane, destination Kemajoran." Dad grabbed Mother by the arm and said, "This plane is safe, so let's go!"

Our family approached the Dakota as it rested on its small rear wheel, the body of the plane sloping markedly down toward the tail. A steel stepladder was placed against the side door. Mother and some other women in our small crowd struggled with the climb, and finally they had to be pulled up under their arms by men standing in the wide opening of the door.

The plane had been outfitted as a paratrooper transport. Inside the cabin were rows of steel seats on either side. The center of each seat was concave. After we were seated, Anton and I turned around on our knees to watch the takeoff through the round windows. One crewmember closed the door. The two engines sputtered into action, one after the other, again flattening the tall grass. Slowly the plane turned into the wind and increased its speed for liftoff. After the plane had risen from the field, we realized that we were staying fairly low, below the cloud deck. The plane cruised between the hills, so I had a rare chance to enjoy the scenery from above. It was our first plane ride, and we boys were exhilarated. We pointed out to my parents all the roads, the rivers, rice fields, different kinds of carts, dogcarts, tjicars, and trucks. Everything looked so peaceful and normal.

Coming over the mountains, we covered the eighty-five miles in slightly less than an hour. The landing at Kemajoran was uneventful. When the door was opened, the humid and stifling air, typical for the hot climate of Batavia, offered us our first welcome.

Korean prisoners of war who had been in Japanese service unloaded the Dakota. They slid the side door open and started to throw the luggage out onto the swampy field. Their casual disrespect made me angry, and I didn't want our last few belongings to be ruined. I told them to be more careful. They pretended not to speak Malaysian. They looked past me and just shrugged their shoulders. Dad told me to simmer down. But when the workers started the same pattern again, I got behind two of them as they stood in the open door and kicked them both in the rear end. They flew out of the plane and landed with their faces in the swampy terrain. I turned to the others with a smirk on my face, and a crewmember nodded his head. The prisoners went on to unload the plane in a careful, orderly way. Dad shook his head disapprovingly, but I could see a grin on his face.

It was late in the day, and there was no further transportation to our destination, Surabaja. We were taken by car to an elongated, one-story metal building in downtown Batavia that was functioning as a motel and had been subdivided into small apartments. Our quarters were good, and the available food was good as well. Most of the occupants were military.

Batavia was miserably hot, with very high humidity. In the afternoons it rained, but even that failed to cool us. At four o'clock we took a shower, only to perspire profusely again within the hour. We boys got bored. We were able to buy a pack of cards for entertainment, but how many games could we play in a day? There was nothing to read. Our waiting time stretched out to a small week. The streets were not safe yet from the revolutionary unrest. That meant that we stayed mostly around our rooms. Occasionally Anton and I would walk down the road, but there was nothing to do or see in the near vicinity.

Anton and I met an Indo woman and her husband, a soldier in the KNIL. They lived a few doors down in the same building. They were very friendly and hospitable, and they invited our family for a real Indonesian dinner one evening. The man had been a cook in the army, and both he and his wife knew how to prepare traditional foods well. What a feast! Since the camps this was the first time that our family had eaten a special Indonesian dinner, and we enjoyed all the different dishes.

Afterward the men lit cigars that Dad had obtained, and the cook became talkative. His wife stated that he had not revealed his ordeals as much as he did that evening, discussing his imprisonment. We listened intently. He had been stationed at Ambon, the major spice island. The town by the same name had a beautiful natural harbor, which the Japanese attacked before their invasion of Java. A contingent of Australian, Dutch, and American soldiers had shouldered the defense of the island. The Americans were withdrawn at the very last moment, along with their navy support, after their commander declared Ambon indefensible. The Japanese navy soon entered the main harbor, where one of their ships was hit by artillery and sunk. This was only the beginning of a difficult struggle, and the Japanese had a hard time taking the island. After days of hard combat the Japanese did finally succeed in forcing the Allied troops to surrender. Most of the Dutch troops were kept on this island as slave laborers. The Japanese executed many Australian and some Dutch prisoners.

Our host took another puff of his cigar and told us how Japanese navy ships would stay out at sea so as not to be trapped in the harbor by Australian bombers. The POWs had to swim out to the vessels to move supplies.

There the Japanese crews dumped supplies overboard, sealed in big drums, as was done throughout the islands all the way into the Solomons. Each POW had to grab two drums and swim, pushing them, until they could land the drums on the beach. The rusty drums would cut their hands. Sharks sometimes were a problem, but the biggest problems were with the currents, which would exhaust the swimmers. Some drums drifted out to sea, and the guards would take this loss out on the prisoners.

In April 1945 a merchant vessel arrived in the harbor displaying a huge gaping hole in its side. Our host said, "Wow, were we excited to see a ship that had received such a beating." Then consternation set in, for the Japanese ordered them to pack up and board this badly neglected hulk of a ship. They were packed in like sardines. Our storyteller considered himself among the lucky ones. He grinned as he explained that his berth was close to the ragged hole. "Getting fresh air was a problem in other parts of the ship."

The edge of the rusting, twisted opening was a foot above the waterline, and the prisoners could see and hear the sea sloshing and swirling by. The occasional spray felt refreshing. This gap also allowed them to get rid of excrement, a big problem in other holds. Nobody was allowed topside.

They disembarked in Batavia, where they were still imprisoned at the time of Japan's surrender. They were probably in the process of being moved to the west in the face of the approaching Allies.

We boys enjoyed this story greatly, but Mother listened with clear sadness reflected in her face. The cook's wife leaned toward him and, placing her hand tenderly on his cheek, said, " I am so glad you made it." I could see tears in her eyes. Dad never said a word. He just listened thoughtfully and attended to his cigar. Then he got up abruptly, grabbed the man's hand, and said, " Let us look forward and work and hope for better times." With that our family said goodnight.

We waited in Batavia for a way to get to Surabaja. Every day Dad went to air transport headquarters, showing the draft telegram from Surabaja, to ask for space on the next flight, but to no avail. He became discouraged and annoyed with the fruitless daily trips.

After five days of this Mother said, "Put on your new RAPWI uniform." The uniform was similar to Marine Corps officer dress. The moment Dad entered the headquarters in that uniform, he was saluted, and transport was made available. All Mother said was, "Clothes make the man." We boys had never heard that expression before. Dad gave full credit to Mother for her astute advice. She knew very well the subtleties of influence and persuasion.

The plane for this trip was a Mitchell, a B-25 bomber. There were a total of eight passengers, my mother the only woman. The last thing we expected was to fly in a bomber with so many people crowded inside, but a ride was a ride. It took some time before our plane was cleared for takeoff. The result was stifling heat inside the plane, but once we were in the air the temperature became very pleasant.

Two of the other passengers Anton and I knew well from Bangkong. They were all too familiar to us, for they were the Dernier brothers, the Belgians who had functioned as hanchos at the patjol fields. By the look on his face, I could tell that Anton was reliving the beating he had received from the younger Dernier, who was as nervous as always. I watched the two men, remembering how these brothers, who had always been so afraid of a beating by the Japanese, had taken their fears out on us kids. I could barely speak to them for the loathing I felt.

My Dad had known the Derniers in Surabaja before the war, and they were soon talking to one another. Johan, the elder of the brothers, asked me, with transparently false solicitude, how the rupture in my groin was. Again he was clearly mistaken about the details, but was still trying to curry favor, this time with my father. As the flight continued, both men tried to act friendly, but Anton and I would have no more of their two-faced manner. We had always considered them cowards, and we could not forget Anton's beating. I barely answered when addressed, and my hostility was very plain. Dad, who was unaware of the men's roles in Bangkong, noticed our resentment and afterward asked for an explanation. It didn't take Anton long to make him understand. In response, he said, " I wish I had known that earlier."

In the meantime, my mother was having a new experience of her own. A Royal Air Force colonel invited my mother to join him in the tail gunner section. He explained that we were going to fly at only two thousand feet, and that he intended to observe various places through his binoculars. He handed her a pair of field glasses, and she lay down in the tight confinement of the gunner's station. The plane flew along the coastline and over the harbors of Cheribon and Semarang. When flying over Cheribon, which was not under British control, the colonel pointed out a ship with a foreign flag, which he said was trading in contraband. He was not sightseeing as my mother was.

Mother told us afterward that she really enjoyed the view and the ride, and I was glad to see that she had overcome her fear of flying. But when we flew over Semarang, thoughts crept in again of Bangkong and Lampersari and her friends there. Strong emotions and vivid memories of these camps nearly spoiled the trip. Speaking with the colonel in a choked voice about Lampersari, Mother had difficulty maintaining her composure. The colonel had spent the war in Australia and since had seen similar women's camps in Batavia, and he responded with compassion.

The teenager in me felt some jealousy that Mother had this marvelous view of the countryside while I could see only metal walls and the faces of the other passengers. The spare aviation fuel tank had been removed, as well as the bombs normally located below it. We fellows sat in a circle with our feet dangling in that empty round space. The bomb space valves, when closed, leave a one-inch gap between the rims, which were my view, between my shoes, all the way to earth. Java slid by like a big blur. Anton's head rested against the desk of the telegrapher, and the constant clicking of the key must have surely resounded in his skull.

Surabaja came into sight after about two hours of flying. We flew over Grissee, a coastal suburb to the west of Surabaja, then made a wide banking turn over the water to land. The moment we touched down two jeeps armed with machine guns drove into position on either side of the plane and accompanied us as we taxied over the fields and tarmac to the gate. There were snipers, we were told. What a welcome to Surabaja! Even after the engines were silenced I heard a drone in my ears, and swallowing did not help relieve this miserable sensation.

After disembarking we were escorted inside a building so empty that one could have fired a cannon inside without doing much damage. There was a large but almost bare desk off to one side. Here we were to check in and obtain further instructions. A RAPWI official tried to find a place for the four of us to be quartered. We stood until our destination was decided, for there was no seating, even for Mother.

The British were finally in almost total control of Surabaja, but they were still facing pockets of revolutionaries on the outskirts of the city. They had landed in October 1945 against stiff resistance from young Pemudas who had in their possession plenty of Japanese weapons.

In Surabaja, the British had had to fight for every street. Especially heavy fighting had taken place downtown, where the railroad crossed over the road by viaduct in front of the government building and then over a dike. Indonesians used this setting to defend the main road, and the fighting severed connections between the harbor and the heart of town. The shelling and burning of the county-city building had the immediate effect of destroying years' worth of records, including my birth certificate. The British lost two thousand men, including Brigadier General Melenby.

After a while we learned about our destination, Hotel Brantas. The hotel was on the Brantas River, close to the Gubeng railroad station, which had been so interesting to me in earlier years. We had to cross much of the town to reach the place we thought to be safe.

A small army truck drove us, a six-by-six, so named from the measurements of the truck bed, a very popular means of transportation. As we worked our way to our final destination, sights around us told many such stories of revolutionary fighting. Going through downtown, we saw where streetcars had been burned out, their electric wires hanging crisscross. The truck had to snake its way around numerous obstacles as we advanced over the major roads. Black spots on the sidewalks and the asphalt road revealed totally or partially burned bodies. The driver told us that in order to combat the stench, the bodies had been doused with gasoline and set afire. In that heat it was not a luxury but an absolute necessity. The downtown area presented a disturbing scene, but most striking, there were no people, no sounds. The city was empty. The four of us became anxiously quiet.

Hotel Brantas was located next to the second bridge spanning the river of the same name, connecting with Gubeng, the name for that district of the city across the river. At the time the bridge was blocked by sandbags and a guardhouse, for it was the outpost, the last piece of land controlled by the British. On the opposite side, including Gubeng, was no-man's-land. Thus, from our hotel room, we had a clear view of the revolutionary territory. Along one side of the hotel was an asphalt road leading toward the bridge, and the sidewalk was totally blackened where burned-out hulks of British lorries rested.

In September 1945 the RAPWI had escorted civilians from various camps back to Surabaja. From there many former employees of the plantations immediately returned to Eastern Java to begin restoring the damage done to the plantations and to try to forget the terrible concentration camps. Before some of them could depart Surabaja, they were rounded up by the Indonesian revolutionaries and imprisoned. Several were severely beaten and others killed, depending on where they were incarcerated.

The British and Indian troops were sometimes very lucky in liberating people, but a group of two hundred former prisoners faced an ironically tragic fate. After they had crossed the Brantas Bridge, their lorries were stopped next to the Hotel Brantas. When they had come to a standstill, Indonesians on the rooftops poured gasoline over the vehicles and ignited them. Those who leaped from the trucks were caught by bamboo spears. There were no survivors; all two hundred died right there. Two boys were from Camp Bangkong, and one I had known fairly well, Itzig Heine. He had left Bangkong the moment the gate had been opened, but he never made it out of Surabaja.

Slowly, in bits and pieces, more was learned about various exploits that had taken place there during October and November. The revolution was beyond the control of the British. Authorities announced over the radio that all Europeans living in Surabaja had to try, on their own during the night, to reach the former concentration camp in the downtown area. From there people would be evacuated to the harbor by truck. The British could offer no help. All those women and children had to track through the dark streets, knowing they might be killed, and in many instances they were turned back by revolutionaries. The ones who made it were trucked from the old camp to the harbor, Tandjung Perak.

The plight of more than two thousand mostly Dutch male prisoners, confined in the Werfstraat jail, came to the attention of a Dutch captain named Boer, who was attached to the British as a translator. He was warned that the Indonesians were planning to poison the prisoners and decided to launch a heroic rescue effort. In order to make a successful raid, he managed to get hold of one tank and was assigned ten Gurkhas. After breaching the gate of the jail, a gunfight and hand-to-hand battle erupted. At the loss of one Gurkha, all the jail guards were killed. Captain Boer found that several prisoners had been tortured, and some had already been executed. The rest successfully got to the downtown camp near the harbor.

From there the refugees boarded a landing craft that took them outside the harbor, going through mined areas to reach a British hospital ship, the *Talma*. On board, many women finally broke down, and some of them became hysterical after all the horror they had experienced. My mother shuddered as she heard this story, but even Anton and I were reduced to silence when we heard the additional rumor that on her return trip the landing craft blew up on a mine.

We were right on the border of hostile territory, so it was no surprise that the British had their heavy mortars stationed directly behind the hotel. They fired mostly at night. It made a distinctive swooshing sound as the projectiles went through different layers of air completing their arcs. At first each firing awakened us with a start; later on we were able to sleep through this noise—or, better, sleep with the noise. We did not welcome this type of music at two in the morning, but we realized that it was part of our protection.

Upon our arrival at the hotel we found very austere conditions, and there were no other guests at first. In the succeeding weeks, though, more people under similar circumstances arrived. Since our family was the first among the Dutch to arrive at the hotel, my brother and I were assigned to a second floor room with a sweeping view of the river and the bridge. Somebody else before us had discovered the value of this room too. Under the windowsill all the bricks had been removed, leaving a gaping ventilation hole, and later we learned that it had been used as a machine gun post. Empty shells were discarded on the floor. The room contained a double bed and a sink that did not function. Nevertheless, we did have a real window with wooden shutters that were never closed unless the wind drove the rain in. Sitting on the windowsill and clasping our feet underneath, we were in a favorite position to enjoy the bridge and river scenes. My parents occupied the room below us.

Service in the hotel was about nonexistent, for just about all Indonesians had fled the city. There was no running water. Any available water was trucked in, and it was like gold. A bath once a week was tough in the tropics, where most people bathed twice a day. Only the bathrooms downstairs were in use, with a bucket of water to flush. The kitchen had the same problem, with its water use also rationed. That situation lasted for months, and we ate food out of cans. There was, however, plenty of hard liquor and beer for the adults, all gratis.

Slowly the situation improved, with fresh food nicely cooked instead of coming out of a can and linens washed. More hotel staff came in to work. After a few months, when the city had been under the control of the British for a while, the water taps started to function again.

Every Saturday at noon we were served a special traditional treat, *rijsttafel*. This Dutch Indonesian specialty was essentially rice with multiple additional dishes, up to forty sometimes, including a variety of sauces and meats. There were plenty of hot spices. Dad would eat a hot pepper paste, called *sambal oelek*, spread heavily over his fish. Even as he was claiming that the taste was exquisite, the tears would run down his cheeks. Anton and I could not tolerate that type of hot food, even when I used my teeth to scrape the food off my spoon.

British and Indian troops, primarily Punjabis and Sikhs, guarded the bridge around the clock. The last group I did not trust at all, and I stayed away from the tall, turbaned men. They would call out loudly to us or make sexual gestures without any embarrassment, hoping to impress us or lure us boys—and these men were our guards.

The British commandant occupied a large mansion on the other side of the road beside the hotel, and every week a military tattoo would take place there, in the front yard. It consisted of music from a military band, in this case with many bagpipes. These events always took place in the evening and were illuminated by torches, which gave a certain added dignity to the occasion. Still, the pomp of the British tattoos could not erase the realities of the revolution going on about us, and we knew we had traded a difficult situation in Bandung for an equally dangerous one here in Surabaja.

chapter twenty-three

SURABAJA RESTORED

We spent the first seven months of 1946 in Hotel Brantas. Mother and Dad tried to restore a normal family life and daily routine for us, although we were still surrounded by the revolution. Dad went daily to work. At first a jeep picked him up, and later on a Chevy sedan. Having a meal together and tea after four o'clock became very meaningful. We had tea on the outside terrace, talking about our circumstances and efforts to understand what lay ahead. Such were the uncertainties that I often tried not to think about more than one day at a time.

Mother and Dad were mostly concerned about the lack of schooling. Many school buildings had been ransacked. Eventually a school system was put into operation, but our school, which had started haltingly in June 1945, never functioned very well. Teachers were in short supply. Gradually a few qualified people trickled into town, some coming back from as far away as Siam. They had been prisoners on the Burma-Siam death railroad. Their health was not good, and of course they had no supplies. As time went on more subjects were added to the curriculum, but it was a far cry from the classes with which we had been challenged in Malang. The hours spent in school were limited. We tried to make up for lost time with extra studying at home.

My dad taught us English from a travel book, which had something to do with a ship that belonged to the P&O line. The described tour started in Egypt, and the ship went through the Red Sea. This was our only English textbook, and it was tough going without a dictionary. We had to rely on making notes about what Dad taught us, especially when it came to pronunciation, and he was often very impatient. Dad was quite fluent in English, but he had been out of touch with the language for more than three years.

One of our new subjects was a class in Malay, a language he spoke very well. In this subject, too, he blew up on many occasions when we did not catch on quickly. A new language, Bahasa Indonesia, was created in an attempt to overlap all the different tongues spoken throughout the Indies. One example was *sapoe*, a broom, which also meant the action of sweeping. In the new Bahasa the motion became *memsapoe*. This new language was on the way to becoming the official written one.

Algebra was another problem, primarily because of the lack of proper books, but also because our Indonesian teacher explained things poorly. He was not entirely fluent in Dutch, and he was impatient with us white boys, who had to get used to discipline again after our camp lives. He was inclined to ignore us. There were Indonesian and Chinese kids in our classes too. My parents shook their heads many times over about our uneven education. Mother, who had the patience of an angel, helped with our French lessons. She grew up attending the church of the French Huguenots in Amsterdam, where only French was spoken.

I turned eighteen in June 1946, but had an education no further than the first six months of the eighth grade, earned back in 1942. But during 1946 I did end up with some knowledge of Dutch, French, English, and Malay, as well as a painfully acquired understanding of human frailties.

Eating better helped us to regain our strength, and Mother put much of her energies to that end. Surabaja was still a beleaguered city. Rations and food out of cans were the mainstay, a situation that improved only slowly. We ate lots of corned beef and Spam. Gradually Indonesian foods were added, providing needed vegetables, and hot peppers supplied the excitement. Alcohol was free for the adults and readily available: beer, gin, whiskey, and Coca-Cola for us younger ones. After six o'clock the adults would sit on the verandah in front of the hotel and have a cool drink. They had a view of the road that ran parallel with the river, connecting with the semicircular driveway of the hotel. Between the road and the river was a grass mat sloping down to the water. This extended the vision across the stream into no-man's-land. That part of the city across the river was cleaned out early during our stay in 1946, making our location somewhat safer, while a brick wall enclosed the back of the hotel grounds.

After several months, a hot little Indo jazz band began to play in the evenings when Saturday night came around. Again we were enthralled by the music of George Gershwin. This music became immensely popular, resulting in lots of dancing. Dad loved to dance and always took to the floor, dragging Mother out of her chair. Military officers were often invited or would just crash the party, lured by the free drinks. The jazz music tempted them to dance, and they brought young women with them from other locations to spice up the evenings.

Mother had been able to lay her hands on colorful paper lanterns for candleholders that she suspended all around the verandah. Later on Dutch marines introduced the jitterbug, which they had learned when they were in training in North Carolina, and there was plenty of room for this wild dance on this large open space. At nine o'clock the younger set was sent to bed, but from our open window on the second floor we looked out over the party. No girls our age were around to make us want to go down and to join the festivities. Besides, Anton and I didn't know how to dance.

The people who gathered on those lively Saturday nights had survived all the bad years and now wanted to let go of their pent-up feelings. Each person there tried to take advantage of that moment and live it up. Even the few teenagers at the hotel were well aware of the uncertain future of the colony.

A friend of ours, Hans, who was one year older than I, and who had also been a prisoner in Bangkong, visited us daily. His family had been just recently reunited and had arrived in Surabaja earlier in the year. Hans's father worked as an engineer for the electrical utility that supplied Surabaja, and he was needed, just as my father was, to get the city's basic infrastructure back in functioning order.

Hans, Anton, and I often swam in the dirty Kali Brantas, whose waters flowed right in front of the hotel. Poor mother was absolutely mortified by the sight of our swimming escapades in that dark brown, dirty water. Sometimes we could see feces float by, for it was an open sewer. The camp experiences had left us with different ideas about what was really dirty.

Upstream of Surabaja, the mighty Brantas formed an extensive delta, one arm, the Kali Porong, flowing east. The northbound arm supplying our city was the Kali Mas, the river of gold. It had no similarity to gold, though, when you looked at the muddy brown water. One morning in March the native servants of the hotel were buzzing with excitement, for the level of the river water had dropped to that of a muddy creek. What could have happened?

Revolutionaries had dammed off the northern arm. The result was a real problem for the smaller boats in a city that relied heavily on light water transport. A great deal of bulk was handled by these ships, called *praus*, undecked Indonesian boats propelled by boom sticks, which were suddenly getting stuck on the bottom. To us boys, however, the situation was a windfall. We waded through all the mud and muck and extracted from the soft bottom several sunken boats: a one-person skiff, in good shape, a two-person canoe, a small flat-bottomed fishing boat, only ten feet long, and a rowboat. Anton found paddles and long oars in a warehouse and in the hotel's garage. We three boys started to organize again, as we had in the camps, and found tools. All three of us spent hours working and repairing our "home fleet," positioning the boats on sawhorses alongside the delivery road of the hotel.

We brought the skiff to tiptop shape again, but tragedy struck. One day an ice delivery truck backed up straight into the bow of the skiff. All the lapstrake planks splintered. Saddened, we declared it firewood. Repair of this skiff was now beyond our capabilities.

After a few weeks, the military blew the dam up, and the water returned to its original level, allowing us to go up and down the river in our boats as well.

Just south of the hotel, a great many reeds grew in the river, covering a substantial area. One afternoon we heard shots among the reeds, not far from where we were in the water, about a hundred yards upstream. Curiosity took us to the spot, where the local police were busy bringing ashore a six-foot crocodile they had just killed. The sight of this predator cooled our spirits. From my earliest years I had understood that the crocodiles were extinct in that river.

We quickly decided to move our swim efforts to the harbor, where there was a beautiful swimming pool and in front of it a sandy beach. Miraculously, this pool had survived all the fighting. Besides, the salt water in the harbor was much cleaner. This area was quite a distance from the hotel, but the streetcars had started to function again, enabling us to travel. Dad obtained free streetcar tickets for us.

One day an Australian PBY, also called a flying boat or Catalina, landed in the waters of the harbor and tied up to a centrally located buoy. We thought it would be fun to pay the crew a visit, even though the distance was substantial. The three of us swam in that direction, but about halfway to the Catalina we noticed a crewmember stepping onto the buoy, waving both arms wildly. We stopped swimming looked at each other a minute, talked it over, and finally decided that we were not welcome out there. On our return swim, as we approached shore, we noticed a crowd standing and waving on the beach. As we waded ashore a fellow shouted, "Hey, boys, didn't you see the sharks?" At first we thought they were joking.

Somebody handed me a pair of field glasses, and I saw several dorsal fins. It made us realize that Surabaja still deserved its old name—city of sharks and crocodiles.

In our favorite canoe, Hans, Anton, and I made several trips down the river to the locks, ending up in the old town, where we could see the ugly backsides of the multiple-level Javanese homes with outhouses on their balconies. Later that season, one day after tea, Anton and I decided to take the canoe and paddle upstream. After quite a distance we elected to reconnoiter one of the creeks coming from the east. We paddled for a while but then suddenly realized that we had wandered into no-man's-land. It was eerily quiet, and nothing was stirring. Anything or anyone could have been lurking in the bushes alongside the creek. The sudden squeal of a bird overhead gave us goose bumps. The sun was just sliding down toward the horizon, and the rapid approach of darkness made us tense. After looking at each other, we turned the canoe around in a hurry, without a word being said.

It was none too soon, either, for unexpectedly mortar shells started coming right into the area we had just left. The noise was terrifying. We paddled like crazy and felt very much relieved to see the river again. Around darkness we made it back to the hotel, our bodies bathed in perspiration. When we confessed to Dad what had happened, all he said was, "Looking at your faces, I can see that you have been punished already. But your adventure was inexcusably stupid."

Another time Hans accompanied us upstream in the fishing boat, where we spotted the bow of a prau among the reeds on the riverbank, a deserted half-submerged Indonesian sampan, partially filled with sand. Circling this craft, we saw that the cabin was partially underwater, the current running through the open windows. There was a green military Gurkha shirt bobbing inside the cabin.

Not expecting a body, I took a bamboo stick and tried to dislodge the shirt by poking around in the collar. When I lifted the tip of my stick, several vertebrae were strung along it, so that my stick occupied the space where normally the spinal cord should have been. It dawned on me that I was confronted with a decapitated soldier of the British army, whose corpse must have been in the boat for some time. I then discovered pale, leached-out flesh, which was decaying and fell apart easily. Startled, I dropped the stick. It was a gruesome discovery, and we hurriedly rowed away. The police received our report with a shrug of the shoulders.

Right after my birthday in June, in the late afternoon, I found Dad sitting on the verandah with a letter in his hands, staring off at nothing. When I sat down next to him, I could see tears in his eyes. About two months before, Mother had sent mail to The Hague in the Netherlands to let the family know that we were alive and where we were located. The letter in Dad's hands had come from there, and was our first such communication after nearly one year of liberation. Dad turned to me and explained in a choked voice that his parents, in their eighties, while living in The Hague, had died of starvation during the winter of 1944–45. I could find no words to comfort him.

Anton and I got our hands on two Japanese bikes under unusual circumstances. Dad got written permission to collect two bicycles from a warehouse, for which he received a key. The three of us had trouble finding this warehouse. After walking several blocks in the afternoon heat, we finally discovered the building in a narrow side street downtown. This warehouse was flanked on both sides by small private homes. Upon entering this alley we saw a sign, intended for military personnel: "Out of bounds."

A rusty padlock secured the warehouse door. As Dad was wrestling with the lock, three Australian soldiers walked into the alley and stopped at the house next door. Two nice-looking young Indo girls answered the door, full of giggles that distracted me. It was soon apparent that the Australians were inebriated. One soldier walked up to us and growled quite belligerently, "You bloody Dutchmen, are you spying on us? If you have the guts to report us I will find you and lay you out!" Dad kept his cool and said, "Why should I report you? I don't want anyone to know what I am doing here either. You enjoy yourselves, and pretty soon we'll be on our way."

Then we rushed to get our bikes, but found only ones with solid tires. Nevertheless, we were glad to have a means of transportation. On our way out, we noticed that the military men were gone, probably into the girls' home.

From that point on Anton and I rode our Japanese bicycles on solid tires, their rubber ends were clipped together with staples. When the staples came loose, a rubber strip was left behind like a snake. Still, we never had to worry about a flat tire.

During the spring of 1946, as the revolution settled into a somewhat predictable presence, the British were withdrawn from Surabaja and replaced by a Dutch marine division. When the southern part of Holland was liberated in 1944, many young Dutch men volunteered for the marines and were trained in North Carolina. These marines landed initially in Singapore in 1945, but at that point the British were unwilling to allow them to progress to Java, clearly for political reasons. Finally, a division of our own countrymen landed in Surabaja. Anton and I went downtown to watch the marines passing through.

Huge GMC trucks pulling trailers loaded with tanks rattled through the narrow streets, barely managing the turns. It was a thrill to see all this equipment.

After the marines had taken over, the patrols across the river became more intense, with the intent to control Surabaja totally. Unfortunately, though, the Dutch troops were inexperienced in this type of activity. One morning at five, we were awakened by trucks driving up to the verandah of the hotel, each carrying wounded soldiers. Stretchers were unloaded and the injured placed on the lounge chairs of the terraces. Two marines were dead and were covered by blankets. The medics were taking care of the wounded. Mother ran out and tried to help them by offering something to drink. Two patrols had run into each other, and without proper identification, both sides started to shoot. The result was two dead and seven wounded. It was a dreadful sight. The soldiers who were not wounded were sitting on the low brick wall at the edge of the patio, mostly in shock from the realization of what they had done. Mother and some of the other women tried to console them but it seemed to have little effect. Ambulances arrived, adding to the chaos and turmoil. The entire commotion had started suddenly, and just as suddenly a deep silence fell over the area when the trucks departed.

The morning coolness faded as the sun started to come up. Many of the women living at the hotel at the time were in tears. The words, "They shot each other," were repeatedly heard. People tried to comfort each other. Most of them were sitting on the low brick wall with an arm around a neighbor's shoulders. Dad just stood there in his kimono and never said a word. Abruptly he turned and went into his room. Anton had been sitting on the windowsill of our bedroom, watching it all in silence. Hardly anybody went for breakfast. Again there was a reminder that for us the war was not over.

Aunt Loes and her daughters had survived the camps. They moved back from Ambarawa to Surabaja in the middle of 1946. They found their home plundered but otherwise intact.

After a thorough effort to clean the place up, my aunt took up her old profession of designing ladies' dresses. Soon she had several seamstresses working for her, as she had before the war, when she provided many dresses for the "upper ten." My aunt's home was again filled with the humming, ticking noises of the foot-paddled Singer sewing machines.

Around July our family of four moved back to my aunt's large house, which gave all of us the closer ties with family that we had been missing. Mother started to work as a secretary for a Hungarian businessman who imported all kinds of distilled drinks, especially wine from Hungary. Her office was all the way downtown and was air-conditioned, a new luxury. The boss's sedan provided her with transportation, for he was aware of her physical frailty. Owning a private car was very rare for that time. She got free alcohol, mostly European imports. Dad obtained free tickets for the movie theaters, passes made available for military and government workers.

One modern air-conditioned theater, the Maxim, was only a block away from Aunt Loes's home. We boys liked to visit this cinema around three o'clock, so we could see the feature movie twice. There were hardly any people at that time of day, and we had the theater to ourselves, occupying the best seats.

The big Hollywood shows in color certainly got our attention, with all the glamorous platinum blondes, and the luxury displayed in the films fascinated us. We saw all the war movies, satisfying our hunger to understand the historical part of World War II. People must have thought it funny to see three boys in an otherwise empty theater, loudly applauding when the enemy was beaten. We wanted to know what had happened in Europe, but mostly we favored the clips where the Japanese were being defeated. We wanted to see those again and again.

chapter twenty-four

TO HOLLAND ON *ORANJE*

One day in August 1946, Dad called us boys and asked us to sit down. By then Anton was fifteen and I eighteen years old. Dad explained that in his opinion our education was extremely inadequate. He thought it would take years before the schools in Surabaja would be back to normal again.

"During the war we were separated for three and a half years, and we've been together again for only ten months," he said. "It will be hard, but Mother and I think you boys should go to the Netherlands to study." Mother had contacted her sister in Haarlem, who did not have children of her own. She replied that she would be willing to lodge us. Anton and I really did not know what to think of that plan, but we respected Dad's judgment and agreed.

Our family had to begun to realize that the future of the Dutch in Indonesia was going to be limited. The revolution was still going on, making travel outside Surabaja an extremely dangerous undertaking. We had just heard recently, for example, about the death of two Danish doctors in Kediri. Bandits stopped them on the road and they were shot in the head at point blank range. There was no law and order in those outlying districts held by the revolutionaries.

Dad had heard that a hospital ship, the *Oranje*, was outside the harbor, lying in the roads for the Westgat. Both channels, the Westgat and the Eastgat, had sanded up during the war, but previously both had provided an entry to the original harbor. The Brantas River brought steady deposits of silt, creating sandbars. As a result, the distance between the harbor and the ship was substantial, and small boats had to be used to reach the hospital ship. The *Oranje* was in need of additional help for simple jobs and was hiring hands. So far, about fourteen boys had signed on. Dad thought that we could earn our passage on this ship, which was bound for the Netherlands.

Oranje, named after the royal family, was a 20,000-ton line ship built in 1939. Before the war it had sailed between Europe and Indonesia. When

Germany invaded the Netherlands, the government in exile converted *Oranje* into a hospital ship equipped with a modern operating room. During the war it sailed across the Indian Ocean, returning wounded Australians and New Zealanders, and was able to accommodate seven hundred patients. *Oranje* was now being used to take sick and injured Dutch citizens to Holland.

One of the many problems the government faced in 1946 was a severe shortage of ships, with long waiting lists for people who were not desperately ill. Some of them were evacuated by 1947. Anton and I, being in good condition, would not have qualified until that year. Working aboard *Oranje* would earn us a hundred guilders each and provide us an earlier departure.

Early one morning in September, when the time arrived for us to leave, we bid a difficult farewell to Aunt Loes and our cousins. Then our family went by truck to the harbor, where we boarded an LCT, one of several heading for *Oranje*. Many hundreds of people were to embark that day. My parents went, as Mother called it, "to push us off." We steamed out of the harbor, and it took the LCTs three hours to come alongside the ship. The situation was still considered unsafe, so the LCTs were armed with cannons. We were escorted as well by two motor torpedo boats and twelve amphibian tanks. Mother remarked that seeing the escort gave her a sense of safety. Only very recently had the Westgat been swept clean of Japanese mines.

Coming alongside the hospital ship and looking up made me realize how big *Oranje* was. After climbing the gangplank, we encountered an officer and stated our names. Immediately we were identified as crewmembers and told to stand aside, for our work was about to begin.

Abruptly we had to say farewell to our parents. Dad then suggested they return on the LCT that had brought us, but it had already headed for the harbor. Mother had hoped she could stay longer, and she was disappointed to have to turn around that soon. On the advice of one of the officers, my parents boarded a returning tugboat. They stood on the bridge, waving at us. Mother was crying, Dad holding her. I would never be able to erase that image from my heart. Slowly they steamed away and out of our lives. We had no idea when we would see them again.

All the new crewmembers were called into the salon, fancy with all its woodwork and shiny brass, and introduced to the steward, who became our foreman. He told us to leave our belongings in the corner of the room until later that day. The purser registered our names and divided us into groups.

My first temporary assignment that day was to help supervise Japanese prisoners. A sailor showed me the way down to one of the holds, where a crane was lowering cargo deep inside the hull. Crates and sacks held together by nets landed on the floor. After unhooking the nets, the Japanese had to stow away the cargo in a certain order. I worked under an apprentice mate, who explained how important it was that cargo not start to roll or shift during bad weather, for it could dramatically increase the risk of capsizing.

There were fifteen Japanese prisoners doing the work of stowing the crates and lashing them down. I had to see to it that the process was done right. The Japanese were not very willing to work and pretended constantly not to understand. I told the mate that I could correct this problem easily, if he would be so kind as to remove himself from the scene. He must have figured what my intention was, and he said, "We are not going to lower ourselves to their standards." This mate was fresh from the Netherlands and had no sense of my feelings toward the Japanese. I was still full of revenge, and his response did not sit well with me. I realized I could never make this mate understand, so grudgingly I set about my work. After the job was done the officer told me to get the Japanese back into an LCT; then he left. I did not feel like driving fifteen unwilling Japanese up the long ladders. After all, it would be difficult to oversee.

I signaled the crane operator to lower a big net, than I spread the meshwork on the floor. After I herded the prisoners onto it, I hooked all four corners of the webbing and secured the clip. At this point I signaled the crane operator to hoist. At first this operator was surprised, but I could see a big grin spread over his face. If looks could have killed, those from the Japanese would have struck me dead. Deeply satisfied, I smiled and bowed and said, "Now you really look like monkeys!" That became their flight to the awaiting LCT, where soldiers took over the duty of guarding them.

That evening we received our permanent assignments. I volunteered to work as an orderly on the third-class deck, on a ward that contained forty shell-shocked soldiers and five patients with leprosy. Once the steward uttered the word "leprosy," nobody wanted to work in that department for fear of contagion. One of our patients was a Catholic priest, whose face was without a nose; you could look straight into the air passage. The priest was in his forties, kind and humane. Often he would just sit there with a smile, watching what I was doing. At first I was not sure what to think of his manner, but soon I realized that it was his way of encouraging me. That made a deep impression on me. I was unafraid. Feeling sorry for all of them and being eager to help made me decide to try to do my best.

When we first boarded the ship, we new workers were quartered as a group right over the three propeller shafts. There was a constant noise from the steady churning of the props, as well as an oppressive heat. We were still in tropical waters, and that made the heat almost unbearable. We asked the steward who supervised us for permission to sleep on the first-class promenade deck at the highest level toward the stern. This was granted.

My brother got the best job ever, working in the pantry, because his health was not yet up to par and he was the youngest. Every evening we had chocolate milk and toast with real butter—a special treat.

The first port of call was Batavia, where we took on more people. This time the ship tied up at the quay. Taking on the sick people took only a short time, compared with the tedious process in Surabaja. Then off we went, through the Strait of Sunda into the Indian Ocean, our destination the Suez Canal. Our ship made good time. The ocean was like a mirror, especially in the Arabian Sea. We spotted some dhows, listless without wind. When I had the chance, I would hang over the railing forward to watch the ship's strong bow split the water, creating a wave that curled over farther down at the side of the hull. It left behind the ship two long lines of vee-shaped white foam. I hunkered down there often, alone at the foremost point. For hours I would breathe in the clean air and enjoy my freedom. The air was warm and the sky an intense blue, with a few puffs of white clouds in the distance. To me this was living again, far away from war and the memories of the camps. If this experience could have lasted forever, I would not have minded.

At dusk the Chinese laundrymen came on deck, talking and laughing in Cantonese and interrupting my reverie. Their work area and sleeping quarters were under decks in the bow. They joined me leaning over the railing. We enjoyed watching a school of dolphins jumping up out of the water just ahead of our ship, always managing to avoid a collision. Flying fish, not larger than a herring, would jump off a swell and sail visibly for several yards through the air, to land with a slight splash. One day at lunch a flying fish flew into the dining room through the open porthole and landed on the table right in front of a woman, who in response dropped her spoon in her soup. This episode drew a great deal of laughter.

The temperatures were high, and much higher yet going into the Red Sea after passing the long, narrow island of Socotra, which then belonged to England. In the far distance, to starboard, we could see Aden on the hazy outline of the coast. With Socotra, it controlled the Strait of Bab el Mandeb, the entrance to the Red Sea.

Before entering the Suez Canal, we dropped anchor portside, toward Egypt. We could make out the shoreline in the distance, a stretch of desert trembling in the heat, and some hills in the hazy distance. We spotted a cluster of Quonset huts alongside a small quay. A flagpole carried a drooping Union Jack. All passengers were to be transported by LCT to shore in the very small harbor of Ataka to be outfitted with winter clothes issued by the Red Cross.

We entered a hut and tried on the available garments. The heat inside was stifling. Only a bureaucrat could set up such a situation, I thought. We were stopped in one of the hottest places on earth to be outfitted with clothes for a cold European winter. Still, we were grateful. German soldiers in gray uniforms, taken prisoner in North Africa, helped us select our clothes: long winter underwear; a woolen shirt; a woolen herringbone suit, heavenly blue like a piece of the sky; a very heavy winter coat that, according to the label, came from New York; and a lined wool jacket. With my winter outfit on and the temperature near 120 degrees, I began to sweat profusely. Watery pearls ran from my forehead, dripped on my glasses and nose. The shirt, wet with perspiration, stuck to my chest. Asked if the suit fit, my immediate answer was, "Yes, yes." I was in a hurry. I wanted to get out of that suffocating outfit. Thank God we also got a coke to drink. Most of the German prisoners were strictly correct but hid every emotion. They packed our new belongings neatly for us to take back aboard ship.

The convoy of which we were a part had to proceed through the Suez Canal single file. Almost halfway, our convoy reached the Bitter Lakes. Here the ships dropped anchor to allow escorted ships heading in the other direction to pass. Some scholars believed that when Moses led his people out of Egypt he crossed the Bitter Lakes area, thought in those days to be an estuary of the Red Sea. It was here that troops of the Pharaoh were caught by the incoming tide. Even though I understood that it might not be true, I loved the story and was interested to see the area.

We continued north to Port Said, where we tied up to a long row of hinging pontoons, originating at the shoreline and floating toward the ship to connect us to shore. There were no facilities for mooring ships. The captain ordered all portholes closed, for in his experience Arabs would try to come aboard. In rowboats they surrounded the ship, looking for ways to come on deck. They came equipped with ropes tied to grappling hooks, which they would throw over the railing for access. Their excuse for coming aboard was always to sell things, such as the trinkets attached to their belts. But they were also known to try to steal.

I was assigned as a guard to the rear deck, all alone. The railing and the deck were in the shape of a crescent, so I had to circle constantly to prevent Arabs from climbing aboard. I heard the clanging of the hooks grabbing the railing. I kept releasing one hook after another. This system worked for a while, until one Arab suddenly jumped over the railing. When I approached him, clearly with the intent to push him overboard, he pulled a knife.

I was not armed. In a flash I remembered a defensive move; I ripped off my shirt and wrapped it around my left arm. He tried to stab, but my shirt protected me from being hurt; besides I was quicker than he in avoiding contact. A woman on a higher deck had an excellent view of the scene and screamed, sounding the alarm. Several sailors came to my rescue, and together we managed to sit on the fellow and confiscate his knife. Then he was wrestled to the gangplank. After being kicked in the rear end, he rolled head over heels downward and landed hard. I was worried that the other Arabs would storm the ship. Instead they laughed and admitted, "He got caught."

I loved my job as an orderly. The insane ward, which used to be the third-class promenade deck, occupied the entire area in the rear. The railing had been extended by welded wire all the way up to the deck above us to prevent depressed patients from jumping overboard. It was a good thing, since there were some very gloomy people among the military patients. Some of the younger soldiers told me that they had served on the island of Bangka. While being on patrol, coming up a steep road, they were ambushed. They suffered heavy casualties, and some of them suffered shellshock. So they ended up on our hospital ship to go back to the Netherlands.

One of my tasks was to feed the catatonic schizophrenics. This required a great deal of patience, for a patient sometimes sat with his mouth full of food but would not chew. As I tried repeatedly to get a patient to eat, my brain memorized American tunes, piped through the ship in the mornings, with popular titles like, "Don't Fence Me In," or "Give Me Five Minutes More."

There were padded cells, with a centrally located peephole in the door. One day a sergeant in such a cell went berserk; he was a very strong man and created a great disturbance. He ripped a steel bed out of the wooden floor to which it had been bolted, than used it as a battering ram against the door. I looked through the peephole, and he spit in my face.

I rang the alarm. A nurse, the doctor, and an orderly came. The nurse handed me a syringe and told me to jab the sergeant with it. He fought us as he tried for the door, and I found myself comparing him with Samson and his long hair. We finally wrestled him to the floor and injected morphine and Phenobarbital into him. The treatment was wild and primitive. At the time there were few effective medicines for such a problem, and tranquilizers as such did not exist. Finally the sergeant passed out on the floor, sedated.

The ship made no stops in the Mediterranean, but around noon our ship passed, on the starboard side, the Italian isle of Pantelleria, a dead volcano with a beautiful symmetrical cone. This grayish-green mountain stood out against the cloudless azure sky. I spotted some low white homes along the shoreline. Pantelleria was the first island taken by the Allies during World War II and was used as a springboard in their attack on Sicily. It was needed for an air base to support the invasion of Italy. From this distance, though, I only saw the beauty of the island and none of the war's evidence.

In the Bay of Biscay a storm hit us, and everybody got seasick. We used mops to clean up, but no pails, because those would slide away on the rolling ship's deck. It was still hard to get rid of the smell, though. By staying busy I was able to overcome my own nausea from the threatening seasickness, except when I had to perform this messy work; holding my own was tough.

If we had an advance warning about an upcoming storm, Anton would make toast in the pantry and bring it to our sleeping quarters. We placed the dry toast under our pillows at bedtime, then ate it before getting up in the morning; that helped settle our stomachs. A sniff of fresh air was also extremely helpful. After cleaning up, I was allowed to come to the bridge and watch the green swells tower high over the structure. Instinctively I ducked, even though we stood behind a glass screen.

By the time we reached Europe in September, the weather we faced was cold and windy. Again we obtained special permission from our steward to set up the huge heavy glass shields on the seaside, hinged on the deck above us. After the shields were lowered, they would lock in place to the floor with pins and protect us from the cold wind. We spread our mattresses on the floor and rolled them up against the wall during the day.

Our destination was Amsterdam. However, as it happened, a passenger liner just ahead of us, the *Christiaan Huygens*, had run over a mine the night before in front of Ymuiden, at the entry to Amsterdam. This created quite a bit of consternation aboard ship. Our ship was instead directed the following morning to Rotterdam, a closer port.

History repeats itself. An excellent example is the Japanese attack on Pearl Harbor without prior declaration of war. The Russo-Japanese war of February 10, 1904, also started with a sudden torpedo attack on the Russian navy at daybreak off Port Arthur, a Russian-occupied city and port of northeast China, only later followed by a declaration of hostilities. The Russian Pacific fleet was destroyed. Following this sudden attack, the Japanese were able to land their troops in Korea and occupy Seoul.

In 1938, the U.S. Navy held an exercise in the Pacific, attacking a harbor with bombers and torpedo planes. This attack, with Pearl Harbor as the target, was an overwhelming success, and it should have erased any sense of security American forces enjoyed in Hawaii. Critical readers might reasonably wonder if the admiralty was aware or cared about these earlier stories in light of the "Day of Infamy," and why so many warnings that Japan was up to something were ignored. The Russians did the same thing in 1945; they cut all communication with the Japanese embassy. The Soviets then attacked in Manchuria and followed up with an official declaration of war.

Cutting off the oil supplies to Japan in 1941 could mean only one of two things: either Japan would withdraw from China, which was entirely against their Bushido ethic, or they would attack. The Jewish people make certain that the Holocaust will not be forgotten, and rightfully so. But so many news media are not publishing information about the Japanese atrocities in the Pacific, considered by some a second Holocaust.

The Japanese High Command secretly tested its own atomic bomb. Were the Allies aware of this threat? On the day of the explosion at Nagasaki, at dawn, the Japanese government sent a small remote-controlled vessel against a small island in the Sea of Japan. The blast leveled the island and several fishing boats. They killed their own people with this low-yield atomic bomb. Japan had only a scant supply of uranium, apparently supplied by Germany, since in May 1945 a German submarine, the U-235, surrendered in the Atlantic Ocean after Germany collapsed. This U-boat was brought into Portsmouth Naval Base at Kittery, Maine, with uranium and mercury aboard. Its original destination had been Japan, and two high-ranking Japanese nuclear physicists in the submarine committed suicide.

In 1990 the Foundation for Japanese Honorary Debts was established by former Dutch prisoners. There is a similar group in Great Britain, Fulcrum, and in Canada, America, Australia, and New Zealand. The POWs were asking $20.000 each. The Japanese government refused, asserting that the Allied governments absolved it of the obligation to pay reparations in the peace treaty of 1952, signed in San Francisco. This absolution was instigated by the United States. However, under the principle of *jus cogens*, incorporated in international law, it is absolutely illegal for a government to sign or give away the rights of its citizens.

During the investigation of Nazi gold being held in Switzerland, a document surfaced revealing a secret contract between Switzerland and Japan. The British and American governments provided the Swiss with 4.5 million francs—today, about $6 million—to help ease the poor circumstances of the British and American prisoners during World War II. Bern made a secret accord with Tokyo. Forty percent of the money was to be used to retrieve Swiss goods from Japan; the rest went to Japan. This money was transferred in 1944. The prisoners never saw any of it. We never knew until now that this money had been made available. Why was it kept a secret by the Allied governments too?

Many Swiss citizens who happened to be in Indonesia during the war were paid in 1955 by the Japanese government. Switzerland was not at war with Japan. These Swiss were never interned but suffered from losses of household goods and confiscated cars and businesses. There were 186 Swiss in Indonesia and several others in Singapore, Hong Kong, China, and elsewhere, and the Japanese killed twenty of them. Japan paid 22,000 Swiss francs to each, along with 1.5 million francs extra for the twenty who had been executed.

Many former prisoners feel betrayed, considering all these events. The payment, through the Red Cross, to former prisoners of Japan was a joke, far below $200. Members of the Dutch armed forces in Indonesia received $70 each in September 1951. The amount of about $85 for the civilians was not paid until 1956. Probably the only way that Japan will agree to an apology and a further reimbursement is when it is made aware of its moral obligation to the world. Japan must improve its human rights record first. Its government is adamant in its denial of the rape of Nanking and other atrocities, even after so much evidence has surfaced. Many apologies have been made by individuals, but never by the Japanese government itself.

Here is the almost forgotten story of Pingfan in Manchuria. This huge camp, under the innocuous name of the Kwantung Army Epidemic Prevention and Water Supply Unit, was nothing more than an experimental laboratory of terrible bacteriological warfare on human beings. At first the Japanese used Chinese and Russian prisoners, later Allied prisoners of war. Unit 731, as it was called, was the brainchild of a physician named Shiro Ishii, who specialized in bacteriology, serology, and pathology. He experimented with biological warfare and chemical applications on live people, such as freezing naked individuals tied to a post. Ishii developed a drug named Labanarin, which increased resistance to cold weather and frostbite. These persons—men, women, and children—were provided by the Kempeitai.

At first Ishii worked at a converted soy sauce distillery outside Harbin. His detachment received the name Togo Unit, after the admiral who defeated the Russian navy at Tsushima in 1905. Later on Ishii moved to Pingfan, a sprawling experimental station where over three thousand Japanese worked. His bacterial warfare was never used against the Allies. However, they came close. The U.S. government learned about Unit 731 in exchange for a promise that none of the scientists involved would be prosecuted.

Pingfan was destroyed at the order of the Japanese government. The Russians captured several scientists and condemned them to death. The American courts threw out Shiro Ishii's case, for it would have revealed the involvement of the Japanese Emperor Hirohito, whom the U.S. government had decided to spare. All these scientists were pardoned and protected by the American government.

The Germans performed operations on living Jews, cutting spinal cords where nerves originating on one side to study the loss of enervation and motor function of the dermatome involved. I remember from medical school that the neurological department refused to obtain and use this type of information, an action with which I wholeheartedly agree. These Japanese scientist war criminals should have been prosecuted.

Most Japanese are not aware of this horrible piece of their history. Queen Beatrix of the Netherlands visited Japan and said, "Many of my fellow Dutchmen did not survive this war. The ones who did come back, are marked by their memories. As a result no end will come to their sorrow." Later on a Japanese cardinal of the Roman Catholic Church stated that the Japanese people had not understood the meaning of the Queen's speech. Did he really think that the Japanese are so naive?

I was once told that I dwell on my memories. It took about twelve years to write them all down. I wanted to write the story as it happened, so that the camps will not be forgotten.

Anyone who experiences as a teenager the things described in this book and still survives will have a mental scar for life. However, I have tried to go on with my life, to roll with the punches, to make the best of it. I reckon it as a rough experience to be integrated into my total attitude. Anything bad happening to us now will never be as bad as things were at that time.

I have been able not to turn bitter. I came close, but that would have eaten away my insides, and I really was afraid of the effect that would have on my five children. I could not let that happen; they would not understand. They have had already enough trouble dealing with my story. The idea that these atrocities actually happened to their own family, their parents and grandparents, was really hard to deal with.

I still have a problem with the older Japanese who caused the war and the monstrous excesses during their occupation of Southeast Asia. It has been estimated that a total of twenty million people died in the Pacific and in China. There is still a great gulf between former Allied prisoners and Japan, which undoubtedly committed crimes against humanity in the way it ran POW camps during World War II. The death rate of the Allied prisoners in Germany was 5 percent—and in Japan 28 percent. It is up to the Japanese to resolve this issue. They must do so not only to make amends for the past, but also to retrieve their honor.

I felt that I may be able to learn to forgive, but it is not possible to forget.

I have nothing against the American Japanese; actually, I want to thank the Nisei who fought the enemies of the United States. That must have been very difficult under their circumstances.

Yes, I am guilty to the extent that there are times when I become very hostile about certain world events, especially if they involve statements of the Japanese government in regard to the war of 1941–1945, its denial of guilt and moral obligation, its ruthless handling of the so-called comfort women whom its army forced into prostitution. A high-ranking Japanese official recently stated, "Those women were making good money." That could not be farther from the truth. Many of those poor souls were tortured, dismembered, and killed, even after Japan had surrendered.

Around the year 1994, many former comfort women came forward to testify before the Diet, the Japanese Parliament. One was a Caucasian woman, a former Dutch national now living in Australia. She stood there among all the Asian females and accused the Japanese of their crimes. As an older teenager, she had been used against her will by Japanese officers in Semarang.

One older Japanese man said to her, "You must have liked it."

The brave woman burst into tears.

The war and the concentration camps delayed my education markedly. I reentered the ninth grade at the age of eighteen to go to school with fourteen-year-olds who I thought were so smart, for I had a hard time integrating and catching up, realizing that I never had attended the second half of the eighth grade. Finally I graduated at twenty-one. I was grateful to be able to finish medical school. I experienced a tremendous satisfaction in practicing family medicine from 1959 through 1996. Often I was asked why I had entered medicine—if this was the result of my experiences during the war. I really do not know. A fact is that my outlook on life and how I dealt with patients was markedly influenced by the internment of the concentration camps. I thought that I understood the circumstances of the poor, often cancelling bills they owed, but I was very tough and intolerant with cheaters. People who needed support with their mental problems were given extra time and consideration. I felt that to listen, to try to understand the background of their feelings, was of the utmost importance. Only after one eye started to impair my function as a physician at age sixty-eight did I say farewell to my patients. I can sincerely say that I missed them so much, especially during the first six months of retirement. But everything comes to an end.

GLOSSARY

(D = Dutch, M = Malay, J = Japanese)

anglo (M), clay pot containing charcoal, like a hibachi
arang (M), charcoal
atap (M), dried double-folded coconut leaves, used for roofing
babi (M), pig
balong (M), fishpond
bango (J), countdown, head count
belanda (M), European
betjak (M), tricycle taxi
blimbing (M), starfruit
bodoh (M), stupid
boeng (M), brother
chabar angin (M), rumor
da-me (J), no good
dilarang keras (M), strictly forbidden
djangkerik (M), cricket
dogcart (M), lit. dog cart, a two-wheeled, horse-drawn vehicle
fundoshi (J), loincloth
furyo (J), prisoner
fushinban (J), night guard duty
gaijin (J), non-Japanese
gajong (M), bucket with a wooden handle on the inside, like the spoke of a wheel
gambir (M), perennial vine (*Uncaria gambir*)
gedek (M), fence made of woven bamboo
goedang (M), storeroom
gula-djawa (M), brown sugar, crystallized in half a coconut shell
hakko ichiu (J), global rule, Japanese doctrine
han (J), camp subdivision
hancho (J), head of a *han*

ianfu (J), "comfort woman," usually forced into prostitution

Indo (D), Eurasian

kabaja (M), blouse

kali (M), river

kampong (M), village

kankung (M), edible marsh plant

katana (J), sword

katjong (M), young boy

kawat (M), barbed wire

keirei (J), command to bow or salute

Kempeitai (J), military police

kepas (M), fan

kepiteng (M), crab

kerandjang (M), woven bamboo basket

katella (M), edible root source of tapioca

kiotsuke (J), attention

klamboe (M), mosquito netting

klontong (M), wooden rattle

Kodo-ha (J), radical nationalist faction in the Japanese army

koelie (M), coolie

komicho (J), assistant to the *hancho*

KPM (Koninklijke Paketvaart Mij) (D), royal merchant-marine freight line

kraton (M), palace of the sultan

kroessi males (M), rattan easy chair

kumpulan (M), gathering of people

kutsu (J), shoes

larong (M), flying termite

loewak (M), common palm civet (*Paradoxurus hermaphroditus*)

mada-mada (J), much more, still more

mata (M), spy, lit., eye

mandi-bak (M), cement washbasin

mandoer (M), foreman

melati (M), fragrant jasmine (*Jasminum sambac*)

merdeka (M), freedom

mesigit or *masdjid* (M), mosque

momok (M), ghost

naore (J), straighten up

oebie (M), edible tuberous plant

pasar (M), market

patjol (M), hoe

Pelopor (M), Indonesian guerrillas

pemuda (M), freedom fighter, lit., young man

pendopo (M), ramada or meeting place

pikoelan (M), yoked baskets

rajap (M), termite

rampas (M), murderous piracy

rampok (M), plunder

razzia (D), raid

romusha (J), slave laborer

rotan (M), rattan

rumah sakit (M), sick room

salto (D), somersault

sawah (M), rice paddy

selamat pagi (M), good morning

senzo owari (J), the war is over

shochi itashimashita (J), I understand

slamatan (M), festive meal

slendang (M), long strip of cotton cloth, strapped over one shoulder, with which
    to carry a burden

slokan (M), gutter or ditch

soenat (M), circumcision

taiso (J), exercise

tampat (M), place

tandoe (or *tanggoeng*) (M), sedan chair, carried by four persons

tenko (J), roll call

toko (M), shop

tomare (J), halt

Volksraad (D), House of Representatives in Batavia

wallang sangit (M), stinkbug

waringin (M), banyan tree

yasume (J), at ease

yosoro (J), yes

WORLD WAR II:
THE GLOBAL, HUMAN, AND ETHICAL DIMENSION
G. Kurt Piehler, *series editor*

1. Lawrence Cane, David E. Cane, Judy Barrett Litoff, and David C. Smith, eds., *Fighting Fascism in Europe: The World War II Letters of an American Veteran of the Spanish Civil War*

2. Angelo M. Spinelli and Lewis H. Carlson, *Life behind Barbed Wire: The Secret World War II Photographs of Prisoner of War Angelo M. Spinelli*

3. Don Whitehead and John B. Romeiser, *"Beachhead Don": Reporting the War from the European Theater, 1942–1945*

4. Scott H. Bennett, ed., *Army GI, Pacifist CO: The World War II Letters of Frank and Albert Dietrich*

5. Alexander Jefferson with Lewis H. Carlson, *Red Tail Captured, Red Tail Free: Memoirs of a Tuskegee Airman and POW*

6. Jonathan G. Utley, *Going to War with Japan, 1937–1941*

7. Grant K. Goodman, *America's Japan: The First Year, 1945–1946*

8. Patricia Kollander with John O'Sullivan, *"I Must Be a Part of This War": One Man's Fight against Hitler and Nazism*

9. Judy Barrett Litoff, *An American Heroine in the French Resistance: The Diary and Memoir of Virginia d'Albert-Lake*

10. Thomas R. Christofferson and Michael S. Christofferson, *France during World War II: From Defeat to Liberation*

11. Don Whitehead, *Combat Reporter: Don Whitehead's World War II Diary and Memoirs*, edited by John B. Romeiser

12. James M. Gavin, *The General and His Daughter: The Wartime Letters of General James M. Gavin to His Daughter Barbara*, edited by Barbara Gavin Fauntleroy et al.

13. John J. Toffey IV, *Jack Toffey's War: A Son's Memoir*

14. Lt. General James V. Edmundson, *Letters to Lee: From Pearl Harbor to the War's Final Mission*, edited by Dr. Celia Edmundson.

DATE DUE

DEMCO, INC. 38-2931